EMERGING POWERS IN THE INTERNATIONAL ECONOMIC ORDER

The Post-War liberal economic order seems to be crumbling, placing the world at an inflection point. China has emerged as a major force, and other emerging economies seek to play a role in shaping world trade and investment law. Might they band together to mount a wholesale challenge to current rules and institutions? *Emerging Powers in the International Economic Order* argues that resistance from the Global South and creation of China-led alternative spaces will have some impact but no robust alternative vision will emerge. Significant legal innovations from the South depart from the mainstream neoliberal model, but these countries are driven by pragmatism and strategic self-interest, not a common ideological orientation nor do they intent fully to dismantle the current ordering. In this book, Sonia E. Rolland and David M. Trubek predict a more pluralistic world, which is neither the continued hegemony of neoliberalism nor a full blown alternative to it.

DR. SONIA E. ROLLAND is Professor of Law at Northeastern University School of Law. She is the author of *Development at the WTO* (2012) and regularly acts as an expert for international and non-governmental organizations including the United Nations, the International Centre for Trade and Sustainable Development and the Indian Institute of Foreign Trade. She has held appointments at Columbia University, Georgetown University and the University of Michigan.

DAVID M. TRUBEK is Voss-Bascom Professor of Law and Dean of International Studies Emeritus at the University of Wisconsin-Madison and a Senior Research Fellow at the Harvard Law School. He is a world renowned expert on law and development, with a regional focus on Latin America. He has published dozens of books and articles, including *Law and the New Developmental State: the Brazilian Experience in Latin American Context* (2013) and *World Trade and Investment Law Reimagined: A Progressive Agenda for an Inclusive Globalization* (2019).

CAMBRIDGE INTERNATIONAL TRADE AND ECONOMIC LAW

Series editors

Dr. Lorand Bartels, *University of Cambridge*
Professor Thomas Cottier, *University of Berne*
Professor William Davey, *University of Illinois*

As the processes of regionalisation and globalisation have intensified, there have been accompanying increases in the regulations of international trade and economic law at the levels of international, regional and national laws.

The subject matter of this series is international economic law. Its core is the regulation of international trade, investment and cognate areas such as intellectual property and competition policy. The series publishes books on related regulatory areas, in particular human rights, labour, environment and culture, as well as sustainable development. These areas are vertically linked at the international, regional and national level, and the series extends to the implementation of these rules at these different levels. The series also includes works on governance, dealing with the structure and operation of related international organisations in the field of international economic law, and the way they interact with other subjects of international and national law.

EMERGING POWERS IN THE INTERNATIONAL ECONOMIC ORDER

Cooperation, Competition and Transformation

SONIA E. ROLLAND

Northeastern University School of Law

DAVID M. TRUBEK

University of Wisconsin School of Law

CAMBRIDGE
UNIVERSITY PRESS

CAMBRIDGE
UNIVERSITY PRESS

University Printing House, Cambridge CB2 8BS, United Kingdom

One Liberty Plaza, 20th Floor, New York, NY 10006, USA

477 Williamstown Road, Port Melbourne, VIC 3207, Australia

314–321, 3rd Floor, Plot 3, Splendor Forum, Jasola District Centre,
New Delhi – 110025, India

79 Anson Road, #06–04/06, Singapore 079906

Cambridge University Press is part of the University of Cambridge.

It furthers the University's mission by disseminating knowledge in the pursuit of
education, learning, and research at the highest international levels of excellence.

www.cambridge.org
Information on this title: www.cambridge.org/9781107129061
DOI: 10.1017/9781316416020

© Sonia E. Rolland and David M. Trubek 2019

First published 2019

Printed and bound in Great Britain by Clays Ltd, Elcograf S.p.A.

A catalogue record for this publication is available from the British Library.

Library of Congress Cataloging-in-Publication Data
Names: Rolland, Sonia E., author. | Trubek, David M., 1935–, author.
Title: Emerging powers in the international economic order : cooperation, competition,
and transformation / Sonia E. Rolland and David M. Trubek.
Description: New York : Cambridge University Press, 2019. | Series: Cambridge
international trade and economic law
Identifiers: LCCN 2019019490
Subjects: LCSH: Law and economic development. | Developing countries – Foreign
economic relations. | Cooperation – Economic aspects – Developing countries. |
International economic relations.
Classification: LCC K3820 .R655 2019 | DDC 343.07–dc23
LC record available at https://lccn.loc.gov/2019019490

ISBN 978-1-107-12906-1 Hardback

CONTENTS

TABLES

PREFACE

This book had a long gestation period. It originated over six years ago when separately we began to explore the significance of the BRICS countries for the future of international economic law. In the ensuing years, the scene we have studied has changed dramatically.

We had come at the issue from different directions. Sonia, who had honed her skills as a trade and investment law expert, looked at the issue from within this field but sought to understand the broader significance of technical debates. Dave, whose expertise lay largely in the economics, politics, and domestic legal issues affecting economic development, sought to understand the role of international legal institutions in the development trajectories of countries like Brazil, India and China. We saw that by pooling scholarly expertise we could carry out an integrated investigation of these trends.

We saw that to one degree or another BRICS country development strategies were in conflict with aspects of world trade and investment law. The rules of the WTO and bilateral investment treaties (BITs) created a system that sought to remove most barriers to the free flow of goods and capital. These rules put pressure on emerging economies to change some of their development policies: China, India, Russia and Brazil all shared heterodox approaches to development frowned on by trade and investment law. We saw that these countries were increasing their share of the global economy and asked whether they might band together with South Africa in the BRICS bloc to resist these strictures and even reverse them.

Six years on these issues are still with us but the scene has changed dramatically and many things we thought might happen did not occur while developments we failed to anticipate are shaking up the landscape. When we started, the advanced countries of the Global North were perfecting the system of market-oriented rules and they expected that emerging economies would gradually accept them. Today the United States has walked away from the liberal system it created and threatens to upend core institutions. When we started, China was an important country but not yet perceived as an economic and political colossus capable of asserting global economic leadership. When we started, many thought China would gradually evolve into a mixed-economy capitalist system: today it is clear it has no intent to abandon state capitalism and Party leadership. When we started, it looked as if China and the United States were on mutually supportive paths: now they may be locked in outright economic warfare. When we started, Brazil was re-establishing its commitment to state-led growth and eager for alliances with other emerging economies: today a newly installed administration promises to reverse those developmentalist policies and rejects any South–South orientation.

As a result, the story that we tell in the book is far more complex than the ideas we had when we started. To be sure, emerging economies still adhere to policies that bring them in conflict with some aspects of international economic law. And in some cases they have taken steps to resist or even change those rules. But no unified approach ever developed and resistance has been largely ad hoc and pragmatic. Emerging economies sought to use as much of the liberal trading order as they could to promote their own export drives while trying to temper its impact on their domestic development strategies. There was some coordinated resistance at the WTO to efforts to expand trade and investment disciplines, but no coherent counter-model ever emerged and the BRICS – as such – never became an effective source of new rules.

As this book goes to press, there are strong indications that the world order that evolved after World War II and took final shape after the collapse of the Soviet Union is coming apart. The most dramatic evidence comes from the actions of the Trump administration, which has questioned the very foundation of that order. But other forces are also at work. Regional differences and policy divergences create centrifugal forces that undermine the global system created by the WTO and BITs The world seems to be moving to a more plural and pluralist system for the governance of transnational economic flows. The emerging economies are playing an important role in the evolution of such an order. We hope our book, which charts their dissatisfaction with the old order, may help the construction of a new one.

The project has required in-depth study over time. We have interviewed and reinterviewed trade officials, lawyers and other actors in several key countries and consulted trade and investment law scholars from the Global North and South. We want especially to thank Michelle Sanchez and Fabio Morosini from the FGV Law School in Sao Paulo. We had excellent research assistants including Sarah Marinho, now a graduate student at the University of Sao Paulo and the University of Wisconsin–Madison, and Sara Higgins, Tidimalo Ngakane, Flora Chang, Andrew Manz-Siek and Amy Pimentel, now graduates of Northeastern University.

We benefited from the opportunity to present parts of the book at various universities and professional conferences including UC–Irvine, Loyola of Chicago, Harvard Law School, the University of Wisconsin–Madison, FGV São Paulo and the American Society of International Law and we acknowledge comments from participants in those events and from David Singh Grewal of Yale Law School.

Sonia acknowledges support from Northeastern University School of Law and Dave from the University of Wisconsin–Madison, Harvard Law School Center for the Legal Profession, and FGV.

TABLE OF TREATIES AND CONVENTIONS

TABLE OF TREATIES AND CONVENTIONS   xxi

TABLE OF CASES

WTO CASES

Argentina – Poultry Anti-Dumping Duties: Panel Report, *Argentina – Definitive Anti-Dumping Duties on Poultry from Brazil*, WT/DS241/R, adopted May 19, 2003, DSR 2003:V, p. 1727.

Argentina – Preserved Peaches: Panel Report, *Argentina – Definitive Safeguard Measure on Imports of Preserved Peaches*, WT/DS238/R, adopted April 15, 2003, DSR 2003: III, p. 1037.

Brazil – Taxation: Panel Reports, *Brazil – Certain Measures concerning Taxation and Charges*, WT/DS472/R, Add.1 and Corr.1 / WT/DS497/R, Add.1 and Corr.1, as modified by Appellate Body Report WT/DS472/AB/R, WT/DS497/AB/R, circulated December 13, 2018.

Canada – Aircraft: Panel Report, *Canada – Measures Affecting the Export of Civilian Aircraft*, WT/DS70/R, adopted August 20, 1999, upheld by Appellate Body Report WT/DS70/AB/R, DSR 1999:IV, p. 1443.

Canada – Aircraft (Article 21.5 – Brazil): Appellate Body Report, *Canada – Measures Affecting the Export of Civilian Aircraft – Recourse by Brazil to Article 21.5 of the DSU*, WT/DS70/AB/RW, adopted August 4, 2000, DSR 2000:IX, p. 4299.

Canada – Aircraft Credits and Guarantees: Panel Report, *Canada – Export Credits and Loan Guarantees for Regional Aircraft*, WT/DS222/R and Corr.1, adopted February 19, 2002, DSR 2002:III, p. 849.

Canada – Aircraft Credits and Guarantees (Article 22.6 – Canada): Decision by the Arbitrator, *Canada – Export Credits and Loan Guarantees for Regional Aircraft – Recourse to Arbitration by Canada under Article 22.6 of the DSU and Article 4.11 of the SCM Agreement*, WT/DS222/ARB, February 17, 2003, DSR 2003:III, p. 1187.

Chile – Price Band System: Panel Report, *Chile – Price Band System and Safeguard Measures Relating to Certain Agricultural Products*, WT/DS207/R, adopted October 23, 2002, as modified by Appellate Body Report WT/DS207AB/R, DSR 2002:VIII, p. 3127.

Chile – Price Band System (Article 21.3(c)): Award of the Arbitrator, *Chile – Price Band System and Safeguard Measures Relating to Certain Agricultural Products – Arbitration under Article 21.3(c) of the DSU*, WT/DS207/13, March 17, 2003, DSR 2003:III, p. 1237.

China – Raw Materials: Panel Reports, *China – Measures Related to the Exportation of Various Raw Materials*, WT/DS394/R, Add.1 and Corr.1 / WT/DS395/R, Add.1 and

ABBREVIATIONS

AB	– Appellate Body
ACP Group	– African, Caribbean and Pacific Group of States
AEC	– Asian Economic Community
AFTA	– ASEAN Free Trade Area
AIIB	– Asian Infrastructure Investment Bank
ALBA	– Bolivian Alternative for the Peoples of Our America
AU	– African Union
APDev	– African Platform for Development Effectiveness
AGOA	– African Growth and Opportunity Act
APEC	– Asia–Pacific Economic Cooperation
ASEAN	– Association of Southeast Asian Nations
BEE	– Black Economic Empowerment (South Africa)
BIT	– Bilateral investment treaty
BNDES	– National Bank for Economic and Social Development (Brazil)
BRICS	– Brazil, Russia, India, China and South Africa
BRI	– Belt and Road Initiative (formerly "One Belt One Road" or OBOR)
CECA	– Comprehensive Economic Cooperation Agreement
CETA	– EU–Canada Trade Agreement
CIFA	– Cooperation and Investment Facilitation Agreements
Cotton-4	– West African coalition comprising Benin, Burkina Faso, Chad and Mali
CBD	– Convention on Biological Diversity
COMESA	– Common Market for Eastern and Southern Africa
Crore INR	– denotes ten million Indian Rupee and is equal to 100 lakh in the Indian numbering system as 1,00,00,000 with the local style of digit group separators (a lakh is equal to one hundred thousand and is written as 1,00,000)
CPTPP	– Comprehensive and Progressive Trans-Pacific Partnership
EAC	– East African Community
ECOWAS	– Economic Community of West African States
EU	– European Union

EPAs	– Economic Partnership Agreements
GSP	– Generalised System of Preferences
FDI	– Foreign direct investment
FET	– Fair and equitable treatment
FTA	– Free trade agreement
GATT	– General Agreement on Tariffs and Trade
GDP	– Gross Domestic Product
ICJ	– International Court of Justice
ICSID	– World Bank's International Center for the Settlement of Investment Disputes
IEL	– International Economic Law
IMF	– International Monetary Fund
INR	– Indian Rupee
IP	– Intellectual Property
ISDS	– Investor-state dispute settlement
JNN Solar Mission	– Jawaharlal Nehru Solar Mission
JV	– Joint venture
LDC	– Least Developed Countries
MERCOSUR	– Mercado Común del Sur
MFN	– most favored nation
MIGA	– Multilateral Investment Guarantee Agency
NAMA-11	– Group of 11 developing countries, working to strengthen Non-Agricultural Market Access
NIEO	– New International Economic Order
NEPAD	– New Partnership for Africa's Development
NGOs	– Non-Governmental Organizations
OECD	– The Organization for Economic Co-operation and Development
PTA	– Preferential trade area
RCEP	– Regional Comprehensive Economic Partnership
R&D	– Research and development
RTA	– regional trade agreements are defined as reciprocal trade agreements between two or more partners
SDT	– Special and differential treatment provisions
SOE	– State owned enterprises
SDR	– Special drawing rights
SADC	– Southern African Development Community
TPP	– Trans-Pacific Partnership
TRIMS	– Agreement on Trade-Related Investment Measures
TRIPS	– Agreement on Trade-Related Aspects of Intellectual Property Rights
TTIP	– Transatlantic Trade and Investment Partnership

UNCTAD	– United Nations Conference on Trade and Development
US	– United States
USTR	– United States Trade Representative
USD	– United States Dollar
UNASUR	– The Union of South American Nations
UNDP	– The United Nations Development Program
UNCITRAL	– United Nations Commission on International Trade Law
WWII	– World War II
WTO	– World Trade Organization
WTO+	– WTO Plus
WB	– World Bank
WIPO	– World Intellectual Property Organization

1

Introduction

This book offers an account of emerging economies' positioning in trade and investment law. We explore the tension between development policies and the demands of the liberal trade and investment ordering, and consider whether a robust alternative vision has or could emerge in the Global South. While our research reveals a constellation of legal innovations from the Global South that depart from the mainstream liberal model, it also concludes that such contributions to law and policy are driven by pragmatism and strategic self-interest rather than more traditional political economy ideological orientations. This in turn has implications for the future of global economic governance. Unlike the socialist-inspired political economy models, or Non-Alignment endeavors, these legal moves do not aspire to coalesce into an alternative ordering for global governance. Emerging countries are not displaying a clear intention to dismantle the current ordering.

We face a watershed moment in international economic law, resulting from the confluence of a number of long-term trends.

First, the field is rife with clashes of values and interests. States in the Global North, encouraged by multinational corporations, push to further open global markets, reduce the role of the state in the economy, and provide special protection for foreign investors. States in the Global South resist some of these pressures in the name of development, maintain a commitment to state-led growth, and demand more control over their domestic markets and opportunities abroad for their exporters. These tensions translate into stalemates over the scope of existing rules, struggles to create new ones, and even fears that the multilateral rule-based system itself will collapse.

Second, the respective weights of developing and developed economies in the world economy are shifting, as the former are overtaking the latter

1

in share of world gross domestic product. Over all this looms China. In recent years, China has become more assertive on the world stage. It has doubled down on its commitment to state-led growth and announced policies that conflict with existing and proposed rules. As its economy grows in both absolute terms and relative to that of the United States and European Union (EU), and it strengthens relations with other developing countries, China's capacity to influence trade and investment policy grows apace.

Third, we are in a time of institutional and governance softening. On one hand, multilateral economic institutions continue to face a legitimacy deficit, and now suffer from relative disengagements from their traditional supporters, the United States and the EU. On the other hand, the large developing countries, sometimes dubbed "middle income" countries by economists, have failed to rise to this governance challenge either individually or collectively.

Could we be witnessing the end of the post-war liberal order and the emergence of a China-led order more supportive of Global South values? It is clear that China will have more and more to say about the multilateral ordering, but it is neither ready nor willing to remake the current system from which it has benefited significantly. Indeed, a closer look at the struggles of China and the rest of the Global South with the liberal trade and investment regime reveals a much more complex picture. Far from trying to overturn the liberal trade order, China and other emerging economies have sought to use it to promote their interests while resisting efforts to extend the regime in ways that challenge their core values and interests. Similarly, while emerging economies have also resisted aspects of the global investment protection system, most have accepted many of its tenets, and some continue to sign Bilateral Investment Treaties (BITs), albeit in modified form.

Despite tensions between the current system of international economic law (IEL) and the policy preferences of many emerging economies, countries of the Global South have managed to achieve some kind of balance between the neoliberal thrust of the system and their desire to pursue strategies that – from a neoliberal viewpoint – are heterodox. The result is a system they can use to further their own ends, and one that intrudes on their policy space only to a tolerable degree.

We might think of this confluence as a "truce" between a radical liberalization/marketization campaign and strong resistance in the name of state-led growth and sovereignty. The truce is acceptable to the countries of the South because the system benefits them to some extent; they lack a clear alternative ordering; and even if they had identified a substitute model, they lack the political structure and discipline to mount a concerted action to implement it. Likewise, the truce is acceptable to the North because it has given those economies sufficient access to lucrative markets in the South, and cheap imports, while ostensibly allowing social protection at home for those dislocated by trade liberalization. That is not to say that this status quo represents a normative, political, social or economic optimum. It is at best a working compromise, an uneasy one fraught with costs that are born unequally by all parties involved.

This truce may be characterized as "embedded neoliberalism" echoing John Ruggie's famous description of an "embedded liberalism" regime that emerged from World War II. Ruggie coined the term to describe the compromise between allowing goods and capital to flow freely around the world as they had in the heyday of the gold standard, and allowing national governments to control such flows and develop social protection systems to protect against destabilizing shocks. Updating the idea of a compromise between discordant policies, we might call today's regime embedded neoliberalism, where free market globalization is governed by a multilateral rule system designed for capitalist market economies but tempered by a series of policies and strategies that allow some deviation from capitalist market organization, and allow some protectionism, along with social protection to cushion import shocks.

While we outline the case that a form of embedded neoliberalism emerged, we argue that it may not endure. It was understood that China and other countries that were committed to state-led growth deviated from the free market capitalist model that the rule system presupposed, but it was assumed they would eventually join the mainstream. What happens when that faith fades? Will the North no longer tolerate the favorable rules, exceptions, avoidance and evasion upon which the truce rested?

There is evidence on both sides that the truce is unraveling. Some of the premises underlying the settlement have come unstuck. China has made it clear that it has no intention of abandoning its state-led model. Systems of social protection in the North are proving inadequate to protect the losers from the shocks of market opening, thus undermining the legitimacy of adherence to the multilateral system as it is currently designed, and creating domestic backlash against the system. The United States now questions many of the trade rules and processes of the post-WWII regime, as does the EU in the field of investment. The World

Trade Organization (WTO) (and the GATT before that), long the lynch-pin of the regime, has largely stalled as a negotiation forum, and its preeminence is being challenged by unilateral moves by the United States, as well as the emergence of competing mega-regional free trade agreements such as the Comprehensive and Progressive Trans-Pacific Partnership (CPTPP) and the Regional Comprehensive Economic Partnership (RCEP). If the truce flounders, can a new equilibrium be found, and what would be its defining features? Alternatively, what would the failure to cooperate between the major trading powers, old and new, mean for the world order and for smaller emerging economies?

I Making the System Work for the South: Embedded Neoliberalism

Behind the theory of embedded neoliberalism lies the claim that developing economies have been able to make use of the liberal trade and investment regime to support their development strategies without having to adopt the full gamut of neoliberal prescriptions. The evidence supports that thesis. A growing number of emerging countries are successfully utilizing the existing trade law system in support of their development policies. Particularly noteworthy are victories in dispute settlement, the use of flexibilities such as trade remedies, and the successful resistance against the expansion of free trade disciplines. On the investment side, the design of traditional BITs involved host countries agreeing to provide extensive protections to foreign investors (post-establishment protections), but host countries typically retain control over access of investors to their markets (limited pre-establishment constraints). In practice, they made extensive use of sectoral exclusions and other policy tools to limit foreign investors in certain parts of their economy, typically in sectors touching on security, energy and what they viewed as government services (health, education). Additionally, countries like South Africa and India have pushed back, while Brazil pursued a different approach altogether, without significantly affecting the flow of foreign direct investment (FDI) to its economy.

A Developing Countries Use the WTO to Gain Access to Markets in the North and South

At the WTO, emerging countries have prevailed in a number of disputes against developed members whose policies restricted their access to markets. The EU lost challenges brought by China, Brazil, Thailand, India, Argentina, Indonesia and Peru. The United States lost against China, Brazil, Thailand, India, Argentina, Indonesia, Venezuela, Chile, Antigua and Barbuda, Ecuador, Mexico and Pakistan. Brazil prevailed over Canada. Indonesia won against South Korea.

However, challenges of implementation in their favor somewhat dampen these apparent victories. Indeed, developing members make up a disproportionate number of complainants in retaliation proceedings and other findings of noncompliance, compared to their proportion in disputes. A number of additional cases were withdrawn or settled without a decision by a panel or arbitrator.

Developing members also successfully challenge each other's trade restrictions. China, Brazil, India, Indonesia, Argentina, Costa Rica, Honduras, Guatemala, El Salvador, the Dominican Republic, Mexico, Guatemala, Panama, Colombia, Turkey, Egypt, the Philippines and Thailand have all been involved in disputes against each other where one party was found in breach of its obligations.

B   Developing Countries Use Trade Remedies and Other Flexibilities to Protect Domestic Industries

A number of avenues exist to modulate general IEL obligations. Some are available to and used by a wide range of states albeit for different objectives. For instance, many developing countries try to maintain industrial policies in the face of neoliberal restrictions thanks to the widespread use of trade remedies such as safeguards, antidumping duties and countervailing duties.

In some cases these measures have been challenged at the WTO and countries have been required to end them. In many more cases, the use of these measures is adjudicated and policed domestically, with international trade law operating as a somewhat remote framework. In the face of massive use of these trade remedies domestically, the international system lacks the capacity to effectively deter strategic abuses.

Trade remedies are not the only escape from restrictions: developing countries avail themselves of additional flexibilities within the WTO trade regime available more specifically to them, including exceptions to most-favored nation obligations for the Generalized System of Preferences, preference programs among developing countries, and ad hoc waivers to other provisions in particular circumstances.

C   In Practice, the Dispute Process Enables Developing Countries to Temporarily Adopt Policies That Contravene the Rules

Even when an exception or waiver is not available, the design of the dispute settlement system results in practice in members breaching their obligations with relatively little economic cost before another member is able to retaliate. The increasingly lengthy WTO disputes settlement process, combined with the fact that a losing party need not offer remedies for past damages, means that several years may pass before a member is forced to withdraw or compensate for a breach.

Developed and developing members make use of this de facto flexibility mechanism. The notorious bananas dispute between various African, Caribbean and Pacific Group (ACP) members and the United States against the EU has been ongoing since the inception of the WTO. More recently, India's solar energy development program continues to offer WTO-incompatible subsidies to domestic producers more than eight years after the inception of the measures challenged by the United States. As India and the United States continue to debate whether and what type of retaliation the latter may be able to impose on India, the program moves steadily toward its forecasted completion date of 2022. In other words, it is possible that India will have designed and implemented a twelve-year-long domestic industrial support program in breach of WTO obligations without providing compensation to affected foreign parties.

China appears to follow a different tactic for creating policy space for its industrial policy. Rather than capitalizing on dispute settlement delays, China makes it difficult for challenges to be brought in the first place. It does so by taking vast ranges of measures that individually, might not be challengeable, and collectively, are difficult to circumscribe. Moreover, measures are often in place for shorter periods of time (although they are in the service of longer-term objectives). Foreign businesses are left to navigate this labyrinthine legal system, identify potential WTO breaches and persuade their governments to bring a complex dispute against a regulatory environment that is constantly shifting.

D   Developing Countries Have Successfully Blocked Extension of the Rules

Lastly, and perhaps most importantly, developing countries have successfully resisted the expansion of the trade liberalization agenda at the

WTO. In the 1990s, they prevailed in largely excluding the "Singapore issues" (investment, competition, government procurement and trade facilitation) from trade negotiations and eventually stalled the launch of a new round of negotiations altogether at the Seattle Ministerial Meeting. In the Doha Work Programme, emerging countries have asserted their voices to limit the scope of negotiations on items they disfavored, and to include topics of interest to them. In the first few years of the round, they gained some concessions on access to medicine and subsidies reduction on cotton from the United States. While the topic of trade facilitation had been one that India and other "refuseniks" of the Singapore Ministerial Meeting had rejected, the disciplines that emerged two decades later likely took a fundamentally different shape thanks to coordinated leadership from several developing countries. The Trade Facilitation Agreement inaugurated a new type of progressive, capacity-based obligation tied to offers for financial support for implementation from richer countries.

Similarly, while emerging economies have resisted aspects of the global investment protection system, most have accepted many of its values, and some continue to sign investment agreements with more restricted investment protections. States opposing the system, most notably Brazil, were able to refrain from entering into BITs while continuing to access global capital markets for investment. Even countries such as India, South Africa, Indonesia and Ecuador, which more recently retrenched from their participation in BITs, do not appear to have suffered significant capital outflow in response.

While we argue that these compromises and strategies resulted in something of an equilibrium, we do not suggest that the international trade and investment law system serves the interests of developing countries adequately or equitably. Moreover, hard-won concessions in favor of emerging countries often revealed themselves to be pyrrhic victories. The status quo was, in many ways, an agreement to disagree, made of a combination of effective resistance to new rules, de jure and de facto derogations, and strategic noncompliance. The post-2008 period, however, called this truce into question.

II Is the Truce About to Be Broken?

From every quarter of the globe, unpredictable political economy choices and normative heterogeneity suggest that we are in a period of legal and

institutional instability. We view changes in Chinese and U.S. trade
policies and development strategies as particularly salient.

A   Trade Policy Changes in the Face of Resurgent Chinese State Capitalism

Far from promising to further move toward market-oriented policies and
liberalization, China has made clear that it is committed to maintaining
its unique form of state-dominated economic strategy. In an effort to
catch up with and surpass the more established economies, China has
announced the "Made in China 2025" action plan, which outlines a ten-
year strategy to build intelligent manufacturing capabilities, enhance
innovation, and upgrade ten key sectors. Many believe this vast new
industrial policy contains numerous violations of WTO law. China is
expanding its influence all over the world, creating new alliances and
institutions and making massive investments. Its rapid upgrading of
industrial and technological skills has allowed it to emerge as a major
competitor to the older industrial powers. Chinese producers and investors' dramatic expansion into Asian, African and Latin American markets is settling into an enduring trend that offers destination countries
new alternatives to their traditional partners.

Strategies in response to this new reality are eroding the embedded
neoliberalism truce. Across the political spectrum in old industrial
powers, progressive and conservative voices, liberal and protectionist
interests concur to cast China as a political, economic and military threat,
a manipulator of the rules. The March 2018 consolidation of power by
China's Xi Jinping further heightened concerns. Taking the lead is the
United States. The first U.S. effort was the Trans-Pacific Partnership
(TPP), which sought to create a more market-oriented space in the
Asian Pacific region. Some saw this as an indirect way to pressure
China to liberalize. After withdrawing from the TPP, the Trump admin-
istration announced a zero-tolerance policy to China's heterodox strate-
gies, in a decisive break from the embedded neoliberal compromise.

Elsewhere, critics differ sharply as to the appropriate response to
China. Some opt to push back on the perceived threats with protectionist
policies, trade litigation, investment restrictions, rapprochement with
like-minded countries and a general hardening of the political discourse.
Others prefer to join China as a new locus of power, influence and
economic opportunity, as demonstrated by the support of the Asian
Infrastructure Investment Bank (AIIB), the Regional Comprehensive

Economic Partnership (RCEP), and Belt and Road Initiative (BRI, formerly known as One Belt One Road). For instance, the collapse of Transatlantic Trade and Investment Partnership (TTIP) negotiations and rise of the AIIB are causing some European countries to shift their negotiation efforts from West to East, while Latin America seeks to maneuver between China, the United States, and Pacific region trade and investment deals.

B Investment Law Is Unsettled

As investment increasingly originates from the Global South and is directed toward old industrialized countries and developing countries alike, the traditional foreign investment legal model is also under attack.

A broad range of legal experimentation is afoot to reframe legal disciplines, the balance of rights of investors and host countries, and the nature and reach of dispute settlement. Countries as diverse as Indonesia, Brazil, South Africa and some Bolivarian-oriented countries (Bolivia, Colombia, Ecuador, Panama, Peru and Venezuela) wish to reassert the preeminence of the state as an arbiter of investment policy and protection. China, which is also a proponent of such policies with regard to inbound investment flows, finds itself more in line with the pro-investor protections enshrined in traditional BITs when it comes to its outward investment.

Investor–state dispute settlement is becoming a highly sensitive pressure point for states. Brazil holds steadfast to its refusal to sign bilateral investment treaties with investor–state dispute resolution clauses. Indonesia, South Africa and others are withdrawing or letting lapse their BITs. The legitimacy of ICSID and other investor–state investment dispute resolution entities is called into question by developed and developing countries alike.

To various degrees, developing countries are manifesting their dissatisfaction with the embedded neoliberalism truce by challenging many traditional features of investment law. These moves may help to reshape investment law. However, the contours of investment law are also shifting, as China, in particular, blurs the lines between public development aid and outward investment. Similarly, rules of origin in trade treaties and some modalities for trade in services are really legal frameworks that condition and affect how and where to locate production, which is a core issue for foreign investment flows.

C   Restricted by IEL, the Social Safety Net Fails to Offset Shocks

International economic regulation implemented in the 1990s, including the proliferation of BITs and trade agreements generally aligned with the WTO, was fundamentally designed to achieve convergence in economic and social policies toward a capitalist, liberal democracy model. Special and differential treatment at the WTO assumes temporary deviations pending full commitment to a mainstream free trade agenda; Washington Consensus policies require privatization and a general curtailing of state intervention in the economy.

The theory was that states would manage and offset the costs of liberalization domestically, as dictated by their particular social contracts. Studies have shown that some states are unable or unwilling to uphold these social contracts. While theories abound as to the reason for such failings, IEL arguably plays a role because it increasingly constrains domestic policy instruments in the name of market opening. For instance, BITs are used to attempt to restrict states' ability to enact regulatory measures in public health, the environment, taxation and other fields. The WTO agreements ostensibly leave it to states to determine the level of regulatory protection they wish to maintain in these areas, but in practice, interpretative standards such as the requirement for the "least trade-restrictive alternative," the expiration of exceptions for certain subsidies, and the tightening of government procurement disciplines, all constrain states' policy options. While robust social safety nets, as cornerstones of the domestic political bargain, tend to be thought of as a Western European feature, they are also mainstays in many middle-income emerging countries. The liberalization of agricultural markets is a major source of concern in India, where food security and government-provided basic food supply are key to social peace and the livelihood of millions of the nation's poorest. The divestment of energy and water supply management to foreign investors in many Latin American and African countries similarly has had a mixed track record in its impact on social stability.

Further, the failure of the social safety net in much of the North fully to cushion trade shocks is one cause of the populist backlash against the trade regime, and provides support for those who want to forego the embedded neoliberal bargain by cracking down on deviations from market principles. At the same time, it poignantly reveals to China and other emerging countries the flaws in liberal capitalism, reducing their incentive to join the system. It was once thought that IEL would manage external liberalization for the greater good and states would mitigate individual costs domestically based on their own policy preferences. But this has not happened: there are many causes for the failure of domestic mitigation, but IEL limitations on states' ability to accomplish the domestic part of the equation have clearly played a role.

III   A New Equilibrium?

If the truce we described in the first part is indeed faltering, what will come in its place? Will emerging countries shift from their old position as rule-takers to a new role as rule-makers of IEL, and if so, with what result?

Transformations of the relationship between development and international economic law stem from the confluence of domestic shifts regarding development economics theory and practice on one hand, and global shifts with respect to the international institutions of economic governance on the other hand.

A   A New Political Economy of Development?

The domestic landscape regarding development economics has changed dramatically over the past two decades. The second half of the twentieth century witnessed the dominance of development economics models including fully or partly planned economies, import substitution strategies, self-reliance and export-led growth. Examples of these strategies are Latin American-style import substitution, promoting "national champions" sometimes based on prestige of a particular sector and cronyism rather than socioeconomic feasibility and desirability, and South Korea-style strict control of imports and domestic consumption to accelerate the development of industrial exports. All were informed by geopolitical ideologies ranging from communism to Wallerstein-inspired center/periphery theories of capitalism. Oil shocks, the fall of the Soviet Union, the end of the Cold War, and the globalization of the economy in the 1990s caused these dogmatic approaches to lose credibility as viable development models. Currency shocks, fiscal crises in emerging countries and the continued decline of the price of raw commodities, combined with the erosion of preferences further undermined post-World War II development policies.

In their place emerged a new developmental state characterized by economic heterodoxy, a more market-oriented understanding of economic development, a drive to innovate in public–private orderings, and efforts to empower certain communities or constituencies (women, youth). A number of states experimented with new industrial policies. Notwithstanding heterodoxy in their political economy, developmental states have in common some acceptance of the liberal order inasmuch as they virtually all seek FDI, they hope to expand their economic opportunities through exports and in many cases integration in global value chains, and they aspire to (and increasingly succeed in) becoming outward investors themselves.

B Alternative Global Governance Paradigms?

In the face of such pressures regarding the political economy of development, the issue of whether and to what extent emerging countries may be able to engage in alternative approaches to trade and investment regulation among themselves and in their relations to developed economies emerges as an important but under-theorized development. We would not expect a broad movement seeking to establish a new ordering, as the Non-Alignment participants had sought to do in the 1970s with the New International Economic Order (NIEO). There is no political drive among emerging countries to create a single alternative model, and the heterogeneous social and economic landscape of middle-income countries militates against a deep consensus for global governance. Any effort to reframe IEL from the Global South is also undermined by increased competition between developing countries. For instance, common economic interests of emerging countries, such as attracting FDI and increasing export markets, often turn into competition. Moreover, successfully implementing a new ordering would also require the participation or at least acquiescence of the old industrial powers, but they are also divided in their response to current developments.

In the early 2000s, the BRICS acronym designating Brazil, Russia, India, China and South Africa helped galvanize a shift in focus toward the impact of these countries and other emerging economies on international economic relations. Economic forecasts of the BRICS' growth, share of world trade, GDP, investment and foreign currency reserve have been somewhat less enthusiastic in the wake of the 2008 financial crisis. Still, the BRICS and other emerging economies are expected to continue to grow faster than old industrialized economies and eventually surpass their share of global GNP. At the political level, developments such as the creation of a BRICS development bank, a common currency reserve fund, and a network of think tanks, suggest, along with legal challenges at the WTO, that they are seeking to sidestep the Bretton Woods system and are making efforts to develop alternative legal and institutional frameworks for international economic law governance.

Such hopeful developments from the emerging powers are often contrasted with the state of play at the WTO, where the Doha Round negotiations appear to be mired in failure for the foreseeable future, or with the International Monetary Fund (IMF) and the Organisation for Economic Cooperation and Development (OECD), which have checkered records in dealing with the 2008 crisis.

Commentators typically offered two reactions to these developments. Some argued that the rise of the BRICS was overplayed and that their leadership aspirations were significantly undermined by ongoing governance problems, insufficient innovation, a questionable development model, and political and social instability. They predicted that the existing world order, created at Bretton Woods and augmented by the creation of the WTO, would continue to prevail. Others saw the dawn of a new era where the tables had turned on the old powers, and a revival of the effort to create a new NIEO. In this view, because the old rules of the game were stacked against emerging economies' development models, these countries would join together to resist the legal status quo, and eventually lead a transformation of the global economic order.

Certainly, transformations of the world order so far have not been as dramatic or as immediate as had been heralded. The BRICS could perhaps have parlayed their growing aggregate economic and political weight into a coherent new deal, but they did not. The 2008 financial crisis and ensuing global protectionist retrenchments, the rise of competing institutions such as the Chinese-led Asian Infrastructure Investment Bank, and political instability resulting from the rise of populism in developed countries all contributed to the demise of the BRICS as a political project, if it ever was. At the same time, the 1990s liberal consensus also became, to some extent, a casualty of the shifting economic and political landscape. The WTO is no longer an effective venue for further liberalization à l'américaine, and the bilateral investment treaty system is suffering a profound legitimacy crisis.

Perhaps the emerging countries' main point of agreement is their desire to reassert the exercise of their sovereignty in economic relations and pull back from the "communautarization" of decision-making in international and intergovernmental organization and their adjudicatory bodies. By nature, this common interest has a centrifugal effect. Broader domestic policy autonomy would allow states to engage in a variety of pathways for development and economic policy. At the same time, the reality of economic interconnection and transboundary value chains still requires states to engage in some degree of international cooperation and coordination. We therefore see a plural normative landscape where groups of countries experiment with different levels and types of joint economic policy making and commitments.

Developed countries also feel the appeal of such a move, thus bolstering the Global South's embrace of a plural normative landscape. The old powers' relative retrenchment from the neoliberal order that they created manifests itself in a number of ways. The EU's drive to create a new investor–state dispute resolution system and to export it to its partners, the resurgence of old-fashioned protectionism in the trail of populist electoral successes, and the fracturing of the liberal social democracy order all contribute to the diversification of IEL. Such trends also mean that there is no longer a powerful, homogeneous core that might galvanize opposition from the Global South. In other words, why would we see an "us" of the Global South if there is no "them" to point at? If that is the case, then the result could be some degree of retreat from global governance rather than a new form of state-centric global governance.

Lastly, international economic relations increasingly bypass the international law framework in ways that affect both the normative content and the institutional role of IEL. Global value chains and their private normative and ordering features have been on the rise since the 1990s. More recently, the boundary between public aid to development and private foreign investment has become blurred with the practices of Chinese outward investment in developing countries under the aegis of the Belt and Road Initiative and other legally soft frameworks. In many instances, such aid/investment uses private legal vehicles and private, domestic commercial law frameworks. It is not the purpose of this book to explore this extremely wide and complex field of public–private orderings and the host of new institutions that support it, ranging from the Dubai International Financial Centre courts to China's newly created International Commercial Court jurisdictions in Shenzhen, Beijing and Xi'an. Rather, this book focuses on trends and transformation in international public regulation, recognizing that the scope and impact of such public ordering is certainly affected by transnational, non-state dynamics.

This book delineates the scope of IEL legal and policy moves in the Global South, offers a narrative of the motivations for such evolutions, and assesses their impact.

Throughout the book we use a range of terminologies to designate different types of countries. Some categories are defined in absolute terms, some in relative economic terms, and some have political connotations.

In the first category lies "Least Developed Countries" (LDCs), which are listed by the United Nations based on composite criteria including both economic and social development factors. In international trade law, "developing country" is a self-designation label, which states may adopt and that typically gives them access to certain rights and exceptions. In the second category, focusing on relative economic descriptions, we place "emerging economies," which describes countries that industrialized since the 1960s and have experienced relatively significant annual economic growth. The third category (political terms) includes both developed and developing countries. These terms have no legal definition in international law, nor do they constitute fixed economic categories. Yet, they are ubiquitous terms in the discourse of international organizations, development agencies, and states themselves. While there is no set definition of these terms, they do reflect broadly understood sets of socioeconomic realities. "Global North" and "Global South" are also politically laden terms with a flawed sense of geography, but nonetheless familiar in law and development epistemological communities. We also use, including in the title of this book, the term "emerging power" to reflect the impact of the growing economic status of emerging economies on world power relations. Yet, this book is not about defining or redefining what constitutes power or who holds power. Rather, we posit that countries acting as agents of institutional change and originators of legal innovation are thus endowed with some measure of power. The book focuses on bringing to light this innovation and institutional change dynamics. Depending on the area of law, whether it be trade, investment, or public aid to development, different countries might be at the forefront of legal creativity or institutional change, and we use the "emerging power" label to include any such country. We are therefore not concerned with theorizing whether a particular country holds all the attributes of power, but instead use the term "power" to recognize actors capable of affecting a legal regime, even if in a limited sense.

The remainder of this book is organized as follows. The next three chapters demonstrate how developing countries position themselves as users and generators of a plural normative landscape. Chapter 2 demonstrates how a veneer of cooperation discourse among developing countries belies deep divergences in their political economy perspectives.

Chapter 3 argues that emerging powers manipulate the liberal ordering by engaging in selective compliance with existing rules and refusing to agree to some proposed liberal disciplines. Chapters 4 and 5 explore how and to what extent developing countries seek to create alternative investment and trade norms with more flexible standards. This in turn informs our concluding perspectives (Chapter 6) on the question of whether the emerging pattern of a plural normative landscape is a transitory phase destined to be displaced by a new consensus or hegemony, or whether it constitutes a steady state for at least the medium term.

2

Cooperation Narratives and Theoretical Divergences

This chapter focuses on the discourse emanating from developing countries regarding international economic law, particularly as it relates to liberalization and development. It highlights tensions between narratives of cooperation among developing countries and domestic realities of diverging interests and priorities. With respect to cooperation, the larger, middle-income countries and some regional groupings emphasize mutual respect for sovereignty and domestic political economy choices. Investment relations among them are ostensibly in support of domestically designed developmental projects and needs. South–South trade groups seek to unlock regional potential free from the political constraints that often accompany North–South trade relations. However, a closer consideration of the domestic discourse and political economy models of Brazil, China, India and African countries (in the context of regional groupings such as SADC- and African Union-sponsored initiatives) denotes significant divergences in objectives for trade and investment relations, as well as in the degree and means of economic liberalization.

The first part of this chapter examines investment relations among emerging countries, followed by a second part that considers trade liberalization dynamics in Brazil, China, India and Africa.

I A Discourse of South–South Cooperation: Investment for Development, Respect for Sovereignty

Some developing countries have heralded the need for South–South investment relationships that are cooperative, compared to what they perceive as the unbalanced, investor-controlled framework arising out of traditional BITs. Some commentators have even decried traditional BITs as a tool of postcolonial anti-communist

17

policies.[1] China's first major foray into foreign investment in the early 2000s was often characterized by a rhetoric of cooperation and mutual assistance. Brazil's new Cooperation and Investment Facilitation Agreements (CIFAs) are also firmly anchored in a discourse of South–South cooperation. However, whether the discourse of cooperation and developmental solidarity actually finds application in legal instruments calls for a nuanced answer. In practice, China blurred the boundaries between aid and development financing on one hand, and foreign direct investment (FDI) on the other hand, in new ways that are now becoming entrenched in the Asian Infrastructure Investment Bank and perhaps the BRICS Bank. Brazil's CIFAs, by contrast, reflect a return to a more diplomacy-led approach to foreign investment relations.

Overall, emerging economies are seeking to differentiate themselves from traditional BIT policies in the framing of foreign investment. Some treaties emphasize investment as a vector for development, understood in a more holistic way than simply a matter of increasing gross domestic product or other aggregate economic benchmarks. In that sense, investment is seen as embedded in social and economic development policies, rather than strictly in the business and finance environment. Additionally or alternatively, some countries prioritize, at least in the discourse, mutual respect for sovereignty and noninterference in domestic policy choices of the parties.

The Preamble to the South African Development Community Model Bilateral Investment Treaty ("SADC Model BIT") released in July 2012 provides an illustration:

> Recognizing the important contribution investment can make to the sustainable development of the State Parties, including the reduction of poverty, increase of productive capacity, economic growth, the transfer of technology, and the furtherance of human rights and human development ... Reaffirming the right of the State Parties to regulate and to introduce new measures relating to investments in their territories in order to meet national policy objectives, and – taking into account any asymmetries with respect to the measures in place – the particular need of developing countries to exercise this right ...[2]

---

[1] See, e.g., Mohammad Mossallam, *Process Matters: South Africa's Experience Exiting Its BITs*, GLOBAL ECON. GOVERNANCE PROGRAMME WORKING PAPER 2015/97 (Jan. 2015), http://dx.doi.org/10.2139/ssrn.2562417 (arguing that the majority of BITs reflect texts developed to promote anti-communist, post-decolonization protection agendas of the 1960s).

[2] See S. Afr. Dev. Cmty., SADC Model Bilateral Investment Treaty Template with Commentary art. 20–22, July 2012, www.iisd.org/itn/wp-content/uploads/2012/10/SADC-ModelBIT-Template-Final.pdf.

This approach is also reaffirmed in the operative, numbered provisions of the treaty such as article 1: "The main objective of this Agreement is to encourage and increase investments [between investors of one State Party into the territory of the other State Party] that support the sustainable development of each Party, and in particular the Host State where an investment is to be located."[3] Also in Africa, the guiding principles for the Pan African Investment Code (PAIC) currently being negotiated under the auspices of the African Union include:

(i) suit the national policies in order to scale up and maintain the Domestic Investment; (ii) create conducive business environment for sustainable growth; (iii) promote African integration process; (iv) ensure that the PAIC tackles the issue of Social Corporate and Environmental responsibility; and (v) attract FDI as one of the vehicles to sustain the development.[4]

The changes in the framing of the India Model BIT over time reveal underlying policy motivations. The Preamble of the 2003 Model BIT was very much in line with traditional BITs. It stated:

[d]esiring to create conditions favourable for fostering greater investment by investors of one State in the territory of the other State; [r]ecognising that the encouragement and reciprocal protection under International agreement of such investment will be conducive to the stimulation of individual business initiative and will increase prosperity in both States ...[5]

By contrast, the Draft 2015 Model BIT emphasized sovereignty and development:

[d]esiring to promote bilateral cooperation between the Parties with respect to foreign investments; and [r]eaffirming the right of Parties to regulate Investments in their territory in accordance with their Law and policy objectives including the right to change the conditions applicable to

---

[3] See id. at art. 1.
[4] See Third Conference of African Ministers in Charge of Integration (COMAI III) held in Abidjan, Côte d'Ivoire, on May 22–23, 2008, excerpted in Press Release, Pan-African Investment Code: African Independent Legal Experts Kicks Off in Djibouti, Press Release No. 292/2014, (Oct. 30, 2014) (describing the gathering of experts to "discuss and review the Pan African Investment Code"); see generally Makane Moïse Mbengue and Stefanie Schacherer, The 'Africanisation' of International Investment Law: The Pan-African Investment Code and the Reform of the International Investment Regime, 18 J. WORLD INVESTMENT & TRADE 414 (2017).
[5] Indian Model Text of BIPA, www.italaw.com/sites/default/files/archive/ita1026.pdf.

such Investments; and [s]eeking to align the objectives of Investment with sustainable development and inclusive growth of the Parties . . .[6]

The final 2016 Model BIT scales back on some of this language and adds the protection of investments as a core feature on par with investment promotion:

[r]ecognizing that the promotion and the protection of investments of investors of one Party in the territory of the other Party will be conducive to the stimulation of mutually beneficial business activity, to the development of economic cooperation between them and to the promotion of sustainable development, [r]eaffirming the right of Parties to regulate investments in their territory in accordance with their law and policy objectives.[7]

A clause in the Draft Model BIT to safe-harbor "the rights of either Party to formulate, modify, amend, apply or revoke its Law in good faith," and specifically that "[e]ach Party retains the right to exercise discretion with respect to regulatory, compliance, investigatory, and prosecutorial matters, including discretion regarding allocation of resources and establishment of penalties," was dropped in the final version. The evolution echoes economic and political developments since the 2003 Model BIT, as India has continued to liberalize conditions of establishment and ownership for foreign investors. The Modi administration, emanating from the more conservative Bharatiya Janata Party that came into power in 2014, has aggressively positioned itself as business oriented.

While Chinese BITs drafted in the 1980s merely included a brief reference to "principles of equality and mutual benefit" in their preambles and emphasized the business relationship between the host and home countries,[8] the following decade inaugurated a shift. The China–Bolivia

---

[6] Model Text for the Indian Bilateral Investment Treaty, www.jurisafrica.org/html/pdf_in dian-bilateral-investment-treaty.pdf [hereinafter Indian Draft Model BIT].

[7] Preamble, Government of India, Ministry of Finance, Department of Economic Affairs, Office memorandum, F. No. 26/5/2013-IC, Annex, Dec. 28, 2015 [hereinafter 2016 Indian Model BIT].

[8] *See, e.g.,* Agreement between the Government of the Democratic Socialist Republic of Sri Lanka and the Government of the People's Republic of China on the Reciprocal Promotion and Protection of Investments, China–Sri Lanka, Mar. 13, 1986, http://invest mentpolicyhub.unctad.org/Download/TreatyFile/781 (indicating that the parties desire "to create favourable conditions for greater economic co-operation between them and in particular for investments by nationals and companies of one State in the territory of the other State based on the principles of equality and mutual benefit" and recognize "that reciprocal encouragement, promotion and protection of such investments will be conducive to stimulating business initiative and increasing prosperity in both states . . . ").

BIT signed in 1992 provides an illustration. Its Preamble notes that the Parties enter into the agreement

> [d]esiring to encourage, protect and create favorable conditions for investment by investors of one Contracting State in the territory of the other Contracting State based on the principles of mutual respect for sovereignty, equality and mutual benefit and for the purpose of the development of economic cooperation between both States.[9]

Variants of this language appear in the 1990 China–Pakistan BIT, the 1989 China–Ghana BIT, the 1991 China–Mongolia BIT, the 1992 China–Philippines BIT and others ratified at various points during the decade.[10] However, not all Chinese BITs reflect the shift in language. Some of the 1990s BITs use the preambular language of the 1980s focused on business relations.[11]

---

[9] Agreement between the Government of the People's Republic [sic] of China and the Government of the Republic of Bolivia concerning the Encouragement and Reciprocal Protection of Investments, Bol.–China, May 8, 1992, http://investmentpolicyhub .unctad.org/Download/TreatyFile/449.

[10] Agreement between the Government of the Islamic Republic of Pakistan and the Government of the People's Republic of China concerning the Encouragement and the Reciprocal Protection of Investment, Dec. 2, 1989, http://investmentpolicyhub.unctad.org /Download/TreatyFile/766; Agreement between the Government of the People's Republic of China and the Government of the Republic of Ghana concerning the Encouragement and the Reciprocal Protection of Investment, China–Ghana, Dec. 2, 1989, http://investmentpolicyhub .unctad.org/Download/TreatyFile/737; Agreement between the Government of the People's Republic of China and the Government of the Mongolian People's Republic concerning the Encouragement and the Reciprocal Protection of Investment, Aug. 8, 1991, http://investment policyhub.unctad.org/Download/TreatyFile/760; Agreement between the Government of the People's Republic of China and the Government of the Republic of the Philippines concern- ing the Encouragement and the Reciprocal Protection of Investment, July 20, 1992, http:// investmentpolicyhub.unctad.org/Download/TreatyFile/769.

[11] See, e.g., Agreement between the Government of the Republic of Chile and the Government of the People's Republic of China concerning the Encouragement and the Reciprocal Protection of Investment, Chile–China, May 23, 1994, http://investmentpolicyhub .unctad.org/Download/TreatyFile/664; Agreement between the Government of the People's Republic of China and the Government of the Republic of Georgia concerning the Encouragement and the Reciprocal Protection of Investment, China–Geor., June 3, 1993, http://investmentpolicyhub.unctad.org/Download/TreatyFile/735; Agreement between the People's Republic of China and the Republic of Turkey concerning the Encouragement and the Reciprocal Protection of Investment, China–Turk., Nov. 13, 1990, http://investment policyhub.unctad.org/Download/TreatyFile/789; Agreement between the Government of the People's Republic of China and the Government of the Oriental Republic of Uruguay concerning the Encouragement and the Reciprocal Protection of Investment, China–Uru., Dec. 2, 1993, http://investmentpolicyhub.unctad.org/Download/TreatyFile/794 (all of the above detailing efforts to improve the financial well-being of both countries through "eco- nomic cooperation").

Brazil's CIFAs also reflect this new trend of framing South–South investment relations as more development oriented, and more mindful of each partner's sovereign policy choices, than the traditional BITs framework. Since 2015, Brazil has signed CIFAs with Angola, Chile, Colombia, Ethiopia, Malawi, Mexico, Mozambique, Peru and Suriname,[12] and has conducted negotiations with South Africa, Algeria, India, Morocco, Nigeria, Thailand and Tunisia.[13] For example, the Acordo de Cooperação e Facilitação de Investimentos entre o Governo da República Federativa do Brasil e o Governo da República de Moçambique (hereinafter "Mozambique CIFA") preamble affirms the development grounding and sovereign autonomy spirit of the agreement: "Recognizing the essential role of investment in promoting sustainable development, economic growth, poverty reduction, job creation, expansion of productive capacity and human development; . . . [r]eaffirming its legislative autonomy and space for public policies," followed by article 1 stating, "This Agreement aims at the cooperation between the Parties to facilitate and promote mutual investment."[14] The recently signed agreement with Mexico, Acuerdo de Cooperacion y de Facilitación de las Inversiones entre la República Federativa del Brasil y los Estados Unidos Mexicanos (hereinafter "Mexico CIFA"), has identical language.

For China and Brazil, the South–South cooperation approach goes beyond investment treaties and involves a multifaceted strategy ranging from overseas development assistance to investment through development finance, infrastructure building, subsidized loans, technical cooperation, and scholarship and cultural exchanges.[15] Brazil, Colombia, India and

---

[12] *Brazil: Bilateral Investment Treaties (BITs)*, United Nations Conference on Trade and Development: Investment Policy Hub, http://investmentpolicyhub.unctad.org/IIA/CountryBits/27 (identifying the countries with which Brazil has signed Cooperation and Investment Facilitation Agreements [CIFAs]).

[13] Brasil, Ministério das Relações Exteriores, Nota 104, Acordo Brasil–Angola de Cooperação e Facilitação de Investimentos (ACFI) – Luanda, April 1, 2015, www.itamaraty.gov.br/pt-BR/notas-a-imprensa/8520-acordo-brasil-angola-de-cooperacao-e-facilitacao-de-investimentos-acfi-luanda-1-de-abril-de-2015.

[14] Acordo de Cooperação e Facilitação de Investimentos entre o Governo da República Federativa do Brasil e o Governo da República de Moçambique, Braz.–Mozam., Mar. 30, 2015, http://investmentpolicyhub.unctad.org/Download/TreatyFile/4717; Acuerdo de Cooperacion y de Facilitación de las Inversiones entre la República Federativa del Brasil y los Estados Unidos Mexicanos, Braz.–Mex., May 26, 2015, http://investmentpolicyhub.unctad.org/Download/TreatyFile/4718, authors' translation (outlining the Cooperation and Facilitation Agreement [CIFA] between Brazil and Mexico).

[15] For Brazil, *see, e.g.*, Paolo de Renzio et al., *Brazil and South–South Cooperation: How to Respond to Current Challenges*, BRICS POL'Y CTR. CENTRO DE ESTUDOS E PESQUISAS, BPC POLICY BRIEF Vol. 3 No. 55, May 2013, http://bricspolicycenter.org/homolog/

other developing countries, with open support from China and the EU, are also considering a multilateral agreement on investment facilitation at the WTO.[16] Many of the standards discussed for such an agreement are similar to CIFA provisions, including the right to regulate, the focal point, and claims for transparency in investment applications.

II Theoretical Debates on the Relationship between Development and Trade

Trade policy debates in emerging countries are inseparable from development discourse in these states. Inasmuch as trade agreements are often criticized for the constraints they place upon developmental policies, the apparent eagerness of developing countries to enter into trade pacts may seem paradoxical. Their stance calls for a deeper analysis of the typical features of recent trade agreements and their relationship with state developmentalism.

A Brazil: A Grand Debate over Trade in a Time of Economic and Political Crisis[17]

Mega-regionals such as the TPP (now incorporated in the Comprehensive and Progressive Trans-Pacific Partnership) are influencing the Brazilian policy elite's debate over whether to seek a neoliberal path aligned with the North and its open trade policies, or whether state-led developmentalism, with its classic policies of domestic industrial support and resistance to unfettered economic liberalism, is the better way to promote socioeconomic growth. Current public discourse includes rhetoric about a need for change, and some calls to align with TPP-type policies. In actual trade negotiations, TPP-type standards influence Brazil's negotiations with the TPP-aligned Pacific Alliance and explorations of a rapprochement with the United States.

uploads/trabalhos/6780/doc/1583232112.pdf (describing Brazil's role in South–South development cooperation and the agencies that work in conjunction with the Brazilian agency for development cooperation).

[16] Joint Ministerial Statement on Investment Facilitation for Development, WT/MIN(17)/59, Dec. 13, 2017; ICTSD, Crafting a Framework on Investment Facilitation (2018), www.ictsd.org/sites/default/files/research/crafting_a_framework_on_investment_facilitation-ictsd-policy_brief.pdf.

[17] As the book went to press, Jair Bolsonaro became president of Brazil and announced a general shift toward more liberal economic policies.

Critics of Brazil's state-led development policies push for alignment with TPP-like standards because they see them as a way to curb the role of the state; "developmentalists" oppose liberalization for the same reason. The right-leaning Temer government announced it would seek trade agreements with "traditional partners," which everyone took to be the United States and European Union, and most understood would mean alignment with TPP-like standards for regulation. The Bolsonaro administration is even more vocal in its desire to reorient Brazil's trade policy toward the United States and the EU. Both the Temer and Bolsonaro administrations called for changes in the Mercosur agreement to allow Brazil to enter on its own into bilateral agreements affecting tariffs. Leading figures in these governments have criticized prior pro-South policies as driven by ideological and partisan goals, not pragmatic efforts that would further the national interest.[18] On the other hand, defenders of Workers' Party Presidents Lula da Silva and Dilma Rousseff pointed to TPP and noted that such an effort would inevitably mean watering down developmental policies that they think have served Brazil well; they urged Brazil to deepen ties with other developing countries in alliances more supportive of heterodox strategies.[19]

These narratives of alignment, global order, and the ways Brazil should participate in such an order are mostly rhetorical. Considering the political instability and the pressures on the economy from a severe ongoing recession, Brazil may have fewer options than the debate suggests. Those who argue for deeper trade relations with the United States may be disappointed: it is unclear whether the United States will offer to sign a preferential trade agreement with Brazil or, if it does, whether Brazil will find the terms attractive. On the other hand, there is no robust and fully developed alternative economic space that Brazil could easily

[18] Speech by Minister José Serra on the occasion of the ceremony in which he took office as Minister of Foreign Affairs, Brasília, May 18, 2016, www.itamaraty.gov.br/en/speeches-articles-and-interviews/minister-of-foreign-affairs-speeches/14044-speech-by-minister-jose-serra-on-the-occasion-of-the-ceremony-in-which-he-took-office-as-minister-of-for eign-affairs-brasilia-may-18-2016; inaugural speech by Paulo Guedes, Minister of the Economy, January 2, 2019, www.poder360.com.br/governo/da-ideologia-de-genero-ao-globalismo-assista-aos-discursos-do-governo-bolsonaro/. *See also* Aloysio Nunes, *Mercosur: más comercio, menos barreras,* EL CRONISTA, October 25, 2017, www.ita maraty.gov.br/pt-BR/discursos-artigos-e-entrevistas-categoria/ministro-das-relacoes-exteriores-artigos/17694-mercosul-mais-comercio-menos-barreras-el-cronista-argen tina-25-10-2017-espanhol.

[19] Celso Amorim, *Guinada à direita do Itamaraty,* FOLHA DE SAO PAULO, May 22, 2016, www1.folha.uol.com.br/mundo/2016/05/1773728-guinada-a-direita-no-itamaraty.shtml.

join. Latin America is split between the Alliance for the Pacific (Mexico, Colombia, Peru and Chile), which has aligned with the TPP, and the Bolivarian alternative, which rejects the United States completely. Brazil and Argentina have held the middle ground but may now be tilting toward the United States. China certainly represents an alternative development model, seemingly trying to use RCEP and the Belt and Road Initiative (BRI) to create an alternative economic space in Asia without the full panoply of TPP-type restrictions, and has made overtures to some countries in Latin America.[20] But given Brazil's geographic profile and export portfolio, an alliance with RCEP would come at the cost of facilitating Chinese imports and investments and likely loosening ties with the United States. Whether such a policy makes sense is questionable even if it proved feasible.

To conclude, it may be that the election in 2018 of right-leaning Jair Bolsonaro as president of Brazil will change this calculus and upend Brazil's foreign economic policy. The new administration talks of abandoning the developmentalist model, opening the economy, reaching out to the United States, and avoiding closer relations with China. All this, however, is easier said than done. China is Brazil's number one export market; the developmentalist model is deeply embedded in Brazilian culture and politics and receives support from groups across the political spectrum; and U.S. trade policy is particularly unpredictable at present.

B   China: State Planning Wins against Liberalism Overtures

The Chinese, like the Brazilians, have engaged in debate about development strategy and trade policy. Like Brazil, the trade debate is closely tied to the debate over development strategy. Those who favor moving further toward a free market economy push for greater engagement with the liberal trade order as a way to gain leverage for economic reform efforts.[21] While these views had substantial effect in the past, helping support China's entry into the WTO, lately the proponents of maintaining state-led development have been more influential. China is unique in the manner in which industrial and economic policies are implemented

---

[20] Jing Tao, *China and TPP: A Tale of Two Economic Orderings?*, in REGULATION CONTESTED: GLOBAL ECONOMIC ORDERING AFTER TPP (Benedict Kingsbury et al., eds., forthcoming Oxford University Press, 2019).

[21] Qingjiang Kong, *Emerging Rules in International Investment Instruments and China's Reform of State-Owned Enterprises*, 3 CHINESE J. GLOB. GOVERNANCE 57 (2017).

and the way the government controls the economy of the country. According to one observer,

> industrial policy is embraced by Chinese policy-makers as a justification of enduring political controls over the economic, sectoral and technological pathways of development. It is legitimized by its core advocates as a golden mean between economically suffocating full state control (as in the former administrative allocation system) and politically threatening market volatilities or dysfunctions (as seen in financial services driven economies).[22]

A particularly salient issue has been the role of state-owned enterprises (SOEs). Chinese SOEs continue to dominate the economy. While many have adopted some commercial practices and participated in competitive markets at home and abroad, Chinese SOEs exercise great market power through the system Mark Wu has called "China, Inc."[23] This involves a complex network of state, party and market relations that operates in ways different than almost any other economy and in which SOEs are at the apex. For trade partners, though, the connection between the state and enterprises generates fears of market manipulation.[24] Concerns include China mandating specific localization of manufacturing, forcing the transfer of technology, the state's control of trade distribution rights, and granting exclusive license to certain firms, thereby limiting other firms' ability to compete.[25]

Pro-market advocates in China have pushed for greater trade liberalization and further integration into the liberal economic order as a way to reduce the powers, often quasi-monopolistic, of the great SOEs.[26] While this line of thinking had support among China's elite at some point, support for privatization of SOEs seems to have waned as some SOEs have become major players in the global economy and key elements in China's current developmental strategy.[27] Chinese scholar Jing Tao notes that while some Chinese elites once accepted the idea that Washington Consensus policies were the road to growth, in recent years China has begun to show more confidence in its own path and to tout the heterodox

---

[22] SEBASTIAN HEILMANN & LEA SHIH, THE RISE OF INDUSTRIAL POLICY IN CHINA 21 (Harvard Yenching Institute, 2013).

[23] Marc Wu, *The China Inc. Challenge to Global Trade Governance*, 57 HARV. INT'L L.J. 261 (2016).

[24] *Id.* at 295.

[25] *Id.* at 297–9.

[26] Tao, *supra* note 20.

[27] *Id.*

"Beijing consensus," which puts state-led growth at the center of devel-opment strategy.[28] As China shows more confidence in its heterodox approach and we come to understand the unique features of China, Inc., it becomes clearer that state-led growth will remain at the core of China's strategy, and efforts to use trade law to reduce the role of the state in the economy will meet stiff resistance.

China's continued adherence to state-led development, and resistance to efforts by the United States and others to limit the role of SOEs, may be affecting its approach to global ordering. In the face of the TPP initiative, China moved to strengthen RCEP, the China-backed Asian mega-regional ordering which, unlike TPP, almost certainly will not impose direct restrictions on SOEs and will be generally more tolerant of indus-trial policy and other aspects of state-led development. With the U.S. withdrawal from TPP, China has stepped up the effort to conclude the RCEP negotiations, and made overtures to the Pacific Alliance coun-tries on the west coast of Latin America. The growing ties between militarist and geopolitical objectives, and economic strategies could lead China to try to move further away from the existing multilateral legal and institutional framework unless such moves are checked by the trade war with the United States.

C   India: Developmentalism Priorities, Liberal Aspirations

India has been moving away from its post-decolonization planned econ-omy model for several decades, largely through incremental changes. The trade liberalization process of the General Agreement on Tariffs and Trade (GATT) and WTO has long been the main venue for India's engagement on the international scene, but the country has also engaged in significant unilateral dismantling of trade barriers beyond what was mandated by multilateral rules.[29] The 1980–5 Five Year Plan put the country on the path to deregulation. Privatization began as a policy in 1991, marking a turning point for India's political economy.[30] India now

---

[28] Id.
[29] Shadan Farasat, India's Quest for Regional Trade Agreements: Challenges Ahead, 42 J. WORLD TRADE 433, 434 (2008).
[30] Ram Kumar Mishra, Role of State-Owned Enterprises in India's Economic Development, OECD Workshop on State-Owned Enterprises in the Development Process, April 4, 2014, at 4, 28, www.oecd.org/daf/ca/Workshop_SOEsDevelopmentProcess_ India.pdf; see also OECD, SOEs IN INDIA'S ECONOMIC DEVELOPMENT IN STATE-OWNED ENTERPRISES IN THE DEVELOPMENT PROCESS (2015); B. S. Chimni, Mapping Indian Foreign Economic Policy, 47 INT'L STUDIES 163 (2010).

boasts a number of large industrial conglomerates that act globally, such as Tata, Mittal, the TVS Group, Reliance Industries, Aditya Birla Group, Essar Group, Bharti Group, and OP Jindal. These companies are capitalized on the market or privately held within families; in many instances, they have bought foreign businesses – Jaguar's acquisition by Tata in 2008 being perhaps the most iconic display of Indian industrial globalization.

The Indian Constitution devotes a number of provisions to the establishment of a "social order for the promotion of welfare of the people" (article 38). It enshrines a development model aimed at promoting social, economic, and political justice, minimizing inequalities, ensuring ownership and control of resources for the common good, and promising "that the operation of the economic system does not result in the concentration of wealth and means of production to the common detriment" (art. 39 (c)). While India's economic and political system is not governed by rigid socialist principles, the country retains its commitment to a progressive vision of socioeconomic development, where growth and competitiveness are seen as tools to be deployed in the service of collective socioeconomic advancement, rather than end goals in themselves. Accordingly, the state remains a key player in the economy. It boosts certain economic sectors with subsidies and local content requirements. It supports its agriculture by providing a minimal guaranteed access to basic foodstuffs. Currency controls remain stringent. State-owned enterprises remain important in certain sectors, and special economic zones help manage industrial and regional development. While India fundamentally adheres to market principles, particularly under the leadership of Prime Minister Modi, its trade policy is driven by developmental imperatives, particularly ensuring food security, providing employment opportunities for its population, and mindfulness of sustainability and the socioeconomic cost of climate change.[31]

---

[31] India's intellectual contributions to trade policy are as diverse as its economic landscape. At one end of the spectrum, Marxist and postcolonial critiques endure with thinkers such as B. S. Chimni (Jawaharlal Nehru University). A range of centrist progressive thinkers includes researchers in academic institutions and think tanks such as James Nedumpara (Jindal Global Law School) and Abhijit Das, Head of the Centre for WTO Studies at the India Institute of Foreign Trade. The WTO Centre is independent but is regularly commissioned by the government to undertake specific research projects. The Energy and Resource Institute (TERI) is another leading progressive think tank. The Indian Council for Research on International Economic Relations is more markedly imbued with liberal economics thinking. Its WTO and Trade Policy Research Programme is chaired by Anwarul Hoda, who formerly served as chief policy coordinator for India during most of the Uruguay Round and became a deputy director general of the WTO in 1995.

Politically, India, while embracing the multilateral trade negotiation process, has been a staunch supporter of special and differential treatment, intellectual property flexibilities (particularly compulsory licensing and limitations on patent protection, such as the requirement to work the patent within a certain period of time), and has pushed hard to renegotiate agricultural commitments and food security protection. In July 2014, India somewhat unexpectedly backed out of the Bali ministerial package of measures, including the Trade Facilitation Agreement, until it reached an agreement with the United States a few months later to extend the "peace clause" whereby the latter would continue to refrain from challenging India's food security programs.[32] Similar issues are now raised in the context of the RCEP negotiations, with some Indian stakeholders voicing concerns about the impact of the agreement on access to medicine, and increased competition with Chinese products.

India's participation in world trade remains strong in the post-2008 era, with an annual export growth rate for merchandise of 6 percent and an annual import growth rate of 4.5 percent over the 2010–14 period.[33] Although such figures are not quite as strong as China's rates, they remain much higher than those of Europe, Australia and Japan, for instance. Regional trade accounts for a significant portion of these figures. In the first few months of 2017, India's exports (in value) to ASEAN countries, Northeast Asian countries[34] and South Asian countries[35] amounted to nearly as much as exports to the EU and United States combined.[36] Imports from these countries amounted to twice the value of imports from the United States and the European Union combined.[37] While the importance of regional trade for India has been an economic reality for the past two decades, it is only after 2000 that these relationships translated into legal trade agreements.[38]

East Asian economic integration schemes prior to 1997 were quite loose political bodies, but are now moving toward more robust institutional

---

[32] *India and US Reach WTO Breakthrough Over Food*, BBC NEWS, Nov. 13, 2014, www.bbc .com/news/business-30033130.

[33] World Trade Organization, International Trade Statistics 2015 (2015), www.wto.org/ english/res_e/statis_e/its2015_e/its2015_e.pdf at 39.

[34] China, Hong Kong, Japan, Korea, North Korea, Macao, Mongolia and Taiwan.

[35] Afghanistan, Bangladesh, Bhutan, Maldives, Nepal, Pakistan and Sri Lanka.

[36] Directorate General of Commercial Intelligence and Statistics, India's Foreign Trade by Economic Region (India) (2017), Table 2A.

[37] *Id.*

[38] Julien Chaisse et al., *The Three-Pronged Strategy of India's Preferential Trade Policy*, 26 CONN. J. INT'L L. 415, 417 (2011).

features, with rule-oriented legal personalities and closer monitoring of members' domestic practices, but still with the desire to preserve the respect for sovereignty that characterized the earlier model.[39] India then moved from PTAs with developing countries to PTAs with OECD countries.[40] India's more "modern" trade agreements include investment and services. The India–Singapore CECA is comparable to trade agreements entered into by the European Union, the United States or Japan. India is building on that experience to negotiate with Indonesia, Malaysia and South Korea.[41]

Indian PTAs increasingly tend to include services and investment as India strives to compensate for losses in trade in goods. Both India and its partners try to protect their goods sector through limited, very targeted liberalization on goods.[42] India's regional trade agreements tend to be defensive, focusing on neutralizing trade diversion by PTAs with third countries, in particular China. In that sense, India pursues a similar tactic to the EU and the United States, which try to avoid being sidelined by each other's PTAs with third countries.[43]

D   Africa: Forging its Own Trade and Development Experimentation at Last?

Having moved from import substitution strategies in the 1970s to neo-liberal "structural adjustment" under the aegis of the World Bank and IMF in the 1990s, a number of African countries have experienced disappointments at both ends of the trade and development relationship spectrum. A number of African countries are currently crafting instrumentalist approaches to trade, framing trade as a tool to help achieve economic growth and human development objectives.[44] In that sense, African perspectives are somewhat resonant with the Indian approach, where the trade discussion is embedded in a broader search for a political and socioeconomic compact grounded in welfare, empowerment and the reduction of inequalities.

---

[39] Zhang Zhiyong, *Economic Integration in East Asia: The Path of Law*, 4 PEKING U. J. LEGAL STUD. 262 (2013).

[40] Chaisse et al., *supra* note 38 at 416.

[41] *Id.* at 453.

[42] *Id.* at 450.

[43] *Id.* at 452.

[44] *See generally* THE INDUSTRIAL POLICY REVOLUTION II: AFRICA IN THE 21ST CENTURY (Joseph E. Stiglitz, Justin Yifu Lin & Ebrahim Patel, eds., 2013).

The discourse from policymakers often emphasizes industrialization,[45] and in some cases, the promotion of trade in services.[46] However, the extent to which domestic industrial policy is aligned with countries' international trade and investment positions is at times weak. A study of Namibia, Ghana and Kenya finds that industrial development policies in these countries are often in breach of WTO obligations, yet these countries do not invoke legal flexibilities that would be available to provide legal cover for some of these policies.[47] Overall, many African economies remain fairly undiversified and continue to rely on extractive industries and exports of raw commodities.[48]

The most promising development may be the continent's renewed interest in regional integration. Visions of a pan-African economic and social space date back to the 1950s,[49] but have been mired in economic, political, social and governance failures. Shifting economic and geopolitical trends due to the entrenchment of China as a major trade and investment partner in the continent, uncertainties regarding the future of relationships with Europe, and a lull in U.S. leadership may now provide a political opportunity for achieving concrete results. Moreover, the engagement of experts and intellectuals such as South African multilateral trade negotiations veteran Faizel Ismail in favor of a continental integration[50] gives some measure of credence to the broad

---

[45] See generally Afr. Dev. Bank Grp., Industrialize Africa (2017); United Nations Econ. Comm'n for Afr., Greening Africa's Industrialization – Economic Report on Africa 2016 (2016); see, e.g., Dept. of Trade and Indus. (South Africa), Industrial Policy Action Plan – IPAP 2016/17 – 2018-19 (2016); Ministry of Industrialization and International Development, Kenya's Industrial Transformation Programme (2015).

[46] Junior Davis, Unlocking Africa's Potential for a Growing Services Sector, AFR. POL'Y REV., May 16, 2016, http://africapolicyreview.com/unlocking-africas-potential-for-a-growing-services-sector/. Business process outsourcing and information technology outsourcing are established sectors in Algeria, Morocco and Tunisia with call centers serving French speakers; and Cameroon, Cote d'Ivoire, Senegal and South Africa are hoping to attract these industries by offering subsidies. Logistics, finance, telecommunications and tourism are also growth sectors.

[47] Colette M. A. van der Ven, Trade, Development and Industrial Policy in Africa: The Case for a Pragmatic Approach to Optimizing Policy Coherence between Industrial Policy and the WTO Policy Space, 10 L. & DEV. REV. 29, 33–34, 46–70 (2017).

[48] Raw commodities made up 72 percent of Africa's exports (with fuel accounting for nearly 60 percent of exports) while manufactured goods amount for 62 percent of its imports. AFRICAN DEVELOPMENT BANK GROUP, INDUSTRIALIZE AFRICA 2 (2017).

[49] Ali A. Mazrui, Pan Africanism and the Intellectuals – Rise, Decline and Revival, in Thandika Mkandawire, ed., AFRICAN INTELLECTUALS. RETHINKING POLITICS, LANGUAGE, GENDER AND DEVELOPMENT (2005).

[50] F. A. Ismail, Advancing Regional Integration in Africa through the Continental Free Trade Area (CFTA), 10 L. & DEV. REV. 119 (2017).

policy statements of the African Union. While the lack of economic diversification remains a concern, the current integration project focuses on improving transportation, communication, and energy infrastructure, as well as legal cooperation and convergence. These subject matters are key prerequisites to creating a more favorable trade environment.

The African Union proposed a common vision for the region's development and "Renaissance" with the adoption of its Agenda 2063 in 2015. This ambitious plan seeks to put into practice the African Union's pan-African vision of "an integrated, prosperous and peaceful Africa, driven by its own citizens and representing a dynamic force in the international arena."[51] More specifically, it announces:

> In this new and noble initiative, past plans and commitments have been reviewed, and we pledge to take into account lessons from them as we implement Agenda 2063. These include: mobilization of the people and their ownership of continental programmes at the core; the principle of self-reliance and Africa financing its own development; the importance of capable, inclusive and accountable states and institutions at all levels and in all spheres; the critical role of Regional Economic Communities as building blocks for continental unity; taking into account of the special challenges faced by both island and land-locked states; and holding ourselves and our governments and institutions accountable for results.[52]

In this framework, trade policy is but one aspect of a holistic approach to socioeconomic development. It recognizes that trade, on its own, is not an economic driver but rather is incidental to a political choice of "[e]conomies ... structurally transformed to create shared growth, decent jobs and economic opportunities for all."[53] The main focus is on establishing a favorable environment characterized by an integrated infrastructure (rail and air transportation are identified as priorities), a qualified and stable workforce that is free from violence and discrimination, a sustainable approach to resource management, the modernization of agricultural practices, investment in science and technology, and development finance. The 2015 Africa Action Plan on Development Effectiveness and the First Ten-Year Implementation Plan 2014–23 stress intra-African trade promotion, aiming to double it by 2022 and triple it

---

[51] AFR. UNION COMM'N., AGENDA 2063 (2015).
[52] Id.
[53] Id. at 3.

by 2023.[54] Concurrently, extensive work has been undertaken by public and private stakeholders in the mining sector to frame a new policy for mineral extraction activities.[55]

III Conclusion

Overall, then, the trade debate in Brazil and India continues to draw on ideological approaches ranging from inward-oriented to export-oriented development approaches. Africa appears to take a less dogmatic path, focusing instead on solving concrete problems such as infrastructure, access to education, and legal frameworks, to create conditions favorable to socioeconomic development.[56] China remains bound to a strong ideological driver domestically but seeks acceptance into liberal economic status from other countries. Mirroring such political ambiguities, emerging powers' trade agenda at times embraces free trade policies, but often includes developmental instruments and policies at odds with liberalism. Chapter 3 explores exactly how far these instruments are from liberal benchmarks such as the TPP. By identifying such discrepancies and assessing how critical they are to the core of state developmentalism, the chapter will also reveal the areas where emerging powers might seek alternative rules, among themselves or in multilateral agreements with industrialized partners.

---

[54] The African Union Comm'n, Africa Action Plan on Development Effectiveness, 2011, www.nepad.org/resource/africa-action-plan-development-effectiveness; First Ten-Year Implementation Plan, The African Union Comm'n, Sept. 2015, www.nepad.org/resource/agenda-2063-first-ten-year-implementation-plan-2014-2023 at 16 and 23.

[55] See Afr. Mining Vision, www.africaminingvision.org/ (Oct. 27, 2017).

[56] See, e.g., Colette M. A. van der Ven, *Trade, Development and Industrial Policy in Africa: The Case for a Pragmatic Approach to Optimizing Policy Coherence between Industrial Policy and the WTO Policy Space*, 10 L. & DEV. REV. 29 (2017); Faizel Ismail & Brendan Vickers, *Reflections on a New Democratic South Africa's Role in the Multilateral Trading System*, in TRADE, POVERTY, DEVELOPMENT: GETTING BEYOND THE WTO'S DOHA DEADLOCK (James Scott & Rorden Wilkinson, eds., 2012).

3

Developing Countries' Love–Hate Relationship with Neoliberalism

For many emerging countries, a fundamental policy question is whether market forces as they are currently channeled and institutionalized are adequate to deliver their developmental objectives. At the core of this inquiry is the role and capacity of the state in managing economic development.

When the liberal trading order was created after World War II, developing countries stood largely outside. They closed their economies to imports, and engaged in import substitution industrialization while seeking special and differential treatment for their exports to developed countries. They banded together to demand a New International Economic Order (NIEO) that would give them greater control of natural resources and a fairer share of global wealth accumulation. To one degree or another, they each adopted state-led development strategies that ranged from full state control of the economy to various forms of state-led capitalism. The core capitalist countries, driven in part by Cold War concerns as well as by development theories that accepted the need for a major state role in developing economies, tolerated these exceptions to the liberal trading regime and the capitalist order. State interventions in emerging countries largely took the form of direct entrepreneurship, through state-owned enterprises, golden shares guaranteeing the government a seat at the corporate governance table; strong national, regional and local development offices that distributed various forms of state assistance; business and trade financing by public entities and development banks; and protectionism from foreign competition through quantitative barriers such as tariffs and quotas.

Changes in the North and South during the 1990s led to modifications in the relationship between developing countries and the liberal trading order. The fall of the Soviet Union was a watershed for everyone. In the North, the collapse of the socialist alternative and prospects for a unified global market economy led to new demands that developing countries adhere to the rules of the trading order. In the South, the decline of the Soviet economy spurred some emerging economies to question state-led growth, and the success of Japan and the Asian Tigers pointed to state-steered export-led growth as preferable to import substitution. China opened to the world and sought membership in the WTO. Emerging economies began to privatize state-owned enterprises, seek FDI from developed counties, promote exports and explore possibilities for investment in developed and developing markets. In order both to attract foreign investment and get access to developed markets for trade and investment, emerging economies entered into bilateral investment treaties (BITs) that gave investors special protection, and accepted trade rules like TRIPS that they had previously avoided. The Washington Consensus required a reduction of the state's role as a major entrepreneur in the economy.

This adoption of more market-oriented development strategies and partial embrace of the liberal trading order did not mean full-scale abandonment of state-led growth. Countries including China, India and Brazil did privatize some sectors and open their economies to foreign goods and investment, but they maintained often robust and usually powerful state-owned sectors and continued to employ various forms of industrial policy. While the nature and extent of their commitment to the policies and instruments of state-led growth varied, all found themselves in conflict with some of the rules of the liberal trading order, and sought ways to limit its impact by manipulating rules, seeking exceptions, avoiding compliance, and proposing new, more development-friendly norms. In other words, the development and political economy debate amounted largely to a tug-of-war between the continuation of state-led entrepreneurship policies and divestment by the state of its economic stake.

While all major emerging economies resisted elements of the liberal order, this resistance was not driven by a common ideology or backed by collective action. There was a common core, including a desire to maintain state ownership in key industries, engage in industrial policy, and limit protection for intellectual property. But the nature and degree of resistance varied, as did the tools used to protect national policy space. These countries found they had significant differences as well as common interests; occasionally their interests conflicted.

Meanwhile, developed countries were moving on to state interventions in the economy that focused on regulation. For example, the EU's regulatory purview expanded dramatically in the 1990s. In response, deregulation became the new clarion call of the neoliberal camp. The mainstreaming of disciplines on technical barriers to trade, sanitary and phytosanitary measures into the WTO, and the rise of the concept of "regulatory expropriation" in international investment law marked significant victories against the administrative state. There are recent illustrations of the continuing debate regarding the appropriate, efficient role of the state in creating and administering a regulatory framework for private economic actors. These include efforts to negotiate a counterpart to the WTO's Trade Facilitation Agreement in the service sector and for foreign investment, and the collapse of TTIP negotiations over issues such as prudential regulation in the financial services sector and automobile production standards. However, when emerging countries also shifted their focus on enhancing development and economic management through regulation, the proponents of deregulation swiftly challenged them. Many developing countries' administrative states are often berated for their inefficiency, lack of sophistication or corruption but neoliberalism proponents push for their curtailment, rather than their improvement. Moreover, private actors who regularly challenge regulatory schemes imposing obligations upon their activities also seek more protection from the administrative state when it comes to their rights, such as intellectual property. At odds with such a trend are consumers of products from global value chains, who worry about food and product safety, quality control and cross-border financial scams as their home countries are unable to effectively protect them.

The clash between proponents of full liberalization and the policies sought by developing countries came to a head in the Doha Round. Developed countries pushed for, among other things, rules that would shrink the role of the state in the economy, extend protection for intellectual property and open developing country markets more fully. Resistance to these moves led to a standoff, and the round petered out.

As the Doha Round waned, the scene became more complex. The growth of China and the rise of the BRICS led some observers to predict a major shift in global economic power, and major changes in the global trading order. There was talk of a second New International Economic Order, possibly led by the BRICS. At the same time, the core capitalist countries, frustrated with WTO negotiations, opened a new front by creating mega-regional trade blocs based on liberal ideas and norms. These efforts culminated with the TPP, which was designed to draw important parts of Asia and Latin America into the liberal camp and isolate China.

Neither of these démarches was successful. The TPP fell apart because the Trump administration, yielding to protectionist pressures, decided to withdraw, thus signaling that the United States was ready to abandon leadership of the liberal order. And while individual BRICS countries continued to challenge aspects of that order, the BRICS have not yet developed common trade and investment policies, nor mounted a systemic campaign to reform the system. Rather, our study shows that most emerging powers are maneuvering within the liberal order by engaging in selective compliance with existing rules, or refusing to agree to some proposed liberal disciplines. At the same time, some seek to create alternative orderings with more flexible standards.

While we recognize that actual development stems from state and private actors, we position our analysis at a public law level, to assess how state-led developmental instruments related to international economic law and policy. In a number of instances, the implications for private actors loom large. For example, whether a country is able to maintain a vast state-owned enterprise network, state-controlled monopolies and price controls dramatically affects the ability of private firms to compete on a market basis with domestic and foreign counterparts. The nature, extent and policing of intellectual property rights will frame how and where corporate research is deployed. Equally, the lack or weakness of international disciplines on corruption affects incentives for domestic actors, both public and private. A study of the effects of international regulation on the entire chain of domestic public and private actors is, however, beyond the scope of our undertaking.

Rather than a wholesale rejection of neoliberalism, emerging powers are engaging in policy eclecticism: adopting some of the tenets of liberal ordering while rejecting others, applying liberal disciplines asymmetrically in pursuit of strategic self-interest, creating other fora for negotiations, and adopting different regulatory priorities. In this chapter, we examine how emerging countries' discontent with the status quo transpired, and what is left of the liberal ordering in the practice of emerging countries. The first part assesses how developing countries are utilizing WTO law to further their own economic policies, but also denotes how they are strategically breaching some rules and resisting the adoption of new disciplines. The second part analyzes how and why bilateral investment treaties and related institutions are falling out of favor with emerging countries after the initial wave of adoption of these instruments. By highlighting the tensions between emerging countries' developmental policies and IEL, along with the more specific clashes that have transpired in recent decades in their practice of trade and investment law, this chapter sets the stage for discussing developing countries' responses in Chapters 4 and 5.

I   A Partial Rejection of the WTO Trade Ordering

Since the Seattle Ministerial Meeting in 1999, developing countries have been a vocal and visible constituency within the WTO. On the one hand, their agenda has been mostly a defensive one, resisting the expansion of liberal disciplines. On the other hand, their engagement with the institution and their use of flexibilities within the system testifies to a willingness to participate in the liberal order. This section analyzes the extent to which emerging countries are attempting to shape and utilize the existing system in furtherance of their developmental policies. It examines how developing countries' institutional participation has grown since the 1990s (Section A). Some emerging countries have become extensive users of flexibilities to modulate their obligations (Section B). However, developing countries' discontent with some existing rules also results in breaches, where a member may fully anticipate that its policy will be challenged, but relies on the years of dispute resolution and the prospective nature of any possible remedy to breach at a relatively low cost, if only temporarily (Section C). At the extreme end of the contestation spectrum, emerging countries are also using their increased voice to block the adoption of new disciplines (Section D).

A   Increased Institutional Participation

1   Expansion of the Green Room Process, Emergence of Developing Country Coalitions

The formal legal equality of member states, each of which is automatically part of every council and committee, the General Council, and the Ministerial Conference, was long belied by a clublike approach to governance. In practice, only members with significant human and financial resources are able to sustain a representation in Geneva that is sufficient to fully participate in the WTO's activities. Many developing country members and LDCs have no permanent representation in Geneva. Meetings of WTO bodies are typically not broadcast by audio or video-conference to members located remotely.

Despite this historical legacy and ongoing political and economic hurdles, emerging countries have undeniably become forces to reckon with. From setting the negotiation agenda to staffing the Secretariat to participating in dispute settlement, developing members and their nationals are increasingly making a mark on the institution.

In the early years of the WTO, the Green Room practice inherited from the GATT years allowed a few powerful players to issue invitations to select counterparts in key negotiations. Ironically, the ill-fated Seattle Ministerial Meeting inaugurated a more inclusive approach to the Green Room process. The 2003 Ministerial Meeting was marked by the establishment of the G20, a group of developing countries that joined forces with Brazil, India and South Africa in the wake of the latters' Brasilia Declaration denouncing the continued protectionism of the EU and the United States, particularly in the agricultural sector. The group took its name from the date of a joint proposal it submitted on August 20, 2003 for an alternative framework on agriculture negotiations. The G20 expanded its activities beyond agriculture and beyond the WTO in subsequent years, until the 2008 financial crisis put in the limelight a very different – yet eponymous – G20 group of central bankers, and put a major brake on developing countries' efforts to develop a coordinated trade agenda.

Nevertheless, a practice of group negotiations has taken hold, allowing greater involvement in Geneva by members with low human and financial resources. While the European Union is the only supranational group granted legal status, the WTO website now makes public a list of groups that are typically active in negotiations.[1] The Secretariat also identifies groups active in specific aspects of the negotiations, in particular in agriculture negotiations, non-agricultural market access negotiations, rules negotiations and TRIPS negotiations, together with any proposal or paper tabled by the groups. This may assist members in mapping their and others' interests and positions, and join like-minded members. A number of groups even include observing countries that are in the process of negotiating their accession, or considering doing so. This is particularly true of the LDC group, the ACP group, the G-90 group (bringing together the ACP, LDC and African groups) and the Pacific Group, all of which represent the most vulnerable and least endowed WTO members.

---

[1] WTO: Groups in the Negotiations, www.wto.org/english/tratop_e/dda_e/negotiating_groups_e.htm.

2   Alignments and Competition in WTO Dispute Settlement

The United States and the European Union maintain the lead in the number of disputes they have been involved in as complainants or respondents. Excluding participation as a third party, the United States has been involved in 276 disputes, the EU in 187. China now comes in third place with sixty-three cases, matching Canada's sixty-two disputes. They are followed by India (fifty-three disputes) and Brazil (forty-nine cases). Argentina, Japan, Mexico and South Korea have accumulated around forty cases each.[2]

At the WTO, emerging countries have prevailed in a number of disputes against developed members whose policies restricted their access to markets. China won cases against the EU[3] and the United States.[4] Brazil won against the EU,[5] the United States[6] and Canada.[7] Brazil and Venezuela won against the United States on reformulated gasoline.[8] Brazil and Thailand won their challenge to the EU's sugar subsidies.[9] Thailand won against the United States[10] and the EU.[11] Brazil, Chile, India, Indonesia and Thailand teamed with the EU, Japan and South Korea in a challenge against the United States.[12] Antigua and Barbuda successfully challenged the United States,[13] as did Ecuador,[14]

---

[2] As of April 28, 2019, the total number of disputes where a request for consultations has been issued amounts to 583.

[3] Panel Report, *EU – Poultry Meat (China)*, WT/DS492/R; AB Report, *EC – Fasteners (China)*, WT/DS397/AB/R; Panel Report, *EU – Footwear (China)*, WT/DS405R.

[4] AB Report, *US – Anti-Dumping Methodologies (China)*, WT/DS471/AB/R; Panel Report, *US – Shrimp and Sawblades*, WT/DS422/R; Panel Report, *US – Anti-Dumping and Countervailing Duties (China)*, as modified by AB Report WT/DS379/AB/R; AB Report, *US – Countervailing Measures (China)*, WT/DS437/AB/R.

[5] AB Report, *EC – Chicken Cuts*, WT/DS269/AB/R (Brazil), WT/DS286/AB/R (Thailand); AB Report, *EC – Tube or Pipe Fittings*, WT/DS219/AB/R.

[6] AB Report, *US – Upland Cotton*, WT/DS267/AB/R.

[7] AB Report, *Canada – Aircraft*, WT/DS70/AB/R; Decision by the Arbitrator, *Canada – Aircraft Credits and Guarantees* – Recourse to Arbitration by Canada under Article 22.6 of the DSU and Article 4.11 of the SCM Agreement, WT/DS222/ARB.

[8] *US – Gasoline* WT/DS2/R, as modified by AB Report WT/DS2/AB/R; *US – Gasoline*, WT/DS4/3 (Brazil).

[9] AB Report, *EC – Export Subsidies on Sugar*, WT/DS265/AB/R (Australia), WT/DS266/AB/R (Brazil), WT/DS283/AB/R (Thailand).

[10] Panel Report, *US – Anti-Dumping Measures on PET Bags*, WT/DS383/R; AB Report, *US – Shrimp* (Thailand) / *US – Customs Bond Directive*, WT/DS343/AB/R / WT/DS345/AB/R.

[11] Panel Report, *EC – Chicken Cuts*, WT/DS286/R (Thailand) as modified by AB Reports WT/DS269/AB/R, WT/DS286/AB/R.

[12] AB Report, *US – Offset Act (Byrd Amendment)*, WT/DS217/AB/R (Chile), WT/DS234/AB/R (Canada).

[13] AB Report, *US – Gambling*, WT/DS285/AB/R.

[14] Panel Report, *US – Shrimp (Ecuador)*, WT/DS335/R.

Indonesia[15] and Mexico.[16] India, Pakistan, Malaysia and Thailand won the Shrimp–Turtles case against the United States.[17] India prevailed against the United States[18] and the EU.[19] Argentina and Indonesia won their biodiesel antidumping case[20] and other cases[21] against the EU and the United States.[22] Pakistan won against the United States and the European Union.[23] Peru won against the EU.[24] Indonesia won against South Korea.[25]

Whether they were successful at bringing about implementation in their favor somewhat dampens these apparent victories. Indeed, developing members make up a disproportionate number of complainants in retaliation proceedings and other findings of noncompliance, compared to their proportion in disputes.[26] A number of additional cases were withdrawn or settled without a decision by a panel or arbitrator.

[15] AB Report, *US – Clove Cigarettes*, WT/DS406/AB/R.
[16] AB Report, *US – Tuna II (Mexico)*, WT/DS381/AB/R.
[17] AB Report, *US – Shrimp*, WT/DS58/AB/R.
[18] AB Report, *US – Carbon Steel (India)*, WT/DS436/AB/R; Panel Report, *US – Customs Bond Directive*, WT/DS345/R, as modified by AB Report WT/DS343/AB/R / WT/DS345/AB/R; Panel Report, *US – Steel Plate*, WT/DS206/R; AB Report, *US – Wool Shirts and Blouses*, WT/DS33/AB/R; AB Report, *US – Shrimp*, WT/DS58/AB/R.
[19] Panel Report, *EC – Tariff Preferences*, WT/DS246/R, as modified by AB Report WT/DS246/AB/R; AB Report, *EC – Bed Linen*, WT/DS141/AB/R.
[20] Panel Report, *EU – Biodiesel (Indonesia)*, WT/DS480/R; AB Report, *EU – Biodiesel (Argentina)*, WT/DS473/AB/R.
[21] Panel Report, *EU – Fatty Alcohols (Indonesia)*, WT/DS442/R, as modified by AB Report WT/DS442/AB/R.
[22] Panel Report, *US – Animals*, WT/DS447/R; AB Report, *US – Oil Country Tubular Goods Sunset Reviews*, WT/DS268/AB/R.
[23] AB Report, *US – Cotton Yarn*, WT/DS192/AB/R; AB Report, *EU – PET (Pakistan)*, WT/DS486/AB/R.
[24] AB Report, *EC – Sardines*, WT/DS231/AB/R.
[25] Panel Report, *Korea – Certain Paper*, WT/DS312/R.
[26] Four out of six complainants in proceedings related to findings of noncompliance were developing members (AB Report, *Canada – Aircraft*, WT/DS70/AB/R; AB Report, *EC – Bed Linen*, WT/DS141/AB/R; AB Report, *Chile – Price Band System*, WT/DS207/AB/R; Panel Report, *Korea – Certain Paper*, WT/DS312/R. Authorization to retaliate were requested and obtained by developing members in seven of the fifteen cases were retaliation was ever sought: Recourse by Argentina to Article 22.2 of the DSU, *US – Oil Country Tubular Goods Sunset Reviews*, WT/DS268/24, May 25, 2007; Recourse by Panama to Article 22.2 of the DSU, *Colombia – Textiles*, WT/DS461/18, Feb. 17, 2017; Recourse to Article 22.2 of the DSU, *US – Offset Act (Byrd Amendment)*, WT/DS217/20 (Brazil), WT/DS217/21 (Chile), WT/DS217/23 (India), WT/DS234/26 (Mexico), Jan. 16, 2004; Recourse by Brazil to Article 4.10 of the Agreement on Subsidies and Countervailing Measures and Article 22.2 of the DSU, *Canada – Aircraft Credits and Guarantees*, WT/DS222/7, May 24, 2002; Recourse by Antigua and Barbuda to Article 22.2 of the DSU, *US – Gambling*, WT/DS285/22, June 22, 2007; Recourse by Mexico to

Emerging countries also challenged each other's trade policies. Brazil prevailed against Indonesia[27] and Argentina.[28] Costa Rica, Honduras, Guatemala and El Salvador successfully challenged safeguard measures[29] and other trade restrictions implemented by the Dominican Republic.[30] Mexico successfully challenged Chinese measures[31] and measures from Guatemala.[32] Panama won against Colombia.[33] Guatemala won against Mexico.[34] Chile won against Argentina,[35] and vice versa.[36] Turkey won against Egypt.[37] India won against Turkey.[38] The Philippines prevailed over Thailand.[39]

About one-fifth of WTO disputes involve the antidumping agreement, and another fifth involve the SCM agreement, though there is significant overlap between these two lists. The Agreement on Agriculture is also frequently featured in dispute settlement, with about 15 percent of cases seeing claims under this agreement. The bulk of disputes between developed and developing countries, as well as disputes between developing countries, involve one or more of these three agreements.

B   Using Flexibilities within Existing Rules

The Uruguay Round's much-touted special and differential treatment provisions (SDT), which were meant to assist developing countries in implementing obligations more gradually, proved largely inadequate and insufficient. Aside from the delayed time period for implementation,

---

Article 22.2 of the DSU, *US – COOL*, WT/DS386/35, June 19, 2015; Recourse by Mexico to Article 22.2 of the DSU, *US – Tuna II (Mexico)*, WT/DS381/29, March 11, 2016.

[27] Panel Report, *Indonesia – Chicken*, WT/DS484/R.

[28] Panel Report, *Argentina – Poultry Anti-Dumping Duties*, WT/DS241/R.

[29] Panel Report, *Dominican Republic – Safeguard Measures*, WT/DS415/R (Costa Rica), WT/DS416/R (Guatemala), WT/DS417/R (Honduras), WT/DS418/R (El Salvador).

[30] AB Report, *Dominican Republic – Import and Sale of Cigarettes*, WT/DS302/AB/R.

[31] AB Report, *China – Raw Materials*, WT/DS394/AB/R / WT/DS395/AB/R / WT/DS398/ AB/R (a case also brought by the United States and the EU).

[32] Panel Report, *Guatemala – Cement II*, WT/DS156/R.

[33] Award of the Arbitrator, *Colombia – Ports of Entry* – Arbitration under Article 21.3(c) of the DSU, WT/DS366/13; Award of the Arbitrator, *Colombia – Textiles* – Arbitration under Article 21.3(c) of the DSU, WT/DS461/13.

[34] Panel Report, *Mexico – Steel Pipes and Tubes*, WT/DS331/R.

[35] Panel Report, *Argentina – Preserved Peaches*, WT/DS238/R.

[36] Award of the Arbitrator, *Chile – Price Band System* – Arbitration under Article 21.3(c) of the DSU, WT/DS207/13.

[37] Panel Report, *Egypt – Steel Rebar*, WT/DS211/R.

[38] Panel Report, *Mexico – Olive Oil*, WT/DS341/R.

[39] AB Report, *Thailand – Cigarettes* (Philippines), WT/DS371/AB/R.

other clauses have been seldom used, and some flexibilities have even been phased out in practice, even though they remain technically available (such as temporary trade measures taken in support of balance of payment constraints). SDT has also seen limited use in dispute settlement as a defense to alleged breaches of obligations, or to claim benefits from developed members. The reasons for such a lackluster record range from the aspirational or vague language of some clauses, to the mismatch between rights announced in some provisions and corresponding obligations on members individually or collectively, and the lack of resources to actually implement most technical assistance provisions.

Even where developing countries successfully asserted a right, as India did in the *EU-GSP* case, the political and legal landscape shifted so as to largely limit the impact of the decision. While India won its argument that the EU's GSP program was not congruent with the Enabling Clause, the EU subsequently designed its trade relations with ACP countries to fall under the scope of GATT article XXIV and GATS article V on free trade areas, rather than under the auspices of the Enabling Clause. The United States and others simply sought and obtained waivers to cover their own noncompliant GSP programs.[40]

Least Developed Countries (LDCs) have been more successful at utilizing SDT waivers and other forms of relief from their obligations, in large part because their impact on trade is so small that other trade partners have not objected to the use of derogations by these countries.

Beyond SDT, then, developing members, particularly the middle-income economies, have turned instead to flexibilities available to all members to support their developmental policies and mitigate the impacts of trade liberalization. In particular, trade remedies play the role of a double-edged sword. Ostensibly, they may be used to counter another member's industrial subsidies or some other industrial policy resulting in dumping, or perhaps causing an import surge that would support the imposition of a safeguard. But, less legitimately, they might also be used (or abused) to help a state maintain industrial policies in the face of neoliberal restrictions. Ultimately, they are a protectionist device that is often used, at least temporarily, to insulate fledgling domestic industries from competing imports and, in practice, can be used to shore up such industries in conjunction with industrial support policies. Either way, between March 2013 and March 2018 Brazil initiated fifty-five

---

[40] *See, e.g.,* Council for Trade in Goods – Africa Growth and Opportunity Act Request for a Waiver, G/C/W/713, July 16, 2015 (Request from the United States).

antidumping investigations and two countervailing duty investigations against various WTO members, resulting in duties imposed
against products from India, South Korea, South Africa, China,
Russia, Thailand, Egypt, Mexico, Saudi Arabia, Japan, the United
States, the United Arab Emirates, Sweden, Germany, the United
Kingdom, Canada, Mexico, the Ukraine, the EU, Germany, Israel,
Italy, Malaysia, Taiwan, France and the Netherlands. Another seventeen trade remedies were terminated during the period, involving the
products from several of the same countries (and a few others).
Quantitatively, China and India were the most frequent targets of
trade remedies imposed by Brazil. Meanwhile, China imposed countervailing duties and antidumping duties on products most frequently
from the EU, Japan, the United States, Korea and India, but also
Singapore, Thailand, Malaysia and Taiwan. China also terminated
duties that had been imposed against other products from some of
these members, from Russia, and from Indonesia. This use of trade
remedies illustrates the competitive tensions among emerging countries, as well as between the Global North and the Global South.

In some cases, these measures have been challenged in the WTO
and countries have been required to end them. But not all efforts to
curb the use of trade remedies have been successful, and the cases
that have reached the WTO are merely the tip of the iceberg when it
comes to trade remedies implemented by emerging countries to
protect their domestic policies and markets. In the face of massive
use of these measures, the system lacks the capacity to effectively
deter everything.

Developing countries avail themselves of additional flexibilities within
the WTO trade regime, including exceptions to most-favored nation
obligations for the Generalized System of Preferences, preference programs among developing countries, and ad hoc waivers to other provisions in particular circumstances.[41]

---

[41] *See, e.g.,* General Council – Decision on waiver relating to special treatment for rice of the
Philippines – Waiver Decision of 24 July 2014, WT/L/932; Ministerial Conference –
Ninth Session – Bali, Dec. 3–6, 2013 – Operationalization of the waiver concerning
preferential treatment to services and service suppliers of Least-Developed countries,
Ministerial decision of Dec. 7, 2013, WT/L/903; General Council – Preferential Tariff
Treatment for Least-Developed Countries – Decision on Extension of Waiver – Adopted
on May 27, 2009, WT/L/759; General Council – Senegal – Waiver on Minimum Values in
Regard to the Agreement on the Implementation of Article VII of the General Agreement
on Tariffs and Trade 1994 – Decision of July 31, 2008, WT/L/735.

The Agreement on Trade Facilitation[42] concluded at the 2013 Bali Ministerial Meeting is of particular note because it inaugurated a new type of progressive, capacity-based commitment. Some negotiators from developing countries were key architects of this deal. Unlike the model of the Uruguay Round agreements, the Agreement on Trade Facilitation builds differentiation of commitments into its core rather than as flexibility at the margins.

Specifically, the agreement creates an à la carte approach to implementation for developing and LDC members. Article 14.3 creates three categories (A, B, C), each carrying increasing time periods for implementation, as well as access to financial assistance and capacity building. Developing and LDC members self-designate which obligation they assign to each category. Category A envisions implementation within a year after the entry into force of the agreement. Categories B and C require members to determine when they plan implementation, with the possibility of further postponing (arts. 17 and 18) and the option to shift obligations between B and C (art. 19) for an even more extended implementation period.

Additionally, the agreement calls for funding support for implementation (art. 21). While such financial assistance is up to donor countries, it creates an incentive for exporting countries with an interest in implementation of specific provisions in certain target countries to essentially "buy" implementation by offering financial support and technical assistance. Implementation of obligations that a country designates under Category C, in particular, is explicitly conditioned on the supply of capacity building and assistance.

The substantive obligations themselves are designed to impose varying levels of constraint. Some provisions are positive obligations, some are progressive best efforts mandates, and some are carve-outs preserving members' regulatory autonomy.

Lastly, the agreement includes a standstill clause on bringing disputes for six years after implementation of Category A obligations, and eight years for Category B and C obligations (art. 20), which further protects low-capacity members' ability to implement progressively.

This agreement became part of the single undertaking in 2017, after gathering two-thirds of the members' ratifications in only four years. In

[42] Agreement on Trade Facilitation, Marrakesh Agreement Establishing the World Trade Organization, Annex 1A, Protocol Amending the Marrakesh Agreement Establishing the World Trade Organization, Annex, WT/L/940 (Nov. 27, 2014), entered into force Feb. 22, 2017 [hereinafter Trade Facilitation Agreement].

the following year, 112 members have notified of their Category A obligations, 61 also designated Category B obligations, and 51 listed obligations under Category C, further testifying to the success of this new approach to trade commitments. A number of LDC members made commitments. By contrast, the amendment to the TRIPS agreement with respect to public health came into force nearly fifteen years after the original 2003 waiver was approved, and was used only once in 2007.

C Strategic Breaches

Even when an exception or waiver is not available, the design of the dispute settlement system may in practice result in members breaching their obligations with little economic cost before another member is able to retaliate. Disputes currently should reach a final panel or Appellate Body decision in a maximum of eighteen to nineteen months, but in practice, it averages over two years from consultation request to adoption. Implementation procedures can take another couple of years before the member in continued breach would be required to begin compensating the affected member. Overall, then, a member could readily implement a subsidy or other industrial policy in violation of WTO law for a duration of four or five years before it would have to withdraw its measure or face economic consequences other than paying the legal fees for defending its measure.

Developed and developing members make use of this de facto flexibility mechanism. Infamously, the dispute regarding bananas pitting various members against the EU has been ongoing since September 1995. More recently, India's solar energy development program was launched in 2010, with a request for consultation by the United States following in 2013.[43] Compliance proceedings are ongoing and although the United States requested retaliation rights in 2018, the matter is still unresolved. Meanwhile, the target for completion of the Indian program is 2022.

China's domestic regulation and institutions have certainly changed considerably in the wake of its WTO accession, but the country is also notable for the extensive use it made of flexibilities inscribed in the agreements, and for strategic breaches resulting in a large volume of litigation. Rather than exploiting procedural delays, China atomizes potential challenges by imposing sectoral trade restrictions, targeted subsidies, and other constantly varying restrictive measures. Business

---

[43] Request for consultations by the United States, *India – Solar Cells*, WT/DS456/1.

entities are left to navigate the regulatory maze, identify potential WTO violations, lobby their governments to consider bringing a dispute, possibly organize the financing of such a dispute and eventually, maybe persuade their government to launch a formal request for consultations or impose a trade remedy, years after the measure was put into place – a process that can be rendered moot or further complicated by a change in the measure or its application in the meantime. Although it vigorously defends challenges to its policies, China typically does not end up facing post-dispute compliance proceedings.

In this perspective, China is not so much a product of a neoliberal international economic law framework, but rather an outlier that succeeded in manipulating the rules to further its own domestic political economy agenda. Far from promising to further move toward market-oriented policies and liberalization, China has made clear that it is committed to maintaining its unique form of state-dominated economic strategy. In an effort to catch up with and surpass the more established economies, China has announced the "Made in China 2025" action plan, which outlines a ten-year strategy to build intelligent manufacturing capabilities, enhance innovation, and upgrade ten key sectors.[44] Many believe this vast new industrial policy contains numerous violations of trade law and fundamentally challenges global trade and investment patterns.[45] China is expanding its influence all over the world, creating new alliances and institutions and making massive investments. Its rapid upgrading of industrial and technological skills has allowed it to emerge as a major competitor to the older industrial powers. Chinese producers and investors' dramatic expansion into Asian, African and Latin American markets is settling into an enduring trend that offers destination countries alternatives to their traditional partners. In part, this evolution was a product of the 2008 financial crisis, which prompted China to accelerate its export market diversification.

D Blocking the Adoption of New Rules

The increase in the quantitative and qualitative participation of developing countries in international economic law governance has some impact

---

[44] *See generally* http://english.gov.cn/2016special/madeinchina2025/.

[45] *See, e.g.,* James McBride, *Is 'Made in China 2025' a Threat to Global Trade?*, COUNCIL ON FOREIGN RELATIONS, Aug. 2, 2018, http://english.gov.cn/2016special/madeinchina2025/; Li Yuan, *Why Made in China 2025 Will Succeed, Despite Trump*, N.Y. TIMES, July 4, 2018, www.nytimes.com/2018/07/04/technology/made-in-china-2025-dongguan.html.

on the functioning of these institutions, both formally and informally. First, developing countries have successfully blocked the expansion of the liberalization agenda. Second, they have been, to some extent, able to reframe the content of the trade liberalization agenda at the WTO. From the reckoning at the Seattle Ministerial Meeting, to the rollback on the so-called Singapore issues at the 2003 Cancún Ministerial Meeting, and the Doha Work Programme, emerging countries have asserted their voices to exclude from the negotiations or circumscribe items they disfavor and include topics of interest to them.

By coordinating coalitions in negotiations and targeted litigation, they improved their outcomes on access to medicine; they extracted subsidies reduction commitments from the United States on cotton; and they maintained agricultural subsidies talks as a linchpin to the negotiations. Developing countries are active in dozens of informal groups, whether gathered by subject matter affinity (e.g., Friends of Fish, NAMA-11, Cotton-4, Friends of Antidumping Negotiations, Tropical Products, G-33/Friends of Special Products, G-10, Cairns Group), by geographic proximity (African Group, Asian Developing members, Pacific Group), preferential trade groupings (APEC, ASEAN, MERCOSUR), economic and developmental interests (LDCs, Low-Income Economies in Transition, Small Vulnerable Economies), or historical and political reasons (ACP, G-90).[46] Many of these groups overlap in terms of membership; some include observer countries and other states that are neither WTO members nor observers. A number of groups include both developed and developing countries.

II   International Investment Protection: Adhesion at a Cost

Measures to protect foreign investment were a key component of the architecture of the grand transformation of the neoliberal order. The architects of the new order saw that flows of foreign investment would be necessary to create the desired integration and the construction of value chains. They felt that it was essential to give investors clear and predictable guarantees against discrimination and expropriation.

Although bilateral investment treaties go back to 1959, when Germany and Pakistan signed the first such agreement, in the 1990s capital-

---

[46] For a summary of groups that have been most active in negotiations, *see* WTO: Groups in the negotiations, www.wto.org/english/tratop_e/dda_e/negotiating_groups_e.htm.

exporting countries began to push BITs throughout the world, and developing countries signed up enthusiastically.[47] By 2000, there were 1,496 BITs in effect around the world. By this date, India had signed twenty-five BITs, China had signed seventy-one, and South Africa fourteen.[48] In a moment of enthusiasm for the regime, Brazil signed sixteen agreements with developed and developing countries alike.[49] Brazil's BITs included fair and equitable treatment, national treatment, freedom of incorporation and management for international investors, compensation standards for expropriations, free cross-border transfer of capital as profits and associated amounts, and investor–state dispute settlement mechanisms whereby the investor usually could choose between international arbitration and judicial remedies. Some of these treaties even allowed investors to switch dispute settlement mechanisms along the way in some cases.[50] Brazil also joined the Multilateral Investment Guarantee Agency (MIGA). But as a harbinger of later resistance by other emerging powers, strong domestic opposition to the regime surfaced immediately after the agreements were signed. As a result, Brazil never ratified any of the BITs it signed,[51] and withdrew from the system altogether (except that it remains a member of MIGA).

The BITs system was promoted as an essential part of development strategy, ensuring the smooth flow of needed investment. Initially, both capital-exporting and developing countries welcomed the system and a vast network of treaties was established. In recent years, however, many

---

[47] José E. Alvarez, *The Return of the State*, 20 MINN. J INT'L L. 223 (2011) (at 232–33, "BITs are not just popular with Western capital exporting nations. Today's leading BIT nations include China and Egypt, as even developing nations have multilateral enterprises requiring protection elsewhere. Cuba has concluded more BITs than the U.S., and today, about a third of the total number of IIAs have been concluded between developing states.").

[48] UNCTAD Investment Policy Hub database, http://investmentpolicyhub.unctad.org/IIA.

[49] http://investmentpolicyhub.unctad.org/IIA/CountryBits/27 listing Brazil–Portugal BIT, Brazil–Chile BIT, Brazil–United Kingdom BIT, Brazil–Switzerland BIT, Mercosur (Protocol of Colonia for protection of investors from member states), Mercosur (Protocol of Buenos Aires for protection of investors from nonmember states) in 1994; Brazil–France BIT, Brazil–Finland BIT, Brazil–Italy BIT, Brazil–Denmark BIT, Brazil–Venezuela BIT, Brazil–South Korea BIT, Brazil–Germany in 1995; Brazil–Cuba BIT in 1997; Brazil–Netherland BIT in 1998; Brazil–Belgium–Luxembourg BIT in 1999.

[50] Débora Bithiah de Azevedo, *Os acordos para a promoção e a proteção recíproca de investimentos assinados pelo Brasil*, Study for the Câmara dos Deputados (May 2001), www2.camara.leg.br/a-camara/documentos-e-pesquisa/estudos-e-notas-tecnicas/arquivos-pdf/pdf/102080.pdf.

[51] Daniela Campello & Leany Lemos, The Non-ratification of Bilateral Investment Treaties in Brazil: a Story of Conflict in a Land of Cooperation, 22 REV. INTL POL. ECON. 1055 (2015).

other emerging economies have begun to reconsider the BITs regime and resist some of its features. Several factors have led to this resistance. Data appeared questioning whether the agreements actually increased the flow of investment, and new ideas about development raised questions about whether these flows were always beneficial (Section A). At the same time, a series of arbitration proceedings pitting investors against host states suggests that BITs may constrain the state's regulatory autonomy beyond what BITs signatories had anticipated. Although the latter experience is not limited to developing host states, this chapter focuses primarily on the experience of emerging economies. As claims mounted, countries began to see that the agreements could severely limit their policy space both as a jurisdictional matter (Section B) and as a substantive matter (Section C). Since traditional BITs provide very limited exceptions, developing country attempts to counter constraints on policy space by making use of the treaties' flexibilities proved of limited effectiveness (Section D). [52]

A   Studies Question the Effect of BITs on FDI Flows

In the 1990s, a dense network of bilateral investment treaties emerged to govern foreign investment. The first generation of BITs in the 1960s was designed to replace traditional diplomatic methods that employed open-ended principles, depended on home states to pursue investor interests, and were unpredictable. In the 1990s the system was dramatically expanded. After two decades of experience with BITs, developing countries began to question the value of many aspects of the regime constructed through this web of bilateral agreements. The benefits from BITs are now in doubt, and their potential social, political and economic costs are becoming increasingly apparent. On the benefit side, some have questioned whether signing BITs really increases the flow of investment, pointing to Brazil as a counter-narrative. Although Brazil withdrew from the regime, for the past twenty years it has been one of the top developing-country recipients of foreign direct investment.[53] At the same time,

---

[52] Part II of this chapter is adapted in part from Sonia E. Rolland and David M. Trubek, *Legal Innovation in Investment Law: Rhetoric and Practice in the South*, 39 U. PENN. J. INTL L. 355 (2017) and Sonia E. Rolland, *The Return of State Remedies in Investor-State Dispute Settlement: Trends in Developing Countries*, 49 LOYOLA U. CHI. L. J. 387 (2017).

[53] *See The World Factbook: Country Comparison, Stock of Direct Foreign Investment*, CENT. INTELLIGENCE AGENCY, www.cia.gov/library/publications/the-world-factbook/rankorder/2198rank.html (ranking Brazil as the fourteenth recipient of foreign direct investment [FDI] worldwide based on 2016 estimates of FDI stock. The only emerging country receiving

as decisions against host countries by ISDS arbitration panels accumulate, and significant damages are awarded, concerns over costs of the treaties for host countries are mounting. Emerging countries fear the effects of the BITs regime on their policy-making capacities, leading them to rethink their commitment to the regime established in the 1990s.

Quantitative and qualitative research has attempted to evaluate the benefits of BITs on host states, in particular developing countries. As early as 1988, a UN study found "no apparent relationship" between BITs signed and the amount of FDI, ultimately calling for econometric research on this issue.[54] Such a study produced by UNCTAD in 1998[55] concluded that "following the signing of a BIT, it is more likely than not that the host country will marginally increase its share in the outward FDI of the source country … The effect, however, is usually small."[56] Overall, it finds that "BITs appear to play a minor and secondary role in influencing FDI flows"[57] whereas gross domestic product, population size, and amount of domestic investment transpire in most economic studies as more important factors in explaining FDI flows.

In other more recent studies, the evidence is similarly mixed and lends itself to divergent interpretations. Developing countries are thought to enter into a bargain when signing BITs in which they give up part of their autonomy regarding investment regulation in exchange for the economic benefits of attracting investment thanks to increased investor protection. Some emerging countries, including Brazil, took the strong policy position that BITs are not essential to attracting investment. In the face of early studies casting doubts whether BITs were at all effective to attract investment,[58] or were only effective for some developing countries,[59]

more FDI is China.). *See also* United Nations Conference on Trade and Development, *World Investment Report 2016, Country Fact Sheet: Brazil*, http://unctad.org/sections/dite_dir/docs/wir2016/wir16_fs_br_en.pdf (comparing Brazil's FDI flows and stock to other emerging countries).

[54] United Nations Center on Transnational Corporations, Bilateral Investment Treaties, U. N. Doc. ST/CTC/65 (1988).

[55] United Nations Conference on Trade and Development, Bilateral Investment Treaties in the Mid-1990s, UN Doc. UNCTAD/ITE/IIA/7 (1998).

[56] *Id.* at 122.

[57] *Id.* at 120.

[58] Mary Hallward-Driemeier, *Do Bilateral Investment Treaties Attract FDI? Only a Bit … and They Could Bite*, in THE EFFECT OF TREATIES ON FOREIGN DIRECT INVESTMENT: BILATERAL INVESTMENT TREATIES, DOUBLE TAXATION TREATIES, AND INVESTMENT FLOWS (Karl P. Sauvant and Lisa E. Sachs, eds., 2009).

[59] Susan Rose-Ackerman & Jennifer Tobin, *Foreign Direct Investment and the Business Environment in Developing Countries: The Impact of Bilateral Investment Treaties*, YALE

Neumayer and Spess attempted to prove that the expected benefits to the host state did in fact materialize.[60] For the period 1970 to 2001, they find a statistically significant positive correlation between the adoption of BITs and the growth of FDI to the signatory countries. Even before the effects of the 2008 financial crisis were felt, an increasing number of commentators became cautious about the impact of BITs on FDI. Skeptics include Gallagher,[61] Hallward-Driemeier[62] and Yackee.[63]

A significant issue is the relationship between BITs and good institutional governance in the host country. If a state offers solid or at least credible warranties regarding the rule of law and the equitable treatment of foreigners, it may be that such a country's BIT commitments are also more credible, albeit somewhat duplicative with existing institutions. FDI may indeed flow more readily to such a state, but the positive effect would not necessarily be ascribable to the BITs alone. A range of economic factors also have been identified as equally or even more important determinants for investment.[64] Even Neumayer and Spess acknowledge that evidence of the positive relationship between FDI and the number of BITs in place is weaker in the case of states with a fragile governance framework. Perhaps most persuasively, BITs are typically thought to have some positive effect, but only in conjunction with improved or solid domestic governance institutions that favor investment.[65]

LAW SCHOOL CENTER FOR LAW, ECONOMICS AND PUBLIC POLICY, Research Paper No. 293 (2005), https://papers.ssrn.com/sol3/papers.cfm?abstract_id=557121.

[60] Eric Neumayer & Laura Spess, *Do Bilateral Investment Treaties Increase Foreign Direct Investment to Developing Countries?*, 33 WORLD DEV. 1567 (2005).

[61] *See, e.g.*, Kevin P. Gallagher & Melissa B. L. Birch, *Do Investment Agreements Attract Investment? Evidence from Latin America*, 7. J. WORLD INV. & TRADE 961 (2006) (finding no evidence or a correlation between signing a BIT between a Latin American or Caribbean country and the United States and FDI flows).

[62] Hallward-Driemeier, *supra* note 58.

[63] *E.g.*, Jason Yackee, *Do BITS Really Work? Revisiting the Empirical Link between Investment and Foreign Direct Investment*, in THE EFFECT OF TREATIES ON FOREIGN DIRECT INVESTMENT: BILATERAL INVESTMENT TREATIES, DOUBLE TAXATION TREATIES, AND INVESTMENT FLOWS (Karl P. Sauvant and Lisa E. Sachs, eds., 2009) (expanding the Neumayer and Spess study but drawing diverging and opposite conclusions).

[64] Pravin Jadhav, *Determinants of Foreign Direct Investment in BRICS Economies: Analysis of Economic, Institutional and Political Factor*, 37 PROCEDIA SOC. & BEHAV. SCI. 1, 5–14 (2012).

[65] Jeswald W. Salacuse & Nicholas P. Sullivan, *Do BITs Really Work?: An Evaluation of Bilateral Investment Treaties and Their Grand Bargain*, in THE EFFECT OF TREATIES ON FOREIGN DIRECT INVESTMENT: BILATERAL INVESTMENT TREATIES, DOUBLE TAXATION TREATIES, AND INVESTMENT FLOWS (Karl P. Sauvant and Lisa E. Sachs, eds., 2009)

In addition to econometric studies that consider BIT signatory countries and the FDI flows between the signatories (dyadic relationships) and aggregate studies, another type of analysis focuses on the signaling effect of BITs. The hypothesis there is that the benefit of BITs resides not so much in the technical protection it grants foreign investors and their assets, but rather in the signal it sends to capital-exporting countries that it is "open for business." In this perspective, signing a BIT with one capital exporter may have positive spillover effects on other capital-exporting countries even though there is no BIT in place with the latter.

Here again, the evidence is mixed. Inasmuch as BITs are more effective or only effective when strong governance structures are in place, and play a duplicative or supplementary effect to such institutions, the signaling effect will logically only operate to attract investment to countries with solid institutions. An often-cited study by Tobin and Busch examines an additional implication of the "open for business" signaling theory: they assess whether the existence of a BIT between a developed and a developing country increases the likelihood that these two countries – or that developing country and other developed countries – will also enter into a preferential trade agreement.[66] They find that while the odds of entering into a preferential trade agreement increase as hypothesized, that trend is reversed when the developing country has entered into more than five BITs with rich countries. This tipping point is lower than the average number of BITs signed by many developing countries. Hence, the drive to sign BITs as a signal that a state is willing to accept "the rules of the game" of international economic law and is open to business may play to its disadvantage in the long run even at the signaling level.

BITs signed with little consideration of their credibility in light of domestic institutions or their role in relation to a country's real economic partnerships, then, appear to play a questionable role as a driver of FDI and trade relations. Contrary to the perception of some developing countries' governments, signing BITs might not be an effective way to earn international credibility and economic dividends; commitments they saw as essentially low-cost may in fact be valued equally cheaply by their partners.

---

[66] Jennifer L. Tobin & Marc L. Busch, *A BIT Is Better Than a Lot: Bilateral Investment Treaties and Preferential Trade Agreements*, 62 WORLD POLITICS 1 (2010).

B   Investor–State Dispute Resolution: Too Much of a Good Thing?

One area of concern for emerging countries (and increasingly, states that were historically capital exporters), is the reach of dispute settlement clauses included in BITs and restricting the scope of safeguards created to protect the domestic jurisdiction of the host state. The 2005 free trade agreement between the United States and Australia was the first agreement to include BIT-like investment protection but no investor–state arbitration.[67] The 2006 Japan–Philippines Economic Partnership Agreement allows ISDS, but only if the host state consents to arbitration after the dispute has arisen.[68]

The award in *Maffezini v. Spain* and its progeny was a watershed in this respect because this line of cases significantly expanded the reach of remedies under BITs. An Argentine investor claimed that his investment in a chemical production facility was lost because of the actions of his joint venture partner, a Spanish public–private entity.[69] The tribunal ultimately found against Maffezini, but the case became notorious because of the tribunal's decision on jurisdiction. In its objection to the tribunal's jurisdiction, Spain argued that the Argentina–Spain BIT obligated the claimant to refer the dispute to Spanish courts for eighteen months prior to seeking an arbitration under the treaty (article X(2)).[70] ICSID tribunals have tended to interpret the fulfillment of such provisions as mandatory, the breach of which would constitute an impediment to the tribunal's jurisdiction.[71] *Maffezini v. Spain* inaugurated a workaround of such "local remedies first" obligations. It found that the MFN clause in the Spain–Argentina BIT allowed the investor to claim the benefit of the more favorable (to itself) provisions of the Spain–Chile

---

[67] Kyla Tienhaara, *Once BITten, Twice Shy?*, 30 POL'Y & SOC. 185, 191 (2017).
[68] *Id.* at 192.
[69] www.italaw.com/sites/default/files/case-documents/ita0481.pdf, Emilio Agustín Maffezini v. Kingdom of Spain, ICDIS Case No. ARB/97/7, (Nov. 13, 2000), 5 ICSID Rep. 419 (2002).
[70] Agreement between the Kingdom of Spain and the Republic of Chile on the Reciprocal Promotion and Protection of Investments, entered into force April 5, 1994, 1774 U.N.T.S. 24. Such a requirement for exhaustion of local remedies is fairly typical of BITs, and may be seen as protective of the host state's sovereignty. It is also in line with earlier investor recourses through diplomatic protection, which also carried a prerequisite of exhaustion of local remedies. Barcelona Traction, Light and Power Company, Limited, Judgment, I. C.J. Reports 1970, p. 3.
[71] *See, e.g.*, Joseph C. Lemire v. Ukraine, ICSID Case No. ARB/06/18, Mar. 28, 2011; Ambiente Ufficio S.p.A. and others v. Argentine Republic, ICSID Case No. ARB/08/9, May 28, 2015.

BIT,[72] which lacked a local-remedies-first requirement. The result was to expand the jurisdiction of the arbitral tribunal beyond what would have been available to the investor if it had decided instead that the MFN clause of the Spain–Argentina BIT did not apply to provisions on local remedies.

The tribunal was persuaded, inter alia, by the claimant's argument that while Argentina in its treaty negotiation practice typically insisted on exhaustion of local remedies clauses, Spain was typically more protective of investors benefiting from a direct access to arbitration. These positions reflected the classic configuration where Argentina expected to play the role of host state, and Spain was seeking to protect its outward investors. The tribunal found that the reversal of roles in this case did not outweigh Spain's prior policy and practice.[73] The consequences of such role reversal are particularly salient in light of emerging countries' increased activity as outward investors. The time elapsed since the *Maffezini* arbitration has proven it to be a quite far-reaching decision, with a number of high-profile awards adopting similar approaches and a few declining to expand investor–state dispute settlement in favor of investors.[74]

---

[72] Agreement for the Reciprocal Promotion and Protection of Investments between Chile and Spain, Chile–Spain, Oct. 2, 1991.

[73] Maffezini v. Spain, *supra* note 69 at ¶ 57–61, 64.

[74] *E.g.*, Pantechniki SA Contractors and Engineers v. Albania, ICSID Case No. ARB/07/21, Final Award (July 28, 2009), www.italaw.com/sites/default/files/case-documents/ita0618 .pdf; Siemens A.G. v. Argentina, ICSID Case No. ARB/02/8, Decision on Jurisdiction, (Aug. 3, 2004) 44 ILM 137 (2005); Gas Natural SDG v. Argentina, ICSID Case No. ARB/ 03/10, Decision on the Tribunal on Preliminary Questions on Jurisdiction, (Nov. 10, 2003); Suez, Sociedad General de Aguas de Barcelona S.A., and InterAguas Servicios Integrales del Agua S.A v. Argentina, ICSID Case No. ARB/03/17, Decision on Jurisdiction, (May 16, 2006); RosInvestCo UK Ltd. v. The Russian Federation, Arbitration Institute of the Stockholm Chamber of Commerce, Case No. V079/2005, Final Award (Sept. 12, 2010), www.italaw.com/sites/default/files/case-documents/ita0719 .pdf. Compare with Plama Consortium Limited v. Republic of Bulgaria, ICSID Case No. ARB/03/24, Decision on Jurisdiction, (Feb. 8 2005), 44 ILM 721 (2005); Salini Costruttori S.p.A. and Italstrade S.p.A. v. Hashemite Kingdom of Jordan, ICSID Case No. ARB/02/13, Decision on Jurisdiction, (Nov. 29, 2004) 20 ICSID REV. – FILJ 148 (2005); Telenor Mobile Communications A.S. v. Republic of Hungary, ICSID Case No. ARB 04/15, Award, (Sept. 13, 2006), 21 ICSID Rev. – FILJ 603 (2006). *See also* İnci Ataman Figanmeşe, *The Impact of the Maffezini Decision on the Interpretation of MFN Clauses in Investment Treaties*, 8 ANKARA L. REV. 221–37 (2011). The *Maffezini* tribunal was willing to break new grounds regarding the interpretation of MFN clauses in BITs; it recognized that its approach "might result in the harmonization and enlargement of the scope of [dispute settlement] arrangement[s]," and that other cases may present public policy considerations warranting a different result. Maffezini v. Spain, *supra* note 69 at ¶ 62.

Current investor strategy suggests that treaty shopping has become a standard legal strategy, not only with the operation of MFN clauses, but also upstream, by channeling investment through shell entities incorporated in state parties of BITs favorable to investors. It would be wise to reassess whether the test for determining how liberally MFN clauses should be interpreted needs to be more stringent than envisioned in *Maffezini*. This issue is taken up in Chapter 4, as some emerging countries have designed new treaty language in response to *Maffezini*. The use of MFN clauses to effectively amend treaty terms reinforces research regarding other risks of entering into multiple BITs without a careful consideration of the relationship between these treaties. Arbitration developments at the procedural level confirm that entering into BITs is not merely a convenient and cost-free political and economic signaling device.

The recent move by a number of developing countries to exit the ICSID system suggests that they have learned that the reach of BITs may be greater than they had thought, and the costs higher than they anticipated. India's case exemplifies how domestic bodies have reacted to pressure from trends in dispute settlement. Since the 1990s India has signed eighty-six BITs. All followed the original BIT model. Initially an enthusiastic participant in the original regime, India is now rethinking its approach to FDI and BITs. This review started in 2013 partially in response to public outcry concerning several cases filed by foreign investors.[75] In 2012 India received an unfavorable decision in *White Industries v. India*. This decision, which was based on delays in the Indian judiciary, caused a major stir in India. Shortly after it was decided, India received another seventeen notices of disputes over claims ranging from the cancellation of licenses to the review of supreme court decisions. All of this caused the Indian establishment to consider redrafting its model BIT in order to balance investor protections with the government's regulatory powers.[76]

South Africa took an even more radical stance in response to what it perceived as overreach from ISDS. In the period following the end of apartheid, South Africa entered into a flurry of BITs without really considering the long-term effects thereof.[77] It was only after the first

---

[75] Prabhash Ranjan, India and Bilateral Investment Treaties – A Changing Landscape, 29 ICSID REV. 419 (2014).

[76] Grant Hanessian & Kabir Duggal, *The 2015 India Model BIT: Is This the Change the World Wishes to See?*, 29 ICSID REV. 3 (2015).

[77] Mohammed Mossallem, *Process Matters: South Africa's Experience Exiting its BITs*, Global Economic Governance Programme Working Paper 2015/97 at 7 (Jan. 2015), https://papers.ssrn.com/sol3/papers.cfm?abstract_id=2562417.

claim by a foreign investor, in the 2007 *Piero Foresti v. Republic of South Africa* case, that the implications of all the BITs the government had entered into received necessary scrutiny.[78] As a result of the *Foresti* claim and a shift in FDI strategy, South Africa embarked on a process of reviewing its BITs. At the end of the review process, South Africa found that most of the BITs it had entered into did not accord with its FDI policy and even with its constitutional mandate.[79] It also found that there was no direct link between a BIT with a particular country and the flow of FDI from that country.[80] Between 2011 and 2014 South Africa gave notice of its intention to cancel existing BITs, and in 2013 formally began the process of terminating its BITs.[81] To date, South Africa has terminated BITs with the Netherlands, Spain, Luxembourg and Belgium, Germany, Switzerland and Austria.

C More than Was Bargained for: Concerns about Regulatory Autonomy

Beyond the procedural and jurisdictional aspects of ISDS, the backlash against the traditional BIT system also stems from interpretation of standard treaty terms in a way that increasingly constrains host states' regulatory autonomy and their control over domestic policies ranging from taxation to public health, environmental protection, access to water, and more. To some degree, it is part of a general shift away from unqualified embrace of globalization by both governments and industrial North and South.[82] But probably the biggest driver has been a reaction to the raft of decisions by arbitrators who have used the often vague language of treaties to craft rulings that pose a threat to the regulatory

---

[78] *Id.* at 10.

[79] SOUTH AFRICAN DEPARTMENT OF TRADE AND INDUSTRY, BILATERAL INVESTMENT TREATY POLICY FRAMEWORK REVIEW (June 2009), http://pmg-assets.s3-website-eu-west-1.amazonaws.com/docs/090626trade-bi-lateralpolicy.pdf. *See also* Jonathan Lang, *Bilateral Investment Treaties – a Shield or a Sword?* (Dec. 13, 2013), www.bowman.co.za/FileBrowser/ArticleDocuments/South-African-Government-Canceling-Bilateral-Investment-Treaties.pdf (detailing the findings of South Africa's Department of Trade and Industry's [DTI] official review of BITs in 2010 and the recommendations made in response).

[80] Mossallem, *supra* note 77 at 10.

[81] *Id.* at 12.

[82] *See The Retreat of the Global Company*, THE ECONOMIST, Jan. 28, 2017, www.economist.com/news/briefing/21715653-biggest-business-idea-past-three-decades-deep-trouble-retreat-global.

autonomy of host countries beyond what signatory states expected when they signed onto BITs. These include use of the concept of "indirect expropriation" to challenge regulatory actions that investors claim significantly diminished the value of their investments. In the so-called indirect expropriation scenario, the investor claims that although the host state did not engage in an outright expropriation or taking of the investment, it took some regulatory measure that had the effect of significantly diminishing or even entirely wiping out the value or expected value of the investment. Expropriation claims in response to regulatory controls[83] have arisen from the telecommunication sector,[84] banking and finance,[85] public health,[86] the environment,[87] access to water,[88] the

---

[83] M. SORNARAJAH, RESISTANCE AND CHANGE IN THE INTERNATIONAL LAW ON FOREIGN INVESTMENT 201 (2015). ("[N]umerous control devises ... were instances of control that the administrative state increasingly employed.")

[84] Republic of Ghana v. Telekom Malaysia Berhad, HA/RK 2004.778, PCA Case Repository 2003–03, (Perm. Ct. Arb. Nov. 5, 2004), www.italaw.com/sites/default/files/case-documents/ita0922.pdf.

[85] Rafat Ali Rizvi v. Republic of Indonesia, ICSID Case No. ARB/11/13, Award on Jurisdiction (July 16, 2013), http://icsidfiles.worldbank.org/icsid/ICSIDBLOBS/OnlineAwards/C1560/DC4512_En.pdf; Abaclat and Others v. The Argentine Republic, ICSID Case No. ARB/07/5, Decision on Jurisdiction and Admissibility (Aug. 4, 2011), www.italaw.com/sites/default/files/case-documents/ita0236.pdf.

[86] Philip Morris Brands Sàrl, Philip Morris Products S.A. and Abal Hermanos S. A. v. Oriental Republic of Uruguay, ICSID Case No. ARB/10/7, Decision on Jurisdiction (July 2, 2013), http://icsidfiles.worldbank.org/icsid/ICSIDBLOBS/OnlineAwards/C1000/DC3592_En.pdf; Achmea B.V. v. The Slovak Republic, PCA Case No 2013/12 (Perm. Ct. Arb. May 20, 2014), www.italaw.com/sites/default/files/case-documents/italaw3207.pdf; United Nations Commission on International Trade Law, Les Laboratoires Servier, S.A.A., Biofarma, S.A.S., Arts et Techniques du Progres S.A. S. v. Republic of Poland, www.italaw.com/cases/1179. Pharmaceutical companies have also claimed expropriation or breach of fair and equitable treatment against host countries with mature regulatory environments, including Canada and the United States; see generally Eli Lilly and Co. v. Gov't of Canada, ICSID Case No. UNCT/14/2, Final Award (Mar. 16, 2017), www.italaw.com/sites/default/files/case-documents/italaw8546.pdf, and Apotex Holdings Inc. and Apotex Inc. v. United States of America, ICSID Case No. ARB(AF)/12/1 (2012), http://investmentpolicyhub.unctad.org/ISDS/Details/456.

[87] Compañía del Desarrollo de Santa Elena, S.A. v. The Republic of Costa Rica, ICSID Case No. ARB/96/1, Final Award (Feb. 17, 2000), http://icsidfiles.worldbank.org/icsid/ICSIDBLOBS/OnlineAwards/C152/DC539_En.pdf, 5 ICSID Rep. 157 (2002).

[88] Biwater Gauff (Tanzania) Ltd. v. United Republic of Tanzania, ICSID Case No. ARB/05/22, Award (July 24, 2008); Aguas del Tunari S.A. v. Republic Of Bolivia, ICSID Case No. ARB/02/3, Decision on Respondent's Objections to Jurisdiction (Oct. 21, 2005), http://icsidfiles.worldbank.org/icsid/ICSIDBLOBS/OnlineAwards/C67/DC1589_En .pdf; Damon Vis-Dunbar & Luke Eric Peterson, Bolivian Water Dispute Settled, Bechtel Forgoes Compensation, INV. TREATY NEWS, Jan. 20, 2006, www.iisd.org/itn/wp-con tent/uploads/2010/10/itn_jan20_2006.pdf.

protection of cultural property,[89] the taxation power of the host state,[90] and socioeconomic policies.[91] Many cases of this type have been brought in recent years, and arbitrators awarded damages in several instances. Even when the claim is dismissed, litigation is costly for the host country. Concepts of "fair and equitable treatment" and "full protection and security" also received expansive readings.

At the outset, it is worth noting that socioeconomic and environmental policy constraints are not solely at issue in BITs between developed and developing country partners:[92] similar issues can arise under South–South BITs. For instance, Uche Eweluka notes that BITs between China and African countries display generally the same trends as North–South BITs with respect to broad definitions of investment, standards of treatment of the investor and investment, protection against expropriation, protection regarding transfer of funds outside of the host country, and investor–state dispute settlement. She points out that "[n]oticeably absent from China–Africa BITs are provisions

---

[89] Malaysian Historical Salvors Sdn, Bhd v. The Government of Malaysia, ICSID Case No. ARB/05/10, Award of Jurisdiction (May 17, 2007), http://icsidfiles.worldbank.org/icsid/ICSIDBLOBS/OnlineAwards/C247/DC654_En.pdf; Parkerings-Compagniet AS v. Republic of Lithuania, ICSID Case No. ARB/05/8, Award (Sept. 11, 2007), http://icsidfiles.world bank.org/icsid/ICSIDBLOBS/OnlineAwards/C252/DC682_En.pdf; VALENTINA VADI, CULTURAL HERITAGE IN INTERNATIONAL INVESTMENT LAW AND ARBITRATION (2014).

[90] Señor Tza Yap Shum v. La Republica del Perú, ICSID Case No. ARB/07/6, Laudo (Sept. 11, 2007), www.italaw.com/sites/default/files/case-documents/ita0881.pdf.

[91] Piero Foresti et al. v. The Republic of South Africa, ICSID Case No. ARB/07/1, Award (Aug. 4, 2010), http://icsidfiles.worldbank.org/icsid/ICSIDBLOBS/OnlineAwards/C90/DC1651_En.pdf; CMS Gas Transmission Company v. The Republic of Argentina, ICSID Case No. ARB/01/8, Award (May 12, 2005), 44 ILM 1205 (2005); Enron Corporation and Ponderosa Assets, L.P. v. The Argentine Republic, ICSID Case No. ARB/01/3, Decision on Jurisdiction (Ancillary Claim) (Aug. 2, 2004), http://icsidfiles .worldbank.org/icsid/ICSIDBLOBS/OnlineAwards/C3/DC502_En.pdf; Sempra Energy International v. Argentine Republic, ICSID Case No. ARB/02/16, Award (Sept. 28, 2007), http://icsidfiles.worldbank.org/icsid/ICSIDBLOBS/OnlineAwards/C8/DC694_En.pdf.

[92] José E. Alvarez, Contemporary International Law: An 'Empire of Law' or the 'Law of the Empire'?, 24 AM. U. INT'L L. REV. 811, 835 (2009) (noting "The changes to the U.S. BIT program over the course of twenty years demonstrate that the investment regime can no longer be caricatured as law designed only to protect the capital interests of the metropole. They show that today's investment agreements, or at least those concluded by the erstwhile leader of the investment regime, are not quite like colonial era capitulation treaties. Today's BITs bite the metropole back.").

pertaining to human rights, labor rights, environmental protection and sustainable development."[93]

M. Sornarajah believes that the dispute settlement process was used to try to weave the multiple bilateral treaties into a common framework that would achieve at least some of the goals sought through the various efforts to create a multilateral investment regime. He says this effort was driven by "the reified belief that a single model of investment protection, mandated by neo-liberalism, was needed to ensure economic progress." To that end, he contends, arbitrators

> ... interpreted phrases in the treaties well beyond the intention of states to create rules of secure investment protection. Thus, the provision on full protection and security was regarded as requiring a stable climate for investment to thrive. The fair and equitable standard was interpreted as requiring that legitimate expectations, created at the time of investment, are not thwarted. Mere depreciation of the value of investments caused by government measures came to be regarded as tantamount to expropriation.[94]

Although ISDS defenders are quick to point out that investors lost a number of these claims,[95] developing countries remain concerned about the chilling effect that the specter of arbitration imposes on their policy autonomy, the resources involved in defending arbitrations against well-endowed investors, and the unstable climate created by uncertainty and at times inconsistency in award decisions.

A number of investor–state arbitral proceedings have highlighted the far-reaching ways in which the terms of many BITs may be interpreted to

---

[93] Uche Eweluka Ofodile, *Africa–China Bilateral Investment Treaties: A Critique*, 35 MICH. J. INT'L L. 131, 159–60 (2013).

[94] SORNARAJAH, *supra* note 83 at 44–55.

[95] *See, e.g.,* Plama v. Bulgaria, ICSID Case No. ARB/03/24, Decision on Jurisdiction, (Feb. 8, 2005), http://icsidfiles.worldbank.org/icsid/ICSIDBLOBS/OnlineAwards/C24/DC521_En.pdf, 20 ICSID Rev.—FILJ 262 (2005) (finding that investors misrepresented their identity and qualifications, which was material to the investment authorization); Suez, Sociedad General de Aguas de Barcelona S.A., and InterAgua Servicios Integrales del Agua S.A. v. The Argentine Republic, ICSID Case No. ARB/03/17, Decision on Liability, ¶¶ 151, 217–218, www.italaw.com/sites/default/files/case-documents/ita0813 .pdf (finding no expropriation but deciding that the state had breached its obligations regarding fair and equitable treatment by refusing to renegotiate the tariff rates for water); Energy Corp., LG&E Capital Corp., and LG&E International Inc. v. The Argentine Republic, ICSID Case No. ARB/02/1, Decision on Liability, ¶ 248 (Oct. 3, 2006), 21 ICSID Rev.—FILJ 203 (2006), www.italaw.com/sites/default/files/case-documents/ ita0460.pdf (rejecting the claims that the respondent had directly or indirectly expropriated claimants' investments and denying the claimants' investments full protection and security).

restrict the host state's ability to design and implement social policy and development programs. By highlighting recent cases mostly involving developing host states, this section explores how BITs as interpreted in investor–state dispute settlement have constrained domestic policy space.

1   The Rise of the Regulatory State versus the Expansion of Indirect Expropriation Claims

The first wave of opening to foreign direct investment in developing countries often took place in a low-intensity regulatory environment, which is in part what made the country attractive to foreign investors. Limited environmental and labor regulation, little or no competition (antitrust) discipline, and scarce consumer protection laws and standards made many emerging markets lower entry-cost environments than industrialized counterparts with their sophisticated administrative states. But that state of affairs tends to change over time as a result of different pressures. Investors themselves may push for a more robust regulatory framework in the area of intellectual property, for instance, and that may have spillover effects inasmuch as it teaches the host state how to develop administrative agencies. They may also want more robust infrastructure in the energy, communication and transportation sectors, which might in turn require more state intervention and the development of oversight agencies. Participation in a regional or global market might result in more robust regulation as domestic producers seek to protect themselves from foreign competition, and conversely, as they seek to meet norms and standards in foreign markets they are hoping to access. Hence, directly or indirectly, membership in trade integration or trade liberalization systems, including the WTO, might lead to some increased regulatory activity and the development of an administrative apparatus to manage new commitments, at least in the area of customs and intellectual property. Pressure from the public, consumers, NGOs or certain sectors (such as the tourism industry) may lead to more stringent sanitary standards. Industrialization also tends to require standardization in processes and inputs, including energy inputs. Socioeconomic development, including securing private property attractive to foreign investors, also usually involves reform of rules governing land ownership and use, with the emergence of planning-permitting schemes and property-recording agencies.

While many of these regulatory developments can lead to a safer, more predictable investment environment and a higher value consumer market, investors regularly lodged claims against the state when they were affected by such changes in the administrative and legal environment regulating their investment. New or different planning permissions, environmental authorizations, or the denial thereof have triggered claims of indirect expropriation using treaty terms that were originally meant to address outright takings and nationalization, such as those that were experienced in oil-producing states in the 1970s. Sornarajah catalogs expropriation claims in response to regulatory controls[96] in the telecommunication sector,[97] banking and finance,[98] health,[99] environment,[100] and protection of cultural property.[101]

An early formulation of the doctrine of indirect expropriation is provided by the Iran–U.S. Claims Tribunal in *Starret Housing Corp v. Iran* and has been cited in numerous arbitration awards since then:

> [I]t is recognized by international law that measures taken by a State can interfere with property rights to such an extent that these rights are rendered so useless that they must be deemed to have been expropriated even though the state does not purport to have expropriated them and the legal title to the property formally remains with the original owner.[102]

In an increasing number of cases, claimants construe expropriation provisions to include regulatory changes that decreased the value of investments, or made it impossible to proceed with the investment as originally planned by the investor. Not all such arguments have been successful. In cases where they are, the balance between property and contracts rights of investors on one hand, and public policy considerations of the host state on the other hand, typically tilted in favor of private rights. In other cases, the arbitrators did find that there was an

---

[96] SORNARAJAH, *supra* note 83 at 201.

[97] Telekom Malaysia v. Ghana, PCA Case Repository 2003–03, (Perm. Ct. Arb. 2003), www.italaw.com/cases/documents/1201.

[98] Rafat Ali Rizvi v. Indon., ICSID Case No. ARB/11/13 (July 16, 2013), www.italaw .com/cases/1188; Abaclat v. Argentina, ICSID Case No. ARB/07/5 (Aug. 4, 2011), www.italaw.com/cases/35.

[99] Phillip Morris v. Uruguay (ICSID), www.italaw.com/cases/460; Achmea v. Slovak Republic, UNCITRAL Case No. 20133/12 (May 20, 2014); Servier v. Poland, UNCITRAL. Pharmaceutical companies have also claimed expropriation or breach of fair and equitable treatment against host countries with mature regulatory environments, including Canada and the United States (Eli Lilley v. Canada and Apotex v. United States).

[100] Santa Elena SA v. Costa Rica, *supra* note 87.

[101] Malay. Salvors v. Malay., ICSID Case No. ARB/05/10 (May 17, 2007); Parkerings v. Lith., ICSID Case No. ARB/05/8 (Sept. 11, 2007). *See generally* VALENTINA VADI, CULTURAL HERITAGE IN INTERNATIONAL INVESTMENT LAW AND ARBITRATION (2014).

[102] Starrett Housing Corporation v. Islamic Republic of Iran, Case No. 24, Interlocutory Award No. ITL 32-24-1, Dec. 19, 1983, 4 Iran–US CTR 122, p. 154.

expropriation but did not award any compensation, typically on the basis that the financial loss was really due to the investor's mismanagement rather than the regulatory measure. In those cases, the consequences for the host state are more limited financially, but the concern is the chilling effect on the state's policy-making autonomy. Indeed, the principle of the state's liability has already been established, and future awards agreeing with the reasoning may well go on to require compensation if the investor had a viable project. Last, in a number of cases, the expropriation claim was not adjudicated because the parties settled, typically with the state making an undisclosed payment to the investor. Some of these cases may be a manifestation of the chilling effect just discussed: rather than risk an adverse finding on the expropriation claim, the state would rather settle and cut the proceedings short.

The case of *Santa Elena SA v. Costa Rica* illustrates the first scenario inasmuch as the government measures initially involved indirect expropriation but the case ultimately turned into a direct expropriation argument. There, the expropriation claim was successful and a significant compensatory amount was awarded to the claimant. The case involved a tourist site development project by U.S. investors in a biodiverse area of Costa Rica. The land had been purchased for close to USD 400,000 and various studies were undertaken thereafter aiming for a tourist resort development. Some eight years after the original purchase, Costa Rica issued several environmental decrees, culminating with decrees extending the neighboring nature and wildlife conservation national park to include the land under development and ultimately also engaged in a direct expropriation of the land with compensation amounting to USD 1.9 million. The tribunal did not dispute the state's right to expropriate, though no analysis was offered beyond a general reference to the international law standard for expropriation.[103] The main contentious issue was compensation. The tribunal merely split the difference between the government's offer for compensation in the final expropriation decree and the claimant's valuation at the time. The sum then was multiplied nearly by four to account for the interest accrued since the date of the expropriation two decades earlier. Since then, the parties had been embroiled in domestic judicial proceedings to resolve their difference regarding the amount for compensation. The arbitral tribunal provided no discussion of the text of the BIT, including whether it had any requirement for exhaustion of local remedies that may have justified

---

[103] Santa Elena v. Costa Rica, *supra* note 87, ¶¶ 55, 71.

such lengthy proceedings of nearly two decades. If there was no such requirement, and the claimant could have requested an arbitration soon after the expropriation, it seems surprising that they would be entitled to vast sums of compound interest thanks to delaying initiation of arbitration proceedings, particularly as no physical development had ever taken place on the land.

Plama v. Bulgaria exemplifies a variant on the second scenario, where the tribunal found that there was no expropriation only because there was no loss of the economic enjoyment of the property since the investment was not yielding a financial benefit in the first place. Most other tribunals tend to treat the indirect expropriation separately from the issue of the financial damage, if any, and address the latter together with the calculation of compensation. In that case, the tribunal identified the following factors to determine whether an indirect expropriation had taken place, which would require compensation by the host state:

> (i) substantially complete deprivation of the economic use and enjoyment of the rights to the investment, or of identifiable, distinct parts thereof (i.e., approaching total impairment); (ii) the irreversibility and permanence of the contested measures (i.e., not ephemeral or temporary); and (iii) the extent of the loss of economic value experienced by the investor.[104]

The public purpose of the regulatory action or its policy rationale is not taken into account in this test. In fact, the law being challenged as an indirect expropriation was passed on a recommendation by the World Bank in an effort to improve the regulatory framework in compliance with the Energy Charter Treaty.[105]

Tza Yap Shum v. Peru illustrates the third scenario, where the tribunal found an indirect expropriation and imposed damages.[106] The Chinese investor's company in Peru was subjected to a tax audit, which the tribunal deemed a routine and justified exercise of the administrative state. However, Peru then imposed some onerous interim measures in response to the tax irregularities it had detected, even though the imposition of such measures was normally justified only in more extraordinary circumstances, presumably beyond merely owing back taxes. As a result of the interim measures, which included an asset freeze and preventing the investor from carrying on normal operations through Peru's banking

---

[104] Plama v. Bulgaria, *supra* note 95 at ¶ 193.
[105] *Id.* at ¶ 218.
[106] Tza Yap Shum v. Perú, *supra* note 90.

system, the business was substantially encumbered, had to be restructured, and eventually lost profitability. In the meantime, the investor challenged the interim measures in domestic courts. The tribunal found that the imposition of interim measures was arbitrary because the authority granting the measures had to abide by their own administrative guidelines and therefore the actions amounted to an indirect expropriation.[107] The tribunal further noted that the interim measures had been ineffective for tax collection purposes, as they only secured assets amounting to around USD 170, compared to the USD 4 million tax debt.[108] The tribunal also found that the investor had been denied due process in his quest to challenge the interim measures in domestic administrative and judicial proceedings.[109]

One puzzling aspect of this decision is the focus on expropriation rather than denial of fair and equitable treatment (FET). Since the tribunal is cautious in multiple instances to affirm the legitimacy of the state's tax regulatory authority[110] and ground its finding of wrongdoing on the arbitrariness and denial of due process in the manner of the application of the state's regulatory and administrative authority to the investor, it would seem that FET would be a more suitable avenue for analysis. Nowhere is there any suggestion of the state's taking of the investor's asset in any way, only that the investment was harmed by the arbitrary application of the tax interim measures. As a result, this decision may hint at the potential for an overbroad expansion of the concept of indirect expropriation that becomes increasingly unmoored from any notion of taking, and blurs the line with other rights recognized under BITs, such as FET.

2 Conflicts between Social Policies, Human Rights and Investment Protection

A significant body of literature explores the problematic intersection of human rights and investment law.[111] A number of cases suggest the

[107] Id. at ¶¶ 171–217.
[108] Id. at ¶¶ 219–22.
[109] Id. at ¶¶ 223–40.
[110] See, e.g., Tza Yap Shum v. Perú, supra note 90 at ¶180 ("[e]ven though the Tribunal recognizes that the regulatory authority of the State deserves deferential treatment, it is essential to do so without losing sight of the reasons why such deference is accorded.").
[111] E.g., HUMAN RIGHTS IN INTERNATIONAL INVESTMENT LAW AND ARBITRATION (Pierre-Marie Dupuy et al., eds., 2009); Bruno Simma & Ted Kill, Harmonizing Investment Protection and Human Rights: First Step towards a Methodology, in INTERNATIONAL INVESTMENT LAW FOR THE 21ST CENTURY: ESSAYS IN HONOUR

practice is tilted in favor of private rights of investors, rather than public policy and human rights. This section provides a few examples.

The 2007 arbitration in *Piero Foresti v. Republic of South Africa* illustrates potential clashes between investor rights and socioeconomic policies that foster economic and social human rights. This case concerned the broad-based Black Economic Empowerment (BEE) provisions of the Minerals and Petroleum Resources Development Act of 2002 (MPRDA). The claimants, several Italian citizens and a Luxembourg corporation, alleged that provisions of the MPRDA, which required mining companies to transfer 26 percent of their shares to historically disadvantaged South Africans, amounted to the expropriation of their mineral rights. The government responded by defending its obligation to promote equality under both international human rights law and the South African Constitution, and argued that the mining policy was aimed at realizing its human rights obligations. The case was ultimately settled, illustrating the third type of case, where an expropriation claim is made but the state settles before the decision on the merits is handed down.

The emerging right to water[112] appears in a number of arbitrations, yet its legal role in interpreting investment treaties remains embryonic at best. The fact pattern typically involves private operators providing subpar water distribution or treatment services, such that the host state eventually finds it necessary to take over operations. In *Biwater Gauff v. Tanzania*, the tribunal found the private investor's loss to be inevitable, as the loss was largely due to the investor's own miscalculation of the financial viability of the operation, but nonetheless found the host state to be in breach of the BIT for having taken over the facility without compensation, even though it found that none was due.[113] This case illustrates another instance, where the tribunal made a finding of expropriation potentially exposing the state to financial liability, but did not award compensation based on the specific facts. A number of other cases involved the price of water supplied by private operators. *Aguas del Tunari S.A. v. Bolivia* involved a series of events that became known as

OF CHRISTOPH SCHREUER (Christina Binder et al., eds., 2009) at 678–79; Ryan Suda, *The Effect on Bilateral Investment Treaties on Human Rights Enforcement and Realization*, in TRANSNATIONAL CORPORATIONS AND HUMAN RIGHTS (Olivier De Schutter, ed., 2006).

[112] Edith Brown Weiss, *The Evolution of International Water Law*, in COLLECTED COURSE OF THE HAGUE ACAD. INT'L L. 308, 332 (2009).

[113] Biwater v. Tanzania, *supra* note 88.

the "Water Wars," leading to major civil unrest and violence relating to a failed privatization of water facilities in the Bolivian city of Cochabamba.[114] After protracted proceedings, the tribunal found that it had jurisdiction, but the parties ultimately settled, with the state buying back the investor's shares for a nominal sum (equivalent to USD 0.25) and providing no additional compensation.[115] In its objections to the tribunal's jurisdiction, Bolivia argued that the subject matter at stake – the conditions for private ownership of the country's resources, including water – required exclusive jurisdiction in Bolivian courts, as a constitutional matter.[116] The tribunal rejected the argument on jurisdiction.

The case of *Suez and Interagua Servicios Integrales de Agua v. Argentina* also involved access to water in a privatized environment. The tribunal did not find any expropriation, but did find that the state had breached its obligations of fair and equitable treatment by refusing to renegotiate the tariff rates for water.[117] The tribunal noted that fair and equitable treatment meant more than the protection of investors' rights, and should instead be read in the context of the object and purpose of the BIT, which included references to economic cooperation and the broader benefits, including technology transfer, to be derived from it.[118] Argentina raised the right-to-water argument in support of its necessity defense.[119] The tribunal did not respond to this argument, and focused solely on the broader necessity defense relating to Argentina's economic crisis prevailing at the time of the events, ultimately rejecting the defense in line with the *CMS v. Argentina* case.

On their face, BITs respect policy and regulatory choices of the host country, particularly if they only address post-establishment investment issues. However, interpretations in arbitrations have become much more inquisitive of state regulation, most notably through an increasingly broad understanding of what is guaranteed by fair and equitable treatment and the type of asset that qualifies as a protected investment, and by a broadening of the definition of expropriation to include regulatory measures with an effect akin to expropriation, much beyond traditional takings. At the same time, the landscape for the treatment of both host

---

[114] William Finnegan, *Leasing the Rain: The World Is Running Out of Fresh Water, and the Fight to Control It Has Begun*, NEW YORKER 43 (April 8, 2002).

[115] Aguas del Tunari S.A. v. Republic of Bolivia, ICSID Case No. ARB/02/3; Damon Vis-Dunbar & Luke Eric Peterson, *Bolivian Water Dispute Settled; Bechtel Forgoes Compensation*, INV. TREATY NEWS, Jan. 20, 2006, www.iisd.org/investment/itn.

[116] Aguas del Tunari v. Bolivia, *supra* note 115 at ¶ 100.

[117] Suez v. Argentina, *supra* note 95 at ¶ 151, 217–18.

[118] *Id.* at ¶ 197–202.

[119] *Id.* at ¶ 232.

states and private investors varies considerably from award to award with regard to substantive rights, as well as possible defenses available to the state. As a result, both sides have complained of inconsistency and unpredictability in the legal environment governing foreign investment.[120] While the trend is true generally, it affects emerging countries particularly when the policies at stake relate to their developmental objectives. In a number of cases, the arbitrators ultimately sided with the state and did not find an expropriation, or did not award damages despite an expropriation finding. The argument here is therefore that beyond outright conflicts between treaty protections and state policies, a vast and perhaps even more concerning gray area is created by the uncertainty as to whether the state policy will ultimately be undermined by a treaty provision. The result is a possibly chilling effect on state policy autonomy, as host states may wonder whether a particular developmental policy will expose them to costly litigation, poor market signaling, and other economic backlash from the investment community.

Since emerging countries often entered into BITs for motivations that were separate from an integrated development plan, discrepancies later surface when the host country seeks to apply new regulatory frameworks, new fiscal or monetary environments, and new socioeconomic policies to foreign investors.

D   Attempts to Use Flexibilities in the Investment Regime

1   Non-preclusion Measures

In the wake of Argentina's 2000–02 financial and currency crisis, exceptions provisions or non-precluded measures clauses have come into the limelight.[121] By way of illustration, the U.S.–Argentina BIT article XI provides:

> This Treaty shall not preclude the application by either Party of measures necessary for the maintenance of public order, the fulfillment of its obligations with respect to the maintenance or restoration of international peace or security, or the Protection of its own essential security interests.[122]

---

[120] Lack of consistency has also been noted with respect to procedural issues. *See, e.g.,* Julie Maupin, *MFN-based Jurisdiction in Investor–State Arbitration: Is There Any Hope for a Consistent Approach?*, 14 J. INT'L ECON. L. 157 (2011).

[121] William W. Burke-White & Andreas von Staden, *Investment Protection in Extraordinary Times: The Interpretation and Application of Non-Precluded Measures Provisions in Bilateral Investment Treaties*, 48 VA J. INT'L L. 307, 337 (2007).

[122] http://investmentpolicyhub.unctad.org/Download/TreatyFile/127.

Since some treaties include fairly detailed substantive exceptions[123] and others provide only limited and generic mentions of "essential security interests,"[124] there is no general jurisprudence of what types of grounds justify a host state's derogation from its treaty commitments, and interpretations vary.[125] A host state wishing to avail itself of the flexibilities of non-preclusion measures will face two types of issues. First, it will have to ascertain whether its contemplated measure is the type of intervention covered by the treaty (such as measures necessary to maintain public order). Second, it will have to determine the legal effect of a qualification of non-preclusion. For example, does it exempt the state from treaty compliance altogether, or does it have a more limited effect? Is the state required to undertake less restrictive measures if they are available? As a subsidiary consideration, should the issue be litigated or challenged in arbitration, further questions may arise as to the allocation of the burden of proof and the level of proof required.

In the Argentine case, different arbitrators issued conflicting interpretations of article XI. Presented with the same facts and arguments, tribunals in five cases reached opposite decisions. In *LG&E Energy Corp. v. Argentina*, the tribunal found that Argentina was justified in invoking the non-preclusion measure based on the severity of the economic crisis and the sociopolitical disruption it caused. This was the first case where a host state successfully claimed that measures taken in response to an economic crisis were needed for the protection of essential security interests.[126] *Continental Casualty Company v. Argentina* also found that the defense of article XI was available and properly invoked by the host state against all but one claim.[127] By contrast, the tribunals in *CMS v. Argentina, Enron v. Argentina* and *Sempra v. Argentina*[128]

---

[123] See, e.g., DR-CAFTA, Article 10.9.3(c) (2004); ASEAN Comprehensive Investment Agreement, art. 17 (2009); US–Uruguay BIT, art. 8(3)(c) (2005); Canada–Egypt BIT, Art. XVII (1996).

[124] Katia Yannaca-Small, *Essential Security Interests under International Investment Law*, in INTERNATIONAL INVESTMENT PERSPECTIVES: FREEDOM OF INVESTMENT IN A CHANGING WORLD (OECD ed., 2007).

[125] Diane A. Desierto, *Necessity and "Supplementary Means of Interpretation" for Non-Precluded Measures in Bilateral Investment Treaties*, 31 U. PA. J. INT'L. L. 827 (2010); DIANE DESIERTO, PUBLIC POLICY IN INTERNATIONAL ECONOMIC LAW: THE ICESCR IN TRADE, FINANCE, AND INVESTMENT (2015), at 326–29.

[126] LG&E v. Argentina, *supra* note 95.

[127] Continental Casualty Company v. Argentina, ICSID Case No ARB/03/9, IIC 511, Final Award (Sept. 16, 2011), www.italaw.com/sites/default/files/case-documents/ita0228.pdf, ¶ 233.

[128] *Supra* note 91.

rejected Argentina's non-precluded measure defense. Inconsistencies in interpretation arose in virtually every aspect of the defense, particularly the analysis of the necessity requirement, the scope of "essential security" and "public order," and the relationship between BIT language and general public international law standards of necessity. Commentators have pointed out analytical, conceptual and interpretative shortcomings of this ensemble of cases.[129]

The scope and availability of non-preclusion measures under treaties of friendship, commerce and navigation also arose in International Court of Justice (ICJ) disputes.[130] Additionally, GATT articles XX and XXI apply to the Agreement on Trade-Related Investment Measures and may, therefore, affect the lawfulness of certain measures relating to foreign investments taken by WTO members. No dispute has yet arisen on that point at the WTO. Some arbitrators and advocates nonetheless refer to reports from panels and the Appellate Body interpreting the notion of necessity under GATT articles XX and XXI in disputes involving the trade of goods rather than investments.[131]

Uncertainty and lack of predictability regarding the legal treatment of major national policies in these cases stoke the smoldering opposition from many emerging countries to the ISDS system and the contour of the rights and obligations under BITs. As the main mechanism for flexibility in BITs, non-preclusion measures offer uncertain and limited leeway for host states to deal with major inflections in their social, political or economic situation. The scarce invocation of non-preclusion measures

---

[129] See, e.g., Andrea Bjorklund, *Emergency Exceptions: State of Necessity and Force Majeure*, in OXFORD HANDBOOK OF INTERNATIONAL INVESTMENT LAW 459 (Peter Muchlinski et al., eds., 2008); William W. Burke-White & Andreas von Staden, *Investment Protection in Extraordinary Times: The Interpretation and Application of Non-Precluded Measures Provisions in Bilateral Investment Treaties*, 48 VA J. INT'L L. 307, 337 (2007); William W. Burke-White & Andreas von Staden, *Non-Precluded Measures Provisions, the State of Necessity, and State Liability for Investor Harms in Exceptional Circumstances*, in LATIN AMERICAN INVESTMENT TREATY ARBITRATION: THE CONTROVERSIES AND CONFLICTS (Thomas E. Carbonneau & Mary H. Mourra, eds., 2008); Desierto, *supra* note 125; Jürgen Kurtz, *Adjudging the Exceptional at International Investment Law: Security, Public Order and Financial Crisis*, 59 INT'L & COMP. L. Q. 325, 326 (2010).

[130] Oil Platforms (Iran v. U.S.), 2003 I.C.J. 161, ¶ 43 (Nov. 6) (involving article XX [1][d] of the Treaty of Amity, Economic Relations and Consular Rights between the United States and Iran); Military and Paramilitary Activities in and Against Nicaragua (Nicar. v. U.S.), 1986 I.C.J. 14, ¶ 223 (June 27) (involving the Treaty of Friendship, Commerce and Navigation between the United States and Nicaragua).

[131] See, e.g., Continental Casualty v. Argentina, *supra* note 127 at ¶¶ 85, 184, 192, 193, 226.

since the Argentina crisis arbitrations may be further indication that host states do not perceive these provisions as significant tools to preserve their ability to regulate.

2 Leveraging Multiple Fora

Host states challenged by investors or dissatisfied with an arbitral award have not limited themselves to ISDS processes and their progeny, including seeking annulment of awards. They have pursued remedies in a range of fora, including the International Court of Justice and domestic courts. This testifies to creative attempts to create flexibilities outside of the traditional channels. Such strategies are seldom deployed and even more rarely successful, and may at times backfire.

Argentina sought to institute proceedings against the United States at the ICJ in August 2014 to dispute U.S. court decisions pertaining to Argentina's sovereign debt restructuring.[132] The application lodged by Argentina may not be entered into the docket unless and until the United States consents to jurisdiction (*forum prorogatum* rule), which it has not expressed as of January 2019.

Forum shopping at times plays against host states. Kyrgyzstan pled *res judicata* to resist claims in an investor–state arbitration under a BIT on the basis that the matter had already been adjudicated in domestic court.[133] The arbitral tribunal concluded that the investor was not precluded from raising claims under the BIT that had not been vented in the domestic proceedings, even though the investor could have raised such claims in the domestic proceedings or in an earlier arbitration.[134] This decision appears to give the investor three opportunities to vindicate a BIT claim while the host state was unable to resist this forum shopping.

Lastly, actions by foreign investors are at times challenged by private parties, rather than the state, also creating opportunities and complications for host states seeking to police investments in their territory. The Chevron–Ecuador dispute provides a recent illustration. In 1993, some thirty thousand residents of the Oriente region of Ecuador and adjoining areas in Peru filed suit in the United States alleging that the oil drilling activities of Texaco's local subsidiary resulted in pollution of the

---

[132] International Court of Justice, Press Release, Aug. 7, 2014, www.icj-cij.org/files/press-releases/4/18354.pdf.
[133] Petrobart Ltd. v. Kyrgyz Rep., Arb. No. 126/2003 (Arb. Inst. of the Stockholm Chamber of Commerce 2005), www.italaw.com/sites/default/ files/case-documents/ita0628.pdf, at p. 38–40.
[134] *Id.* at 66–68.

rainforests and rivers in this area.[135] Texaco won dismissal on the basis of *forum non conveniens* and international comity. It had the support of a letter from Ecuador's ambassador to the United States arguing that the "Government of Ecuador considered the suit an affront to Ecuador's national sovereignty."[136] Litigation in Ecuador resulted in a USD 18 billion judgment against Chevron (which had, by then, acquired the relevant Texaco entities), later reduced to some USD 8 billion. The plaintiffs promptly sought to enforce the judgment in various jurisdictions including Canada, Argentina, Colombia and Brazil.[137] Meanwhile, Chevron initiated proceedings in U.S. courts to block recognition of the Ecuadorean judgment should the plaintiff attempt to enforce it in the United States. After lengthy proceedings, the plaintiffs were barred from enforcing the judgment in the United States, and found liable for costs to Chevron due to bribery, extortion and other fraudulent behavior during the proceedings in Ecuador.[138] Throughout this saga, Ecuador continued to participate in the proceedings. It sued as intervenor plaintiff, together with Petroecuador, the state-owned oil company, in the original action;[139] it provided affidavits;[140] it submitted numerous amicus curiae briefs, including when the U.S. Supreme Court was asked to opine on whether federal courts could entertain a preemptive collateral estoppel attack on a judgment from a foreign court.[141]

---

[135] Aguinda v. Texaco, Inc., Dkt. No. 93 Civ. 7527 (S.D.N.Y. filed Nov. 3, 1993).

[136] Aguinda v. Texaco, Inc., No. 93 Civ. 7527, 1994 WL 142006, at 2 (S.D.N.Y. Apr. 11, 1994) and Aguinda v. Texaco, Inc., 303 F. 3d 470 (2nd Cir. 2002).

[137] Howard Erichson, *The Chevron–Ecuador Dispute, Forum Non Conveniens, and the Problem of Ex Ante Inadequacy*, 1 STAN. J. OF COMPLEX. LITIG. 417, 417 (2013).

[138] Chevron Corp. v. Donziger, 768 F. Supp. 2d 581, 660 (S.D.N.Y. 2011), rev'd and remanded sub nom. Chevron Corp. v. Naranjo, 667 F.3d 232 (2d Cir. 2012), Chevron Corp. v. Donziger Nos. 14-0826(L), 14-0832(C), 2016 WL 4173988 (2d Cir. Aug. 8, 2016).

[139] Intervenor-Plaintiffs the Republic of Ecuador and PetroEcuador's Complaint Maria Aguinda et al., Plaintiffs, v. Texaco, Inc., Defendant, 1996 WL 33670831 (S.D.N.Y.).

[140] Affidavit of Ambassador Edgar Teran, 1996 WL 33670825 (S.D.N.Y.); Affidavit of Ambassador Edgar Teran, 1996 WL 33670827 (S.D.N.Y.); Affidavit of Ambassador Edgar Teran, 1994 WL 16188160 (S.D.N.Y.).

[141] Brief for the Republic of Ecuador as Amicus Curiae in Support of the Petition for Certiorari, 2017 WL 1682687 (U.S.); Brief of the Republic of Ecuador as Amicus Curiae, 2001 WL 34369154 (2d Cir.); Supplemental Brief Amicus Curiae of the Republic of Ecuador, 1996 WL 33670826 (S.D.N.Y.); Brief Amicus Curiae of the Republic of Ecuador, 1994 WL 16188165 (S.D.N.Y.).

III   Conclusion

Both trade and investment rules, and the institutions that undergird them, are facing growing criticism from emerging countries.

In the trade arena, developing countries' practices span a spectrum ranging from increased participation in the institutions and use of flexibilities within the system, to breaches of the system and resisting the creation of further rules. Overall, though, there does not appear to be a radical contestation of the existing system. For instance, no developing country is threatening to leave the WTO. This foreshadows developing countries' moves to create other trade rules or regimes that are meant to complement or overlap with the existing framework, rather than amount to a complete alternative. Chapter 5 will explore the steps taken in response to developing countries' perceived and experienced difficulties with the current trade law regime.

The BITs system, which promised to be predictable, fair, and development friendly, is not delivering on those promises. The ISDS system is not generating clear and general rules; its fairness is questioned because adjudicators are drawn from a narrow spectrum of business-oriented lawyers; and restrictions on development policy space clash with important policy initiatives. Since arbitrators have substantial discretion to interpret general terms, and there is no method to impose uniformity, they have interpreted BITs in ways that leave a high degree of uncertainty concerning the scope of these agreements. Because at least some arbitrators have tended to favor private interests over public policies, and have stretched treaty language to that end, the price in policy space foregone has been increased beyond anything that might have been anticipated when the agreements were signed. Even when developing countries have successfully defended policy initiatives, opinions have included language that could be used in subsequent cases to restrict their actions. Faced with uncertain and ill-defined risks to policy measures, developing states may increasingly hesitate before initiating controversial actions.

While emerging economies have been the most vocal critics of international investment law, some in capital-exporting countries also question the agreements now that they find themselves on the receiving end of investment, playing the role of host state. As emerging economies become capital exporters, developed countries face challenges to their own regulatory autonomy and are coming under pressure from multinational corporations. For example, in the debates over the Trans-Pacific

Partnership (TPP) and the Transatlantic Trade and Investment
Partnership (TTIP), strong voices in the United States and Europe
spoke out against the use of ISDS. With opposition to the BITs regime
developing in both the North and the South, it may be that a broader
global shift is underway that could lead to new standards of, and new
processes for, foreign investment regulation. Notably, the agreement
between the United States of America, the United Mexican States and
Canada (USMCA) (revised NAFTA) will preclude traditional ISDS
between the United States and Canada beyond the first three years of
the agreement.[142] Instead, investors will need to press their claims in
domestic courts. As between the United States and Mexico, investors will
need to pursue local remedies in domestic courts for thirty months before
being able to trigger an investor–state arbitration[143] and at any rate,
claims will be limited to expropriation and nondiscrimination. Fair and
equitable treatment is no longer an available claim under the
agreement.[144] Chapter 4 explores the alternative frameworks and legal
standards promoted by emerging countries in response to their critique
of the current international investment law system.

---

[142] Agreement between the United States of America, the United Mexican States and
Canada (USMCA), Chapter 14 and Annex 14-C, art. 3, https://ustr.gov/sites/default/
files/files/agreements/FTA/USMCA/Text/14_Investment.pdf.
[143] *Id.* Annex 14-D, art. 14.D.5.
[144] *Id.* Annex 14-D, art. 14.D.3.

4

Seeking a New Balance of Rights and Obligations in International Investment Law

As Chapter 3 discussed, the nature of developing countries' resistance to the traditional BITs regime varies. Some states are withdrawing from existing agreements[1] or related systems such as the World Bank's International Center for the Settlement of Investment Disputes (ICSID). Others call for changes in the scope of new BITs, and yet others promote radical alternatives. If Chapter 3 was the "diagnosis" regarding discontent with the international investment regime, this chapter examines the "cure" proposed by emerging powers in response.[2]

Recent BITs signed by emerging countries, and the Model BITs they have developed, offer a departure from the consensus of the 1990s and early 2000s, from the treaty coverage to the nature of the rights and obligations of host states and investors. For instance, South Africa enacted a Protection of Investment Act in 2015, which seeks to replace bilateral treaties with domestic legislation stipulating the rights and obligations of the government and of all investors, both local and foreign.[3] Brazil, which has traditionally relied on domestic law to manage

---

[1] Indonesia's and South Africa's policy is to notify partners of its intent not to renew BITs that reach the ten- or fifteen-year period for initial validity. The first South African treaties to lapse under this type of sunset clause were the BITs with the Belgium-Luxembourg Economic Union (2012), with Switzerland (2013), with the Netherlands (2013), with Spain (2013), with Germany (2014), with Austria (2014), with France (2014) and with Denmark (2014). South Africa also plans to reconsider its BIT with China when the initial ten-year validity period comes to term (in 2018). Indonesia has terminated BITs with Norway (2001), Egypt (2014), Bulgaria (2015), China (2015), France (2015), Italy (2015), Lao People's Democratic Republic (2015), Malaysia (2015), Netherlands (2015), Slovakia (2015), Cambodia (2016), Romania (2016), Turkey (2016) and Vietnam (2016). Additionally, the Indonesia–Argentina BIT was terminated by mutual agreement.

[2] This chapter is adapted in part from Sonia E. Rolland and David M. Trubek, *Legal Innovation in Investment Law: Rhetoric and Practice in the South*, 39 U. PENN. J. INTL L. 355 (2017) and Sonia E. Rolland, *The Return of State Remedies in Investor–State Dispute Settlement: Trends in Developing Countries*, 49 LOYOLA U. CHI. L. J. 387 (2017).

[3] *See generally* Protection of Investment Act 22 of 2015 (S. Afr.).

foreign investment, has now adopted a new form of bilateral treaty called Cooperation and Investment Facilitation Agreements (CIFAs), which defines investment more narrowly than traditional BITs, limits the scope of protection, stresses investment facilitation and dispute avoidance, and eschews ISDS. In 2012, Indonesia undertook a review of its international investment agreements in reaction to high-profile arbitration claims in the banking and mining sectors. Meanwhile, India and others have released new Model BITs that depart from the traditional framework quite significantly. China, after evolving through several Model BITs, now proceeds largely on an ad hoc basis.

The process for defining negotiating positions also has evolved to be more inclusive and more deliberative. The new Indian Model BIT illustrates these trends. In 2015, the Indian government published a draft Model BIT and requested comments from the public. The draft Model BIT deviated significantly from prior Indian Models and from BITs already signed by India. Observers noted that the draft Model represented a radical policy shift by the Indian National Congress-led government that had worked on it until May 2014. The government seemed to wish to assert a narrower meaning for key terms in response to the flood of claims filed since 2012, many based on very liberal readings of the original BITs.[4] Noting that the draft severely restricts the potential impact of ISDS on policy space, some argued that the goal was to foreclose the kinds of claims the country had faced recently.[5] It is no surprise, therefore, that it inspired a rather heated debate and submission of formal comments from groups as diverse as the Indian Law Commission and the U.S. National Association of Manufacturers (NAM). The NAM compared the draft Indian Model to "global standards," and found it sorely lacking in almost every way.[6] The NAM's brief

---

[4] *See* Grant Hanessian & Kabir Duggal, *The 2015 India Model BIT: Is This the Change the World Wishes to See?*, 30 ICSID REV. 729, 731 (2015) (proliferation of claims after 2012 "caused the Indian establishment to consider redrafting its model BIT ... ").

[5] *See* DMD Advocates, *Why India's Draft Model Bilateral Investment Treaty Is a Bit of a Misnomer*, LEGALLYINDIA (May 11, 2015), www.legallyindia.com/views/entry/why-india-s-draft-model-bilateral-investment-treaty-is-a-bit-of-a-misnomer. ("The changes brought in the Draft Model BIT grant minimal protection to investors and are more protective of India's interests than of the investors.")

[6] *See* NAT'L ASS'N OF MFRS., COMMENT ON DRAFT INDIAN MODEL BILATERAL INVESTMENT TREATY 1 (2015), www.nam.org/Issues/Trade/ISDS/NAM-Comments-on-Draft-India-Model-Bilateral-Investment-Treaty-Joint-US-EU-Business.pdf ("[T]he NAM finds that there are many aspects of the draft Indian Model BIT that deviate substantially from global standards ... ").

claims that India had departed from established international investment standards: the coverage of investment was much too narrow; compulsory licensing of intellectual property would undermine efforts to attract high-quality investment; exclusion of a broad commitment for fair and equitable treatment violated international norms and created a lower standard for investors under any new agreements signed in the future; the definition of expropriation was too narrow and "far below international standards"; and ISDS deviated from global best practice as illustrated by the U.S. Model BIT because of an exhaustion-of-remedies requirement, jurisdictional limits and exclusion of review of host state use of exceptions.[7] The final version of the Model, amended under the Modi administration, addresses a number of these industry concerns, and to some degree realigns India with more traditional BIT-drafting practices. Some commentators argue that the adopted 2016 Model BIT, while ostensibly still seeking to reclaim policy space for regulators and limit exposure to arbitration, fails on both counts.[8]

This section explores changes to key aspects of investment agreements: the definition of investments and investors (A), the rights and protections granted to investors (B), exceptions and derogations to protect host states' regulatory prerogative (C), and obligations of investors and home states (D).

I Redefining Investment and Investor

FDI might have been understood in the 1980s and 1990s as a brick-and-mortar establishment into a host country funded and managed by a company located and operating in another country, but the current reality of foreign investment is considerably different. Today, much of what counts as foreign investment consists of intangible assets such as intellectual property, and financial instruments such as stocks and bonds.[9] The nature of investors, too, has changed as various shell

[7] *See id.* at 2–7 (listing "the most concerning aspects" of the draft Model Indian BIT).
[8] *See* Prabhash Ranjan & Pushkar Anand, *The 2016 Indian Model Bilateral Investment Treaty: A Critical Deconstruction*, 38 Nw. J. Int'l L. & Bus. 1 (2017) (discussing how India has not been able to balance investment protection with the host state's right to regulate in the 2016 Model BIT).
[9] Global Investment Trend Monitor 2 (UNCTAD ed., 2005), http://unctad.org/en/PublicationsLibrary/webdiaeia2016d1_en.pdf (noting that 2015 marked the strongest year for FDI flow since the 2008–09 economic crisis, but these flows "lack[ed] productive impact," as they mostly consisted in mergers and acquisitions and other corporate reconfigurations, rather than greenfield investment projects).

subsidiaries are used to route investments through several countries in order to decrease tax exposure, take advantage of favorable regulatory frameworks, limit legal liability and fulfill other strategic motivations. Traditional treaty terms are now interpreted to include these ever-broadening and increasingly amorphous notions of investment and investor, far beyond what the original negotiations had envisioned.

A number of emerging countries that have traditionally been in the host-country position now question the implications of the diversification of conduits for foreign investment, and the treaty protections these investments receive. In an emerging policy consciousness, these states wish to attract and protect only certain types of investment. One set of issues relates to what does and should qualify as a foreign investment. The debate often focuses on the purported investment's contribution to the local economy. If the investment is short-term, precarious, or purely a pass-through entity, should it really be considered as an investment, and benefit from the full range of treaty protections? At a more fundamental level, if the investment does involve some real and long-term local assets, but the benefits to the local economy are minimal or negative, should the operation be treated differently than investments having positive local impact, or at least deliver what it was contractually bound to produce? Is it appropriate to extend BIT benefits to investments and investors that may be of a considerably different nature than those the treaties were originally drafted to protect? In response, new Model BITs from India, Brazil and elsewhere engage in efforts to restrict the definition of investment and investors.

This section analyzes the solutions offered to these challenges by a number of new Model BITs or other investment instruments from India, China, the SADC, Brazil and South Africa. This list offers a full spectrum of approaches to foreign investment regulation: India uses a full-fledged Model BIT; China now negotiates BITs on an ad hoc basis but had model BITs until about a decade ago; the SADC offers a looser Model consisting of menus of options for each typical provision; Brazil customizes its CIFAs; South Africa relies on domestic legislation.

A   Circumscribing the Scope of Investments Qualifying for Protection

1   India

Compared to older Indian BITs, the 2016 Model uses a much more specific definition of investment, alongside a list of exclusions, and more detailed criteria regarding the definition of an investor. Most of the criteria and exclusions are aimed at covering greenfield investments and other investments that involve real and productive economic activity in the host state, with a genuine and direct link to the home state of the investor. The detailed definition provisions are clearly meant as a rollback on the expansive interpretations of terms in traditional BITs and a response to some of the investor–state litigation and arbitration proceedings, such as those involving government bonds in Argentina.

An investment is defined as "an enterprise constituted, organized and operated in good faith by an investor in accordance with the law of the Party in whose territory the investment is made, taken together with the assets of the enterprise, has the characteristics of an investment such as the commitment of capital or other resources, certain duration, the expectation of gain or profit, the assumption of risk and a significance for the development of the Party in whose territory the investment is made."[10] Additional qualifiers of the term "enterprise" from the draft Model BIT have been abandoned. These included the requirement that an enterprise had "its management and real and substantial business operations in the territory of the Host State."[11] The following did not count for purposes of showing "real and substantial business operations": presence and arrangements mainly for purposes of avoiding tax liabilities; passive holding of financial instruments, land or other property; and ownership or lease of real or personal property in a trade or business.[12] Conversely, a real and substantial business operation required at least "a substantial and long term commitment of capital in the Host state," a "substantial number of employees" locally, the assumption of "entrepreneurial risk," and "a substantial contribution to the development of the Host State through its operations [along with] transfer of technological knowhow, where applicable."[13]

The 2016 Model BIT does, however, categorically exclude a long list of "assets" from the definition of an investment. As a result, the listed tangible and intangible properties and interests are excluded from the ambit of the treaty and may not benefit from its provisions, including

---

[10] Preamble, Government of India, Ministry of Finance, Department of Economic Affairs, Office Memorandum, F. No. 26/5/2013-IC, Annex, art. 1.4, Dec. 28, 2015 [hereinafter 2016 India Model BIT].

[11] Model Text for the Indian Bilateral Investment Treaty, art. 1.2(ii), www.jurisafrica.org/html/pdf_indian-bilateral-investment-treaty.pdf [hereinafter Indian Draft Model BIT].

[12] *Id.* art. 1.2.2.

[13] *Id.* art. 1.2.1.

dispute-settlement clauses. Such assets would presumably be solely covered by domestic law and potentially any residual customary international law protection not displaced by the treaty. The list of exclusions covers government bonds and other debt instruments (likely in reaction to the 2001 Argentina debt default),[14] portfolio investments, any pre-establishment expenditures (likely in response to claims such as *Santa Elena SA v. Costa Rica*),[15] claims resulting from commercial contracts for the sale of goods or services, goodwill, brand value, market shares (perhaps in response to claims by Philip Morris in Australia[16] and elsewhere where intellectual property claims were really a proxy for protection of the brand), and money judgment or arbitral award recovery.[17]

2   China

China has historically defined investment and investor rather broadly in BITs to which it subscribed (the first generation spanning 1982–98 and second generation 1998–2008), and the most recent investment agreements as well as the draft fourth Model BIT mostly carry on that

---

[14] Among the dozens of claims and proceedings, the following cases garnered the most attention: CMS Gas Transmission Co. v. Argentine Republic, ICSID Case No. ARB/01/8, Award (May 12, 2005), 44 I.L.M. 1205 (2005); CMS Gas Transmission Co. v. Argentine Republic, ICSID Case No. ARB/01/8, Decision of the ad hoc Committee on the Application for Annulment of the Argentine Republic (Sept. 25, 2007), http://icsidfiles .worldbank.org/icsid/ICSIDBLOBS/OnlineAwards/C4/DC505_En.pdf http://icsid.world bank.org/ICSID/FrontServlet?requestType=CasesRH&actionVal=showDoc& docId=DC687_En&caseId=C4; LG&E Energy Corp. v. Argentine Republic, ICSID Case No. ARB/02/1, Decision on Liability (Oct. 3, 2006), 21 ICSID Rev. 203 (2006); Enron Corp. Ponderosa Asset, L.P. v. Argentine Republic, ICSID (W. Bank) Case No. ARB/01/3, Award (May 22, 2007), http://ita.law.uvic.ca/documents/Enron-Award.pdf; Sempra Energy Int'l v. Argentine Republic, ICSID Case No. ARB/02/16, Award (Sept. 28, 2007), www.italaw .com/sites/default/files/case-documents/ita0770.pdf. *See generally* William W. Burke-White, *The Argentine Financial Crisis: State Liability under BITs and the Legitimacy of the ICSID System*, 3 ASIAN J. WTO & INTL HEALTH L. & POL'Y 199 (2008); José E. Alvarez & Kathryn Khamsi, *The Argentine Crisis and Foreign Investors – A Glimpse in the Heart of the Investment Regime*, 2008–09 YEARBOOK INTL INVEST L. & POL'Y. 379 (2009).

[15] Compañía del Desarrollo de Santa Elena, S.A. v. The Republic of Costa Rica, ICSID Case No. ARB/96/1, Final Award (Feb. 17, 2000), http://icsidfiles.worldbank.org/icsid/ ICSIDBLOBS/OnlineAwards/C152/DC539_En.pdf, 5 ICSID Rep. 157 (2002).

[16] Philip Morris Asia Ltd. (H.K.) v. Austl., PCA Case Repository 2012–12 (Perm. Ct. Arb., 2012), www.pcacases.com/web/view/5. *See generally* Inaê Siqueira de Oliveira, *Corporate Restructuring and Abuse of Rights: PCA Tribunal Deems Philip Morris's Claims Against Australia's Tobacco Plain Packaging Rules Inadmissible*, INV. TREATY NEWS, Aug. 10, 2016, www.iisd.org/itn/2016/08/10/philip-morris-asia-limited-v-the-commonwealth-of-australia-pca-case-no-2012-12/ (providing a summary of the case).

[17] 2016 India Model BIT, *supra* note 10, art. 1.4.

tradition with respect to the definition of investment. However, some argue that a number of other clauses are drafted more restrictively.[18] Third-generation BITs or recent FTAs addressing investment sometimes exclude certain types of business transactions, such as commercial contracts for the sale of goods or services, and certain classes of assets, such as certain loans and debts.[19] However, China tends to retain a fairly broad definition of investment even in its third-generation agreements. For instance, the fourth draft Model BIT defines investments broadly and provides a non-exhaustive illustrative list that includes shares, stocks, debts, rights under contracts, intellectual property rights, rights conferred by concessions or licenses, and other tangible and intangible property.[20] Recent Chinese BITs and trade agreements including an investment chapter reflect this broad definition.[21]

3   SADC Model BIT

Rather than draft a Model BIT, strictly speaking, the SADC developed a range of recommended drafting options, with commentary detailing some of the pros and cons of each option. With respect to the definition of investment, it offers three formulae: an enterprise-based definition that focuses on corporate establishment or acquisition (inspired by the

---

[18] See Elodie Dulac, *Chinese Investment Treaties: What Protection for Foreign Investment in China*, in DISPUTE RESOLUTION IN CHINA 237, 242–43 (Michael Moser, ed., 2012).

[19] *Id.* at 256; Karl Sauvant & Michael D. Nolan, *China's Outward Foreign Direct Investment and International Investment Law*, 18 J. INT'L ECON. L. 893, 918 (2015) (discussing China's exclusions in its new definition of investments). *See, e.g.*, Agreement between the Government of Canada and the Government of the People's Republic of China for the Promotion and Reciprocal Protection of Investments, Can.–China, art. 1.k, Sept. 9, 2012, http://investmentpolicyhubold.unctad.org/Download/TreatyFile/3476 (applying exclusions to the term "investment").

[20] *See* Draft New Model BIT, China, art. 1.3, *reprinted* in NORAH GALLAGHER & WENHUA SHAN, CHINESE INVESTMENT TREATIES: POLICIES AND PRACTICE app. V (2009) [hereinafter China Draft Model BIT].

[21] *See, e.g.*, Accord de Cooperation entre le Gouvernement de la République du Congo et le Gouvernement de la République Populaire de Chine sur la Promotion et la Protection des Investissements, China–Congo, art. 1, Mar. 20, 2015, http://investmentpolicyhubold .unctad.org/Download/TreatyFile/3586; Free Trade Agreement between the Government of Australia and the Government of the People's Republic of China, Austl.–China, art. 9.1, June 17, 2015, http://investmentpolicyhubold.unctad.org/ Download/TreatyFile/3453; Free Trade Agreement between the Government of the People's Republic of China and the Government of the Republic of Korea, China–S. Korea, art. 12.1, June 1, 2015, http://investmentpolicyhubold.unctad.org/Download/ TreatyFile/3462; Agreement Among the Government of Japan, the Government of the Republic of Korea and the Government of the People's Republic of China for the Promotion, Facilitation and Protection of Investment, Japan–S. Korea–China, art. 1, May 17, 2014, http://investmentpolicyhubold.unctad.org/Download/TreatyFile/2633.

commercial presence definition in the WTO's General Agreement on Trade in Services); an asset-based definition with a limitative, exhaustive list of qualifying assets (based on the Canadian Model BIT); and a broader asset-based definition with an illustrative, non-exhaustive list (based on the U.S. Model BIT). The commentary ultimately recommends the first option (enterprise-based definition) as more likely to "promote investment that is supportive of sustainable development, which development policy suggests means business that brings constructive economic and social benefits."[22] By contrast, it strongly advises against the third option (open list of assets) because it gives much discretion to arbitral tribunals in determining what qualifies as an investment, typically playing out in favor of the investor, and creating much uncertainty for the host state.

Like the Indian draft Model BIT (but unlike the 2016 India Model BIT), the SADC text provides some language regarding long-term establishment, and attempts to prevent shell corporations from benefiting from treaty provisions. The recommendation is a slightly modified version of the *Salini* arbitration award[23] stating that "[i]n order to qualify as an investment under this Agreement, an asset must have the characteristics of an investment, such as the [substantial] commitment of capital or other resources, the expectation of gain or profit, the assumption of risk and a significance for the Host State's development." Although the language is not as pointed as in the Indian version, the objective of limiting treaty protection to "productive" investment is common to both texts and reflects language promoted by UNCTAD.

4   Brazil CIFAs

The new series of Brazilian Cooperation and Investment Facilitation Agreements ("CIFAs") appears to experiment with slightly varying investor and investment definitions. The Brazil–Angola agreement stands out, as it leaves the definitions of investment and investor to be determined under the domestic law of the respective countries.[24]

---

[22] SADC Model Bilateral Investment Treaty Template with Commentary 13 (2012) [hereinafter SADC Model BIT].

[23] Salini Costruttori S.p.A. and Italstrade S.p.A. v. Morocco, ICSID Case No. ARB/00/4, Decision on Jurisdiction (July 23, 2001), 42 I.L.M. 609 (2003).

[24] Acordo de Cooperação e Facilitação de Investimentos entre o Governo da República Federativa do Brasil e o Governo da República de Angola, Braz.–Angl., art. 3, Apr. 1, 2015, http://investmentpolicyhubold.unctad.org/Download/TreatyFile/4720 [hereinafter Brazil–Angola CIFA].

The Mozambique CIFA, the first of the series, indicates that to qualify, an investment must involve the establishment of a long-lasting enterprise that will produce goods and services.[25] As in the India Model BIT, portfolio investments, sovereign debts, and money claims arising out of commercial contracts for the sale of goods and services are excluded. This language is reflected in other CIFAs, with the exception of Angola, noted earlier.[26] The intent seems to be to limit coverage to new investments that expand the nation's productive capabilities. Intellectual property is not explicitly included in the illustrative list of assets that may constitute an investment, but nor is it excluded either in the CIFAs with Mozambique and Malawi. The later CIFAs with Mexico, Colombia and Chile do include intellectual property as a possible investment asset and incorporate by reference the WTO's Trade-Related Aspects of Intellectual Property Rights ("TRIPS") Agreement for purposes of determining what qualifies as intellectual property.[27]

5 South Africa

With respect to countries not covered or no longer covered by a BIT, South Africa's Protection of Investment Act provides a domestic law framework governing pre- and post-establishment matters, many of which traditionally would have been addressed by a BIT. Under section 2 an investment within the meaning of the Act requires the establishment of an enterprise under South African law, which "commit[s] resources of

[25] Acordo de Cooperação e Facilitação de Investimentos entre o Governo da República Federativa do Brasil e o Governo da República de Moçambique, Braz.–Mozam., art. 3.1, Mar. 30, 2015, http://investmentpolicyhubold.unctad.org/Download/TreatyFile/4717 [hereinafter Brazil–Mozambique CIFA].

[26] Investment Cooperation and Facilitation Agreement between the Federative Republic of Brazil and the Republic of Malawi, Braz.–Malawi, art. 2.1, June 25, 2015, available at http://investmentpolicyhubold.unctad.org/Download/TreatyFile/4715 [hereinafter Malawi CIFA] (stating in art. 2 that the term "investment" does not include debt securities issued by a government, portfolio investments, or claims to money arising solely from commercial contracts).

[27] Acuerdo de Cooperacion y de Facilitación de las Inversiones entre la República Federativa del Brasil y los Estados Unidos Mexicanos, Braz.–Mex., art. 3.1.2(e), May 26, 2015, http://investmentpolicyhubold.unctad.org/Download/TreatyFile/4718 [hereinafter Brazil–Mexico CIFA]; Acordo de Cooperação e Facilitação de Investimentos Entre a República Federativa Do Brasil e a República da Colômbia, Braz.–Colom., art. 3.1.2(e), Oct. 10, 2015, http://investmentpolicyhubold.unctad.org/Download/TreatyFile/4714 [hereinafter Brazil–Colombia CIFA]; Acuerdo de Cooperación y Facilitación de Inversiones entre la República Federativa del Brasil y la República de Chile, Braz.–Chile, art. 1.1.4(f), Nov. 24, 2015, http://investmentpolicyhubold.unctad.org/Download/TreatyFile/4712 [hereinafter Brazil–Chile CIFA].

economic value over a reasonable period of time, in anticipation of profit."[28] Share in such an enterprise also qualifies as an investment. That language can be interpreted broadly or narrowly, and therefore does not offer much guidance to investors. For instance, it is unclear whether preliminary scoping and feasibility studies would qualify as "resources of economic value" such as to trigger the protection of the law. Resources expended to conduct environmental impact assessments or other surveys in anticipation of obtaining permits have been used to trigger investor–state arbitration claims under BITs in the past, but the Act's language is ambiguous in that respect. The Indian Model BIT, by contrast, specifically excludes such expenditures from the ambit of the investment definition. The "reasonable period of time" for the investment is also a looser standard than the long-term requirements present in some other Models. Particularly if pre-establishment surveying and business model studies are included as a qualifying "resource of economic value," and are used to demonstrate the "anticipation of profit," the mere amount of time needed to obtain such studies, typically over one year, may arguably also satisfy the "reasonable period of time" criterion. In that scenario, the proposed law might serve little to change investors' behavior, compared to traditional BITs.

B   Defining Foreign Investors

1   India

The Indian draft Model BIT attempted to tackle the issue of investments nominally owned by a shell company set up in a country with a BIT solely to take advantage of favorable treaty provisions, avoid certain legal liabilities, evade taxes, etc. An "investor" was required to conduct "real and substantial business operations" in the home state if it was a legal entity, or to be a natural person of the home state.[29] It also addressed the problem of natural persons who possess several nationalities: the test was the "dominant and effective nationality,"[30] in alignment with the general public international law principle recognized by the International Court of Justice in the Nottebohm case.[31] The 2016 Model BIT does away with

---

[28] Protection of Investment Act 22 of 2015 § 2 (S. Afr.), www.gov.za/sites/www.gov.za/files/ 39514_Act22of2015ProtectionOfInvestmentAct.pdf (including lawful enterprises in South Africa within the definition of "investment").

[29] *Id.* art. 1.9.

[30] *Id.* art. 1.12.

[31] *See* Nottebohm (Liech. v. Guat.), 1955 I.C.J Rep. 4 (Apr. 6) (establishing nationality by the presence of a real link between the naturalized person and the naturalizing state).

these requirements[32] and does not address the question of dual citizens. Provisions excluding dual citizens from the ambit of the treaty protections are typically meant for two purposes. First, they serve to exclude the application of a BIT vis-à-vis dual citizens of the host and home state. Second, in the case of dual citizens of the home state and a third state, they restrict the treaty's application to situations where the home-state citizenship is the effective nationality. This limits a dual citizen's ability to engage in treaty shopping. Since India does not allow dual citizenship,[33] the first scenario would not arise in practice, and the second scenario would only come up when India is the host state.

2 SADC Model BIT

With respect to investors, the SADC proposals also aim to protect only genuine investors of the home state, rather than pass-through, shell entities incorporated in a particular state only for legal convenience. Investors who are dual citizens must be "predominantly a resident of the Home State," and the SADC Model also suggests excluding dual citizens who hold the citizenship of the host state. Regarding juridical persons, the SADC text proposes a number of alternative clauses. The first relies on the simple formality of incorporation in the home state, which would not resolve issues relating to investment or taxation treaty shopping. Three other proposals add to legal incorporation a requirement of effective ownership and control by a juridical person of the home state, and possibly a requirement of substantial business activity in the home state. The commentary makes it clear that states concerned about treaty shopping should adopt one of the more robust versions rather than the simple incorporation test.

Although it references the Common Market for Eastern and Southern Africa (COMESA) as an example of a legal framework for an investor definition that includes the substantial business test, the 1993 Treaty Establishing the COMESA[34] does not include such a definition, and in fact adopts a very traditional and investor-friendly approach to the definition of investment.[35] Ongoing negotiations are underway at the

---

[32] 2016 India Model BIT, *supra* note 10, art. 1.5.

[33] *See* INDIA CONST. art. 9. ("No person shall be a citizen of India . . . if he has voluntarily acquired the citizenship of any foreign State.")

[34] Treaty establishing the Common Market for Eastern and Southern Africa, Nov. 5, 1993, 2314 U.N.T.S. 265.

[35] *See id.* art. 159.2 (listing the activities to be considered as investments under the agreement).

African Union to design a Pan African Investment Code that would likely result in a text closer to the features of the SADC Model than to chapter 26 of the COMESA Treaty. The hope is that such a text would also serve as a Model for regional groupings and BITs involving African countries.[36]

3   Brazil CIFAs

The definition of investor varies perhaps more significantly across CIFAs. The Mozambique CIFA merely relies on formal incorporation criteria for juridical entities: the state of incorporation suffices to determine whether an entity qualifies as an investor under the treaty.[37] The Mexico CIFA adopts a somewhat more stringent approach, requiring formal establishment in the territory of the parties, as well as having "its headquarters and the center of its economic activities in the territory of that Party."[38] The Malawi CIFA adds a third requirement that the "property or effective control belongs, directly or indirectly, to nationals or permanent residents of the parties."[39] A slightly different approach prevails in the Colombia CIFA requiring juridical investors to have substantial business activities in the territory of the home state party,[40] as does the Chile CIFA.[41] Hence, while the Mozambique treaty would not exclude shell entities set up for purposes of treaty shopping, the Malawi, Chile, Colombia and Mexico CIFAs would make it harder for such entities to be used. It is likely that the drafting changed after the first CIFA with Mozambique was released and critiqued. Only one CIFA addresses the dual nationality issue for natural persons: the Colombia CIFA excludes investors who hold the nationality of both parties, except if they have continuously maintained their residence outside of the state where they are making the investment.[42]

4   South Africa

The investors seem to be equated with "an enterprise making an investment in the Republic regardless of nationality," and an enterprise is

---

[36] Makane Moïse Mbengue and Stefanie Schacherer, *The 'Africanisation' of International Investment Law: The Pan-African Investment Code and the Reform of the International Investment Regime*, 18 J. WORLD INVESTMENT & TRADE 414 (2017).
[37] Brazil–Mozambique CIFA, *supra* note 25, art. 3.2.
[38] Brazil–Mexico CIFA, *supra* note 27, art. 3.1.3.
[39] Brazil–Malawi CIFA, *supra* note 26, art. 2.1.
[40] Brazil–Colombia CIFA, *supra* note 27, art. 3.1.5.
[41] Brazil–Chile CIFA, *supra* note 27, art. 1.1.7.
[42] Brazil–Colombia CIFA, *supra* note 27, art. 3.1.4.1.

further defined as "any natural person or juristic person whether incorporated or unincorporated."[43] The law intends to regulate domestic and foreign investors alike, so long as they make an investment in South Africa. Dual nationality issues where the investor is South African and holds another citizenship are therefore inapposite.

C   Common Trends

Although a number of different strategies are emerging in recent BITs and Model BITs drafted by emerging countries, a common trend is the attempt to circumscribe who qualifies as an investor and what counts as a protected investment. As we have seen under new-style agreements in several countries, investors, which used to qualify merely on the basis of incorporation in the home state (and at times an additional requirement that the seat of the company be in the home state), are now subject to the additional requirements of conducting substantial business activity in the home state, or of being owned or controlled by nationals of the home state.[44] Such restrictions may also apply if an investor seeks arbitration under the ICSID Convention, thereby facing the jurisdiction requirements of article 25(1)[45] and its jurisprudence, including the *Salini* test. Like India, the SADC and others, China implements such restrictions to avoid the treaty-shopping phenomenon, where shell companies are set up solely for purposes of qualifying under a taxation treaty, a BIT, or a free trade agreement including an investment chapter.

Moreover, there are some clear learning patterns, where states take stock of arbitral developments, particularly those involving them directly, and are aware of other states' practices on the issues of investor and investment definitions. This is suggested, for instance, in the evolution of the Brazil CIFA drafting, which incorporated more specific language in later drafts in line with the type of provisions, or at least issue awareness, prevalent in other emerging-country BITs. Regional and

[43] Protection of Investment Act 22 of 2015, *supra* note 28, § 1.
[44] Dulac, *supra* note 18, at 250.
[45] Convention on the Settlement of Investment Disputes between States and Nationals of Other States, art. 25(1), Mar. 18, 1965, 17 U.S.T 1270, T.I.A.S 6090, 575 U.N.T.S. 159. ("The jurisdiction of the Centre shall extend to any legal dispute arising directly out of an investment, between a Contracting State [or any constituent subdivision or agency of a Contracting State designated to the Centre by that State] and a national of another Contracting State, which the parties to the dispute consent in writing to submit to the Centre. When the parties have given their consent, no party may withdraw its consent unilaterally.")

international organizations, in particular UNCTAD, also play a key role in sharing and disseminating current practices.[46]

The push in a number of emerging countries toward narrowing the definitions of investors and investment in BITs or investment chapters in FTAs is also reflected in the 2004 U.S. Model BIT. The EU–Canada Trade Agreement ("CETA") also follows this trend. It specifies that investment means "[e]very kind of asset that an investor owns or controls, directly or indirectly, that has the characteristics of an investment, which includes a certain duration and other characteristics such as the commitment of capital or other resources, the expectation of gain or profit, or the assumption of risk," followed by a non-exhaustive list of assets.[47] Like several of the newer emerging-country Models discussed previously, the CETA also excludes from qualifying investment "claims to money that arise solely from commercial contracts for the sale of goods or services by a natural person or enterprise in the territory of a Party to a natural person or enterprise in the territory of the other Party, domestic financing of such contracts, or any related order, judgment, or arbitral award."[48] Regarding investors, the CETA specifies that juridical investors must be enterprises that are "constituted or organised under the laws of that Party and [have] substantial business activities in the territory of that Party; or an enterprise that is constituted or organised under the laws of that Party and is directly or indirectly owned or controlled by a natural person of that Party or by an enterprise mentioned under paragraph (a)."[49]

II   Defining and Constraining Investor Protections

This section analyzes the spectrum of positions taken by emerging economies on the nature and extent of the protections offered to investors. As we

[46] *See, e.g.*, UNCTAD, Rep. of the Investment, Enterprise and Development Commission on Its Seventh session, ¶ 3, 8–10, TD/B/C.II/31, (2015), http://unctad.org/meetings/en/SessionalDocuments/ciid31_en.pdf (providing an example of the UNCTAD's role in signaling arbitral developments); *see generally* Investment Policy Framework For Sustainable Development, UNCTAD/DIAE/PCB/2015/5 (UNCTAD, ed., 2015), http://unctad.org/en/PublicationsLibrary/diaepcb2015d5_en.pdf; Rep. of the Expert Meeting on the Transformation of the International Investment Agreement Regime: The Path Ahead, TD/B/C.II/EM.4/3 (UNCTAD, ed., 2015), http://unctad.org/meetings/en/SessionalDocuments/ciiem4d3_en.pdf.

[47] Comprehensive and Economic Trade Agreement, Can.–EU, art. 8.1, Oct. 30, 2016, http://ec.europa.eu/trade/policy/in-focus/ceta/ceta-chapter-by-chapter/.

[48] *Id.*

[49] *Id.*

saw for the definitions of investment and investor, these provisions can be found in several sources, ranging from the traditional form of bilateral investment treaties (India, China and SADC), to alternative investment instruments (Brazil) and domestic approaches (South Africa). This section focuses on notions of standard of treatment (A) and expropriation and compensation issues (B).

A Standard of Treatment

1 India

The 2016 Model BIT spells out rights and protections for investors in great detail. Article 2.3 appears to displace customary international law by limiting parties' obligations to those explicitly stated in the treaty (and in some cases, the treaty terms do incorporate customary international law by reference).[50] This can be seen as an attempt to control efforts by arbitrators to expand the scope of otherwise broad terms such as "fair and equitable treatment."

Unlike most traditional BITs, the draft India Model BIT did not include a general guarantee of "fair and equitable treatment" or of "full protection and security." Instead, article 3 on standard of treatment protected foreign investments from denial of justice under customary international law, "egregious violations of due process," and "manifestly abusive treatment involving continuous, unjustified and outrageous coercion or harassment."[51] This eliminated the possibility of using the fair and equitable treatment language to create a right to protection of "legitimate expectations." The 2016 India Model BIT does include "full protection and security," albeit limited to "a Party's obligations relating to physical security of investors and to investments made by the investors of the other Party and not to any other obligation whatsoever."[52] Additionally, article 4 provides for national treatment but indicates that the assessment of "like circumstances" depends on "the totality of the circumstances, including whether the relevant treatment distinguishes between investors or investments on the basis of legitimate regulatory objectives.[53] These circumstances include, but are not limited to, (a) the goods or services consumed or produced by the investment; (b) the actual

---

[50] 2016 India Model BIT, *supra* note 10, art. 2.3.
[51] Indian Draft Model BIT, *supra* note 11, art. 3.
[52] 2016 India Model BIT, *supra* note 10, art. 3.2.
[53] *Id.* art. 4.

and potential impact of the investment on third persons, the local community, or the environment, (c) whether the investment is public, private, or state-owned or controlled, and (d) the practical challenges of regulating the investment."[54]

There is no most-favored-nation section in the India Model BIT, and no explanation for its absence. This is probably the result of the *White Industries v. India* arbitration where an Australian investor used a clause in the India–Kuwait BIT to expand protection for an Australian company. It reflects a general concern among emerging economies of the use of MFN to expand jurisdiction and substantive content beyond the intended scope of a specific BIT.

Also absent from the 2016 India Model BIT is an umbrella clause guaranteeing that the parties will abide by their contractual commitments with foreign investors. Breaches of contract between the host state and the foreign investors would not typically be actionable under a treaty, but some ICSID arbitrations interpreted umbrella clauses to elevate contractual breaches to treaty breaches. Such reasoning allowed investors to circumvent choice-of-forum clauses in the underlying contract (particularly where the designated forum was a domestic court of the host state) and instead bring an investor–state arbitration claim under the treaty.[55]

Last, the Model treaty's standard-of-treatment clause must be read in the context of provisions regarding the state's ability to apply its law. Article 2.3 excludes from the ambit of the treaty claims "arising out of events which occurred, or claims which have been raised prior to the entry into force of this Treaty."[56] Additionally, article 2.4 carves out from

[54] *Id.* fn 2.
[55] *See, e.g.*, SGS Société Générale de Surveillance S.A. v. The Republic of Para., ICSID Case No.ARB/07/29, (Feb. 10, 2012), www.italaw.com/sites/default/files/case-documents/ita law1525.pdf. But see SGS Société Générale de Surveillance SA v. Islamic Republic of Pakistan, ISCID Case No ARB/01/13, Decision on Objections to Jurisdiction, (Aug. 6, 2003), 8 ICSID Rep. 406 (2005) (holding that article 11 of the Pakistan–Switzerland BIT, which deviated from standard umbrella clause formulations, did not permit the elevation of the contractual breach to a treaty claim), http://icsidfiles.worldbank.org/icsid/ ICSIDBLOBS/OnlineAwards/C205/DC622_En.pdf; Compania de Aguas del Acqunija SA et al v. Arg., ICSID Case No. ARB/97/3, Award, (Nov. 21, 2000), 40 ILM 426 (2001); Compania de Aguas del Acqunija SA et al v. Arg., ICSID Case No. ARB/97/3, Decision on Annulment, (Mar. 3, 2001) and Award (Aug. 20, 2007), 6 ICSID Rep. 340 (2004) (finding that contractual violations do not necessarily amount to a BIT breach), www.italaw.com/sites/default/files/case-documents/ita0215.pdf; CMS Gas Transmission Company v. Arg., ICSID Case No. 01/08, Award (May 12, 2005), 44 I.L.M 1205 (2005).
[56] 2016 India Model BIT, *supra* note 10, art. 2.3.

the treaty local government measures (a vast exclusion for a federal state like India), any measure related to taxation, and a number of other issues such as compulsory licenses of intellectual property rights, government procurement, and subsidies.[57] The draft Model BIT included the same exclusions and safe-harbored existing laws and regulations or their progeny from challenges under the treaty.[58]

2 China

The content of investor protection varies to some degree in China's three generations of BITs, and from one individual BIT to another. Likewise, China's treatment of references to international law in BITs has evolved over time. Reluctance to accept customary international law wholesale has been a longstanding position of China, which views international law as largely the product of capitalist imperialist legal systems.[59]

The inclusion and treatment of fair and equitable clauses illustrates these dynamics. Some Chinese BITs omit such clauses altogether;[60] a number include a commitment to treat investments fairly and equitably, without specifying what such treatment might entail.[61] Starting in 2001, some Chinese BITs refer to international law in reference to fair and equitable treatment, in different formulae ranging from a restrictive "fair and equitable treatment in accordance with applicable principles of international law recognized by both Contracting Parties,"[62] to a more general but ambiguous "fair and equitable treatment, in accordance with principles of international law."[63] The more recent China–Mexico BIT

---

[57] *Id.* art. 2.4 (stating that the treaty does not apply to local government measures).

[58] India Draft Model BIT, *supra* note 11, art. 2.1 (mirroring the exclusions to local government measures of the 2016 Model BIT).

[59] Dulac, *supra* note 18.

[60] *Id.* at 266.

[61] *See, e.g.,* Agreement between the Government of the Republic of India and the Government of the People's Republic of China for the Promotion and Protection of Investments, China–India, art. 3.2, Nov. 21, 2006, http://investmentpolicyhubold.unctad .org/Download/TreatyFile/742. ("Investments . . . shall at all times be accorded fair and equitable treatment.")

[62] Agreement between the Government of the Hashemite Kingdom of Jordan and the Government of the People's Republic of China on the Reciprocal Promotion and Protection of Investments, China–Jordan, art. 3.2, Nov. 15, 2001 (not in force), http:// investmentpolicyhubold.unctad.org/Download/TreatyFile/748.

[63] Accord Sur la Promotion et la Protection Réciproques des Investissements entre le Gouvernement de la Republique de Madagascar et le Gouvernement de la République Populaire de Chine, China–Madag., art. 3.1, Nov. 21, 2005, http://investmentpolicyhu bold.unctad.org/Download/TreatyFile/758. ("[C]hacune des Parties Contractantes s'engage à assurer, sur son territoire défini plus haut, un traitement juste et équitable,

(2008) inaugurates an even broader recognition of fair and equitable treatment and full protection and security, defined as the protection required "by the international law minimum standard of treatment of aliens as evidence of State practice and *opinio juris*."[64] The clear reference to international customary law was subsequently reinforced in the 2009 China–Peru BIT.[65] The joint phrasing for fair and equitable treatment and full protection and security in reference to customary law, as illustrated by the China–Mexico BIT, is fairly typical of third-generation Chinese BITs[66] and is reflected in the latest draft Model BIT.[67]

While older BITs, especially second-generation treaties from the late 1990s and 2000s, often include an umbrella clause that extends protection to contracts entered into between the investor and the host government,[68] the more recent third-generation BITs make no such undertaking.[69] This position, held in common with some other emerging countries, is likely in reaction to arbitral interpretations elevating contractual violations to treaty breaches through the use of umbrella clauses.[70]

Most-favored-nation treatment clauses have been a relatively common feature of Chinese BITs, with varying language.[71] The 2003 Model BIT's

conformément aux principes du Droit international, aux investissements des nationaux et sociétés de l'autre Partie Contractante et à faire en sorte que l'exercice du droit ainsi reconnu ne soit entravé en droit, ni en fait.")

[64] Agreement between the Government of the United Mexican States and the Government of the People's Republic of China on the Promotion and Reciprocal Protection of Investments, China–Mex., art. 5.2, July 11, 2008, http://investmentpolicyhubold.unctad.org/Download/TreatyFile/759.

[65] Free Trade Agreement between the Government of the Republic of Peru and the Government of the People's Republic of China concerning the Encouragement and Reciprocal Protection of Investments, April 4, 2009, http://investmentpolicyhubold.unctad.org/Download/TreatyFile/2586.

[66] Dulac, *supra* note 18, at 270.

[67] China Draft Model BIT, *supra* note 20, art. 3.

[68] For a history and interpretation of umbrella clauses in Chinese first- and second-generations BITs, *see* Dulac, *supra* note 18, at 277–79; Wenhua Shan, *Umbrella Clauses and Investment Contracts under Chinese BITs: Are the Latter Covered by the Former?*, 11 J. WORLD INV. & TRADE 135, 136–45 (2010) (discussing umbrella clauses in Chinese BITs and their legal implications).

[69] *See* Sauvant & Nolan, *supra* note 19, at 919 (noting that China has followed the example of the United States and other nations in abandoning umbrella clauses).

[70] *Id.* (discussing how China has revised its Model dispute settlement clause in response to claimants' attempts to elevate contract breaches to international treaty violations).

[71] *See id.* at 922 ("It was the regular practice of drafters of China's BITs . . . to include a most-favored nation [MFN] clause."); John Savage & Elodie Dulac, *Chinese Investment Treaties and the Dispute Resolution Opportunities Offered by Most Favored Nations Provisions*, 2008 STOCKHOLM INT'L ARB. REV. No. 3, at 1, 10, 29–33 (discussing the various wordings of MFN clauses in Chinese BITs).

National Treatment clause reads: "Neither the Contracting Party shall subject investments and activities associated with such investments of the other Contracting Party to treatment less favorable then that accorded to the investments and associated activities by the investors of any third State."[72] China is clearly aware of the *Maffezini* line of cases and the controversy about whether to use MFN clauses to import broader dispute resolution clauses from other BITs. The investment chapter of the 2008 China–New Zealand Free Trade Agreement explicitly excludes dispute resolution from the ambit of the MFN clause.[73] This approach, and other exclusions, is also reflected in the new draft Chinese Model BIT.[74]

By contrast to the relatively ubiquitous and traditional MFN clauses, China resisted national treatment clauses in its early BIT negotiating history. Such clauses became more standard since the late 1990s, though at times with the restrictive note that such treatment is only granted "in accordance with [China's] laws and regulations."[75] Moreover, national treatment is often restricted to post-establishment treatment, even where the treaty also covers admission of the foreign investment. The 2003 Model BIT's National Treatment clause states: "Without prejudice to its laws and regulations, each Contracting Party shall accord to investments and activities associated with such investments by the investors of the other Contracting Party treatment not less favorable than that accorded to the investments and associated activities by its own investors."[76] Although the 2003 Model BIT mentions that the parties "shall encourage investors of the other Contracting Party to make investments in its territory and admit such investments in accordance with its laws and regulations,"[77] the remainder of the treaty obligations focus on post-establishment rights and protections. By contrast, the subsequent draft

---

[72] Chinese Model BIT Version III, China, art. 3, *reprinted in* NORAH GALLAGHER & WENHUA SHAN, CHINESE INVESTMENT TREATIES: POLICIES AND PRACTICE app. IV (2009) [hereinafter 2003 China Model BIT].

[73] *See* Free Trade Agreement between the Government of New Zealand and the Government of the People's Republic of China, China–N.Z., art. 139.2, Apr. 7, 2008, 2590 U.N.T.S. 101 ("[T]he obligation in this Article does not encompass a requirement to extend … dispute resolution procedures … ").

[74] China Draft Model BIT, *supra* note 20, arts. 4.2, 4.3 (excluding treatment granted in regional trade agreements and "arrangements for facilitating small scale frontier trade in boarder [sic] areas.").

[75] Dulac, *supra* note 18, at 285; Cai Congyan, *China–US BIT Negotiations and the Future of Investment Treaty Regime: A Grand Bilateral Bargain with Multilateral Implications*, 12 J. INT'L ECON. L. 457, 471 (2009).

[76] 2003 China Model BIT, *supra* note 72, art. 3.2.

[77] *Id.* art. 2.1.

Model BIT would extend national treatment protection to the admission of investments to the extent of a yet-to-be-drafted annex.[78]

With respect to standards of treatment, then, the current Chinese BIT policy seems to be more aligned with the traditional BITs framework, albeit with some modifications to take account of recent arbitral developments. Overall, though, China seems to be increasing the scope of protection for foreign investors in its agreements, which represents a move away from its earlier, more restrictive position. In this sense, China seems to be bucking the trend among emerging economies, many of which are trying to restrict the scope of their BITs. However, the picture is quite complex because China's current policy is to negotiate on a case-by-case basis, which may account for the variety of drafting approaches in its latest BITs.

3   SADC

The SADC Model BIT focuses mostly on post-establishment rights and obligations. The only clause dealing with admission of foreign investors references domestic law as the applicable framework.[79] While such a provision appears to fully protect state regulatory autonomy, its inclusion in the treaty might allow investors to elevate a violation of domestic law by state authorities, normally only challengeable in domestic fora, to a treaty breach subject to remedies available under the treaty and customary international law. The SADC Commentary also notes that including such a clause may hinder the host state's ability to modify the conditions of admissions (such as excluding sensitive sectors) subsequent to entering into a BIT.[80] The overall recommendation, therefore, is not to include such a clause, and the language is only provided for illustrative purposes should a state choose to include some pre-establishment provision.

Article 4 guarantees national treatment for post-establishment protection, but requires an assessment of a number of factors related to the nature and impact of the foreign investment, which could result in the foreign investment not being comparable to a domestic investment, and

---

[78] China Draft Model BIT, *supra* note 20, art. 5.2.

[79] SADC Model BIT, *supra* note 22, art. 3. ("The State Parties shall promote and admit Investments in accordance with their applicable law, and shall apply such laws in good faith.")

[80] *Id.* at 16 (noting that certain investment liberalization clauses may restrict a state's ability to close or restrict entry into a sector once it has been opened to foreign investors).

hence warranting a different treatment.[81] In contrast, the Model omits MFN treatment. It also excludes the export of the Model BIT provisions to existing bilateral or regional trade or investment agreements. Hence, more favorable treatment in other treaties cannot be imported under the Model BIT (whereas a traditional MFN clause could allow such import from another treaty), nor can any advantage or concession from the Model BIT be exported to other treaties that might have an MFN clause. Should a state still wish to include an MFN clause in its treaty, the SADC Drafting Committee still recommends excluding legal exports to other treaties as it does with respect to national treatment.[82] This would essentially result in a one-way MFN clause, where investors under the Model BIT could benefit from advantages granted under other trade and investment agreements, but the parties to the latter would not be able to benefit from treatment granted under the Model BIT.

Like India and China, the SADC Drafting Committee is wary of general fair and equitable treatment clauses. In response to arbitral awards that have expanded the concept, the recommendation is not to include such a clause, and to prefer instead a "Fair Administrative Treatment" clause.[83] This is an innovative approach that limits protections to due process guarantees in domestic administrative, legislative and judicial proceedings. Should a country nonetheless choose to include a more traditional fair and equitable treatment clause, the proposed drafting circumscribes such treatment in reference to "customary international law on the treatment of aliens." This fairly traditional formulation[84] leaves space for evolving interpretations of what norms might be – or become – part of customary law.

4 Brazil

Article 11 of the Brazil–Mozambique treaty guarantees that foreign investors will be allowed to establish their investment and conduct business on terms no less favorable than those available to domestic investors.[85] Nondiscrimination between domestic and foreign investors is also provided with respect to restitution, indemnification or compensation in the

---

[81] *Id.* arts. 4.1, 4.2.

[82] *Id.* art. 4.1.

[83] *Id.* art. 5, option 2.

[84] The wording may be traced to Neer v. Mexico, 4 R.I.A.A. 60 (General Claims Commission 1926).

[85] Brazil–Mozambique CIFA, *supra* note 25, art. 11.

case of losses suffered as a result of exigent circumstances including war and uprising.[86]

Brazilian CIFAs exclude fair and equitable treatment, full protection and security, and umbrella clauses, and also limit the scope of protection to national treatment and a most-favored-nation provision. The MFN clauses are carefully circumscribed. Investors of one of the parties will not be treated less favorably than other foreign investors with respect to conditions of establishment and conduct of business. However, most-favored-nation treatment does not include any benefit or preferential treatment that accrues to other investors under a free trade agreement, customs union, or common market scheme, or double taxation treaty in force that may be entered into by Brazil or Mozambique in the future. The MFN clause is designed to avoid any ratcheting effect of present and future treaties that might include more liberal concessions.

5   South Africa

The two main changes brought about as a result of the 2015 Protection of Investment Act are a) the exclusion of the principle of fair and equitable treatment (FET), as it was deemed to be too widely framed and subject to controversial interpretation; and b) reformulation of investor protection from expropriation in line with provisions of the South African Constitution.

Omitting any mention of FET does not, however, absolve South Africa of any obligation in this area. International customary law on minimum standards of treatment would still apply, as the Act recognizes in clause 9.[87] Moreover, since the content of customary law is shaped by state practice and *opinio juris*, it is possible that the formulation of FET in bilateral and multilateral agreements and its interpretation in arbitrations[88] would now be considered to form part of customary law, and thus still bind South Africa to a higher standard than the Act suggests. South Africa's active stance in terminating BITs and rejecting broad notions of FET could perhaps be cast as a persistent objection to

---

[86] *Id.* art. 12.

[87] Clause 9 on "Physical security of property" assures that foreign investors and their investments will be provided the level of physical security "as may be generally provided to domestic investors in accordance with minimum standards of customary international law and subject to available resources and capacity." Protection of Investment Act 22 of 2015, *supra* note 28, §9.

[88] OECD, *Fair and Equitable Treatment Standard in International Investment Law*, OECD WORKING PAPERS ON INTERNATIONAL INVESTMENT 2004/03, 8–22, https://doi.org/10.1787/18151957.

such a development. In practice, though, this may provide little solace to either investors or South Africa as a host country, since the contours of minimum standards of treatment under customary law are in flux, and the outcomes of litigation or arbitration on the issue are highly uncertain.[89]

B Expropriation and Compensation

1 India

The 2016 India Model BIT narrows the concept of expropriation. The draft follows prior practice by stating that a party shall not nationalize, expropriate, or take "measures having an effect equivalent to expropriation" except for a public purpose, in accordance with the procedure established by law, and "on payment of adequate compensation."[90] While "public purpose" cannot be defined specifically, the Model offers a non-exhaustive list whereby certain measures are automatically considered to constitute a public purpose: nondiscriminatory measures (including "awards by judicial bodies") to protect public health, safety, and the environment,[91] and measures relating to land that conform to the law relating to land acquisition (for India).[92] Public purpose is defined by implication in contrast to "action[s] taken by a Party in its commercial capacity,"[93] which are deemed not to count as "public purpose."

Further, the 2016 Model BIT establishes strict limits on what constitutes a "[m]easure ... equivalent to expropriation," which aims at circumscribing claims for indirect expropriation. An indirect expropriation occurs if a state's measure "substantially or permanently deprives the investor of the fundamental attributes of property in its investment, including the right to use, enjoy and dispose of its investment.[94] However, the mere fact that a state measure has an adverse economic impact on an investment is not sufficient to prove that an indirect expropriation has occurred.[95]

---

[89] *See generally* IOANA TUDOR, THE FAIR AND EQUITABLE TREATMENT STANDARD IN THE INTERNATIONAL LAW OF FOREIGN INVESTMENT 54–63 (2008) (discussing the customary framework of the FET along with the international minimum standard that defines the rights states are obliged to extend to foreigners).

[90] 2016 India Model BIT, *supra* note 10, art. 5.1.

[91] *Id.* art. 5.5.

[92] *Id.* art. 5.1; *Id.* fn 3.

[93] *Id.* art. 5.4.

[94] *Id.* art. 5.3(a)(ii).

[95] *Id.* art. 5.3(b)(i).

Monetary awards for expropriation and other claims by investors are circumscribed to "the loss suffered by the investor," reduced by any mitigating factors including restitution made by the state, repeal or modification of the measures at stake, and possibly "current and past use of the investment, the history of its acquisition and purpose, compensation received by the investor from other sources, any unremedied harm or damage that the investor has caused to the environment or local community or other relevant considerations regarding the need to balance public interest and the interests of the investor."[96]

No doubt that the devastating social and environmental impact of oil concessional developments in the Niger delta in Nigeria and in the Amazon region of Ecuador, or the Bhopal industrial disaster in India, loomed large in the drafters' minds with respect both to the scope of legitimate expropriations and to the measure of compensation. The difficulty that aggrieved communities and individuals have had in vindicating their claims[97] clearly militates for an ex ante treatment of the issue at the BIT and establishment level, combined with the possibility for the host state to intervene post-establishment should the need arise. The Model BIT does not address the possibility of the "mitigating factors" resulting in a negative valuation of compensation, that is, where the investor would be found to owe money rather than the host state.

Whereas the draft Model BIT implicitly posited foreign investment as a privilege that may be revoked or curtailed if it is exercised in a way that adversely impacts the local socioeconomic or environmental context, the 2016 final version of the Model BIT is less insistent on rebalancing investment protection and the host state's socioeconomic development. It is less geared toward encouraging investments aligned with development priorities and discouraging investments that bring little or no developmental value. Nonetheless, some of the more controversial language of the draft was maintained in the final version, albeit in footnotes.[98]

---

[96] *Id.* art. 26.3; *id.* fn 4.

[97] *See e.g., Kiobel v. Royal Dutch Petroleum Co.,* 621 F.3d 111 (2d Cir. 2010) (holding that a claim that corporate actors aided human right abuses did not fall within the Alien Tort Claims Act); *Wiwa v. Royal Dutch Petroleum Co.,* 226 F.3d 88 (2d Cir. 2000) (holding that the United Kingdom was a more appropriate forum for a claim involving human rights violations in Nigeria by companies with more substantial business contacts with the United Kingdom than with the United States); *Chevron v. Donziger,* 974 F. Supp. 2d 362 (S.D.N.Y. 2014) (holding that the Racketeer Influenced and Corrupt Organizations Act [RICO] could be applied extraterritorially due to substantial contacts with the United States).

[98] Compare 2016 India Model BIT, *supra* note 10, fn 4 with Draft Indian Model BIT, *supra* note 11 at arts. 5.6, 5.7 and related Explanatory Notes.

2 China

A comparison of the 2003 Model BIT and the subsequent draft Model suggests increased caution on the part of China in preserving regulatory space, particularly in light of arbitral trends on indirect expropriation. Whereas the 2003 Model included standard language on expropriation, nationalization or "other similar measures," guaranteeing compensation, nondiscrimination and due process, and that expropriation could only be for (undefined) "public interests,"[99] the subsequent draft Model specifically defines "non-discriminatory regulatory actions by a Party that are designed and applied to protect legitimate public welfare objectives, such as public health, safety and the environment" as not amounting to an indirect expropriation.[100] Here, China's policy is much closer to the positions taken by India in its 2015 Draft Model BIT.[101] The 2011 China–Uzbekistan BIT reflects the draft Model. While article 6.1 includes indirect expropriation, defined as "[m]easures the effects of which would be equivalent to expropriation or nationalization," within the ambit of the treaty, article 6.3 states that "[e]xcept in exceptional circumstances, such as the measures adopted severely surpassing the necessity of maintaining corresponding reasonable public welfare, non-discriminatory regulatory measures adopted by one Contracting Party for the purpose of legitimate public welfare, such as public health, safety and environment, do not constitute indirect expropriation."[102]

Compensation is calculated as "the fair market value of the expropriated investment immediately before the expropriation occurred."[103] The draft does not include mitigations of monetary awards such as those defined in the India Model BIT,[104] nor does it specify how future profits or past expenses should be accounted for in the calculation of fair market

---

[99] 2003 China Model BIT, *supra* note 76, art. 4.1.

[100] China Draft Model BIT, *supra* note 20, art. 7.3.

[101] Indian Draft Model BIT, *supra* note 11, art. 5.4 ("non-discriminatory regulatory actions by a party that are designed and applied to protect legitimate public welfare objectives such as public health, safety, and the environment shall not constitute expropriation").

[102] Agreement between the Government of the People's Republic of China and the Government of the Republic of Uzbekistan on the Promotion and Protection of Investments, China–Uzb., arts. 6.1, 6.3, Apr. 19, 2011, http://investmentpolicyhubold .unctad.org/Download/TreatyFile/3476.

[103] China Draft Model BIT, *supra* note 20, art. 7.2(a).

[104] Indian Draft Model BIT, *supra* note 11, art. 5.7 (describing various mitigating factors, including the current and past use of the investment, that reduce compensatory damages).

value. The 2011 China–Uzbekistan BIT illustrates such positions,[105] as does the China–Canada BIT.[106]

3   SADC

Article 6 of the SADC Model BIT sets out the general framework for expropriation:

> 6.1. A State Party shall not directly or indirectly nationalize or expropriate investments in its territory except:
> (a) in the public interest;
> (b) in accordance with due process of law; and
> (c) on payment of fair and adequate compensation within a reasonable period of time.[107]

The interpretation of "fair and adequate compensation," however, is where opinions differ, with the Model BIT offering three options ranging from the "equitable balance between the public interest and interest of those affected" taking into account all circumstances and context, to "fair market value of the expropriated investment immediately before the expropriation took place" with or without reference to the public interest and surrounding circumstances regarding the investment and expropriation.

---

[105] Agreement between the Government of the People's Republic of China and the Government of the Republic of Uzbekistan on the Promotion and Protection of Investments, China–Uzb., art. 6.4, Apr. 19, 2011, http://investmentpolicyhubold .unctad.org/Download/TreatyFile/3357. ("The compensation mentioned in Paragraph 1 of this Article shall be equivalent to the fair market value of the expropriated investments immediately before the expropriation is taken or the impending expropriation becomes public knowledge, whichever is earlier. The compensation shall also include interest at a reasonable commercial rate until the date of payment. The compensation shall be made without unreasonable delay, be effectively realizable and freely transferable.")

[106] Agreement between the Government of Canada and the Government of the People's Republic of China for the Promotion and Reciprocal Protection of Investments, Can.–China, art. 10, Sept. 9, 2012, http://investmentpolicyhubold.unctad.org/Download/ TreatyFile/3476. ("Covered investments or returns of investors of either Contracting Party shall not be expropriated, nationalized or subjected to measures having an effect equivalent to expropriation or nationalization in the territory of the other Contracting Party [hereinafter referred to as "expropriation"], except for a public purpose, under domestic due procedures of law, in a nondiscriminatory manner and against compensation. Such compensation shall amount to the fair market value of the investment expropriated immediately before the expropriation, or before the impending expropriation became public knowledge, whichever is earlier, shall include interest at a normal commercial rate until the date of payment, and shall be effectively realizable, freely transferable, and made without delay.")

[107] SADC Model BIT, *supra* note 22, art. 6.

A few terms and carve-outs are noteworthy. First, the Model BIT states "Awards that are significantly burdensome on a Host State may be paid yearly over a three-year period."[108] However, some governments from developing countries, and practitioners working on their behalf, caution that overly onerous awards might simply not be paid, thereby shifting the burden on investors to try to overcome sovereign immunity and seek attachment or seizure of state assets abroad. Since this would likely be a futile endeavor, the threat of nonpayment really acts as a message to arbitrators and investors alike that overly generous awards may amount to purely pyrrhic victories for investors. Second, the Model BIT confirms the state's right to issue compulsory licenses and other restrictions on intellectual property rights made in accordance with international law and the corollary that these would not be considered an expropriation. Third, article 6.7 narrows the scope of indirect expropriation by excluding from its ambit any "measure of a State Party that is designed and applied to protect or enhance legitimate public welfare objectives, such as public health, safety and the environment."[109]

Lastly, although the SADC Model BIT did not recommend including an ISDS clause as a general matter, it does provide the right of investors affected by an expropriation to seek "review by a judicial or other independent authority of that State Party of his/its case and the valuation of his/its investment in accordance with the principles set out in this Article."[110] In other words, the preferred recourse according to SADC is for an investor to vindicate its rights in domestic courts or arbitration in the host country, with that body applying and interpreting the BIT provisions.

4 Brazil

The Brazilian agreements signed so far include commitments by state parties to not nationalize or expropriate without adequate and effective compensation, defined as the fair market value of the expropriated investment immediately before the expropriation, to be provided in a liquid and transferable payment method.[111] The instruments referred to may, in some cases, include public bonds with practical limitations on

---

[108] Id. art. 6.4.
[109] Id. art. 6.7.
[110] Id. art. 6.8.
[111] Brazil–Angola CIFA, supra note 24, art. 9; Brazil–Mozambique CIFA, supra note 25, art. 9; Brazil–Malawi CIFA, supra note 26, art. 8; Brazil–Mexico CIFA, supra note 27, art. 6; Brazil–Colombia CIFA, supra note 27, art. 6; Brazil–Chile CIFA, supra note 27, art. 7.

liquidity and transfer that are required by Brazilian constitutional law.[112] Balance-of-payments considerations may be taken into account under some agreements.

Brazilian agreements limit the concept of expropriation to direct takings. Early agreements did not explicitly exclude indirect expropriation (as the U.S. Model BIT of 2012 does), but the omission of the term was taken to mean it was not covered. Subsequently, the Chilean agreement featured a clause explicitly excluding indirect expropriation.[113]

5   South Africa

Clause 10 on the "Legal protection of investment" guarantees that "[i]nvestors have the right to property in terms of Section 25 of the Constitution." The latter provides:

(1) No one may be deprived of property except in terms of law of general application, and no law may permit arbitrary deprivation of property.
(2) Property may be expropriated only in terms of law of general application –

    (a) for a public purpose or in the public interest; and
    (b) subject to compensation, the amount of which and the time and manner of payment of which have either been agreed to by those affected or decided or approved by a court.

(3) The amount of the compensation and the time and manner of payment must be just and equitable, reflecting an equitable balance between the public interest and the interests of those affected, having regard to all relevant circumstances, including –

    (a) the current use of the property;
    (b) the history of the acquisition and use of the property;
    (c) the market value of the property;
    (d) the extent of direct state investment and subsidy in the acquisition and beneficial capital improvement of the property; and
    (e) the purpose of the expropriation.

---

[112] According to art. 100, Brazilian government branches can only pay their debts through a public bond called "precatórios." To expropriate property, the state must first file a suit and government branches then pay precatórios received from the courts. For this reason, there is no certainty over the date a precatório is due. CONST. FEDERATIVE REP. BRAZ., art. 100.

[113] Brazil–Chile CIFA, *supra* note 27, art. 7.5.

(4) For the purposes of this section –

    (a) the public interest includes the nation's commitment to land reform, and to reforms to bring about equitable access to all South Africa's natural resources; and

    (b) property is not limited to land.

(5) The state must take reasonable legislative and other measures, within its available resources, to foster conditions which enable citizens to gain access to land on an equitable basis.

(6) A person or community whose tenure of land is legally insecure as a result of past racially discriminatory laws or practices is entitled, to the extent provided by an Act of Parliament, either to tenure which is legally secure or to comparable redress.

(7) A person or community dispossessed of property after 19 June 1913 as a result of past racially discriminatory laws or practices is entitled, to the extent provided by an Act of Parliament, either to restitution of that property or to equitable redress.

(8) No provision of this section may impede the state from taking legislative and other measures to achieve land, water and related reform, in order to redress the results of past racial discrimination, provided that any departure from the provisions of this section is in accordance with the provisions of section 36 (1).

(9) Parliament must enact the legislation referred to in subsection (6).[114]

The public interest standard is typical for expropriations, and the requirement that the expropriation be carried out pursuant to a law of general application provides some safeguards against discriminatory targeting of foreign investors. However, the standard for compensation is very flexible and does not reflect customary international law. As with FET, it may be that South Africa is in fact bound by a more stringent international obligation with respect to compensation for the expropriation or nationalization of foreign investments than is enshrined in its Constitution. The issue then becomes how international customary law and treaty obligations interact with the South African Constitution and legislation. South Africa's incorporation of international law in its domestic legal order is bifurcated: treaties appear to be incorporated in a dualist fashion, whereas customary international law "is law in the Republic unless it is inconsistent with the Constitution or an Act of Parliament."[115] Customary international law

[114] S. AFR. CONST., 1996, chapter 2, section 25.
[115] Id. ch. 14, §232.

standards regarding minimum standards of treatment, expropriation and compensation are therefore of direct application in South Africa, but subordinated to the constitution and legislation. However, section 39, which applies to all the Bill of Rights provisions including those on expropriation, provides that "a court, tribunal or forum – ... (b) must consider international law." Overall, then, the Protection of Investment Act and the South African Constitution make it very difficult to ascertain how much and what kind of protection foreign investors and their investments would be awarded, and how that compares with the treatment of their domestic counterparts.

C Extending or Creating Carve-Outs and Exceptions

This section analyzes the spectrum of positions taken by emerging countries, ranging from the familiar form of bilateral investment treaties (India, China and SADC) to alternative investment instruments (Brazil) and domestic approaches (South Africa).

1 India

The 2016 India Model BIT lists topics that are excluded from the definition of indirect expropriation. The list includes government procurement, subsidies, grants, taxation, and compulsory licenses of intellectual property.[116] In addition, article 32 on General Exceptions appears to be loosely inspired by article XX of the GATT. It states that "[n]othing in this Treaty shall be construed to prevent the adoption or enforcement by a Party of measures of general applicability applied on a non-discriminatory basis" deemed necessary to maintain public morals or public order, protect human, animal or plant life or health, conserve the environment and natural resources, protect cultural artifacts, or manage a Party's financial system including exchange rate policies.[117]

2 China

Chinese BITs recently entered into force offer a range of carve-outs and exclusions. Some carve-outs are designed to limit the rights of foreign investors under national treatment or MFN clauses. For instance, the China–Congo BIT, the China–Mali BIT and the China–Uzbekistan BIT exclude investors of one party from benefiting from any advantage or

---

[116] 2016 India Model BIT, *supra* note 10, art. 2.4. *See supra* Section II.B.1.
[117] *Id.* art. 32.

privilege deriving from customs unions, free trade zones, international tax agreements, and agreements facilitating cross-border trade with neighboring countries that may be signed by the other party.[118] This provision would appear to cover export processing zones and the special status of territories such as Hong Kong. Similarly, the China–Canada BIT excludes from the ambit of its MFN clause:

> (a) treatment by a Contracting Party pursuant to any existing or future bilateral or multilateral agreement:
>> (i) establishing, strengthening or expanding a free trade area or customs union; or
>> (ii) relating to aviation, fisheries, or maritime matters including salvage;
> (b) treatment accorded under any bilateral or multilateral international agreement in force prior to 1 January 1994.[119]

Nondiscriminatory treatment is also at times excluded with respect to government procurement and subsidies, including government-supported loans, guarantees and insurances, and grants.[120] Other clauses protect existing nonconforming measures and their future amendments or renewals.[121]

The China–Canada BIT includes a GATT article XX-type list of general exceptions, though limited to measures "(a) necessary to ensure compliance with laws and regulations … ; (b) necessary to protect human, animal or plant life or health; or (c) relating to the conservation of living or non-living exhaustible natural resources if such measures are made effective in conjunction with restrictions on domestic production

---

[118] Accord de coopération entre le Gouvernement de la République du Congo et le Gouvernement de la République Populaire de Chine sur la promotion et la protection des investissements, China–Congo, Mar. 20, 2015, Art. 3(4); Accord sur la promotion et la protection réciproques des investissements entre le Gouvernement de la République du Mali et le Gouvernement de la République Populaire de Chine, China–Mali, Feb. 12, 2009, Art. 3(4); Agreement between the Government of the People's Republic of China and the Government of the Republic of Uzbekistan on the Promotion and Protection of Investments, China–Uzb., Apr. 19, 2011, Art. 4.2; Agreement between the Government of the United Mexican States and the Government of the People's Republic of China on the Promotion and Reciprocal Protection of Investments, China–Mex., July 11, 2008, Art. 10; Accord entre le Gouvernement de la République française et le Gouvernement de la République Populaire de Chine sur l'encouragement et la protection réciproques des investissements, China–Fr., Nov. 26, 2007, Art. 4. See also Agreement between the Government of Canada and the Government of the People's Republic of China for the Promotion and Reciprocal Protection of Investment, Can.–China, Sept. 9, 2012, art. 14 [hereinafter Canada–China BIT] (regarding certain tax exclusions).

[119] Canada–China BIT, supra note 118, art. 8(1).

[120] Id. art. 8(5).

[121] Id. art. 8(2).

or consumption."[122] Additionally, a prudential exception relating to financial markets[123] most likely reflects Canada's recent policy orientations with respect to BITs and an exception for measures relating to "cultural industries," which caters to China's state censorship and other forms of control over publications and broadcasting.[124]

Several China BITs include a denial-of-benefits clause for investments only nominally held by an entity of the BIT signatory countries.[125] This is a response to the forum-shopping trend among investors who look for the treaty offering the most favorable terms and incorporate a shell

---

[122] *Id.* art. 33(2). Compare with Marrakesh Protocol to the General Agreement on Tariffs and Trade 1994, Apr. 15, 1994, Annex 1A, 1867 U.N.T.S. 187; 33 I.L.M. 1153 [hereinafter GATT] art. XX ("nothing in this Agreement shall be construed to prevent the adoption or enforcement by any [Member] of measures:

   (a) necessary to protect public morals;

   (b) necessary to protect human, animal or plant life or health;

   (c) relating to the importations or exportations of gold or silver;

   (d) necessary to secure compliance with laws or regulations which are not inconsistent with the provisions of this Agreement, [. . .];

   (e) relating to the products of prison labour;

   (f) imposed for the protection of national treasures of artistic, historic or archaeological value;

   (g) relating to the conservation of exhaustible natural resources if such measures are made effective in conjunction with restrictions on domestic production or consumption;

   (h) undertaken in pursuance of obligations under any intergovernmental commodity agreement [. . .];

   (i) involving restrictions on exports of domestic materials necessary to ensure essential quantities of such materials to a domestic processing industry during periods when the domestic price of such materials is held below the world price as part of a governmental stabilization plan [. . .];

   (j) essential to the acquisition or distribution of products in general or local short supply [. . .].").

[123] Canada–China BIT, *supra* note 118, art. 33(3). *See also* Canada–China BIT art. 33(4) (concerning other restrictions to protect monetary and exchange rate policies); art. 33(6)(a) (regarding the confidentiality of customers of financial institutions). *But see* Bilateral Agreement for the Promotion and Protection of Investments between the Government of the Republic of Colombia and the Government of the People's Republic of China, China–Colom., Nov. 22, 2008, art. 13 (discussing the prudential measures in the financial sector).

[124] Canada–China BIT, *supra* note 118, art. 33(1).

[125] Agreement between the Government of the People's Republic of China and the Government of the Republic of Uzbekistan on the Promotion and Protection of Investments, China–Uzb., Apr. 19, 2011, art. 10(1)(c), (2); Canada–China BIT, *supra* note 118, art. 16.

corporation in a state party to that treaty in order to benefit from the BIT, while really controlling the investment from another country that might not have a BIT with the host country, or might have a less favorable BIT.

Alongside these varied and sophisticated clauses designed to preserve regulatory autonomy of the host state, some China BITs are rather bare-boned. For instance, the 2009 China–Malta BIT is traditional and unre-markable in its drafting.[126] The 2009 China–Mali BIT is also fairly representative of traditional BITs, as are the 2008 China–Mexico BIT and the 2007 China–France BIT. Some provisions are in direct conflict with more recent Chinese BITs, for instance those provisions regarding whether treaty provisions apply if diplomatic relations between the signatory states are interrupted.

The range of drafting of China BITs over the past ten years supports China's claim that it tailors treaties to each particular negotiation, and is amenable to using the Model BIT of the other party if need be. However, BITs signed around and after 2012 demonstrate much more detailed exceptions and safeguard clauses to protect regulation of the host state. Still, there is little consistency across these newer BITs about what exceptions are included. Overall, most of the exception and exclusion clauses reflect current debates about preserving policy space, in particular debates on subject matters such as public health, thwarting investor forum-shopping strategies, and the effect of MFN clauses from other economic law agreements.

3 SADC

The Model SADC BIT encourages states to create a schedule of non-conforming measures that might violate the nondiscrimination provi-sion and would be excluded from scrutiny under that clause.[127] Similarly, the Model BIT provides for the negotiation of a schedule of sectors or subsectors to be excluded from national treatment. National treatment would also be restricted to any investments protected under the BIT, and would not be extended to other BITs or free trade agreements signed by the parties.

The capital and profits repatriation clause includes a number of exclu-sions to the principle of the freedom of repatriation, mostly dealing with moneys connected to a public interest (taxes, public or other compulsory

---

[126] Agreement between the Government of the People's Republic of China and the Government of Malta on the Promotion and Protection of Investments, China–Malta, Feb. 22, 2009.
[127] SADC Model BIT, *supra* note 22, art. 4.3.

retirement schemes, money judgments, etc.).[128] Additionally, the host states reserve the right to enact restrictions on the movement of capital for balance payment purposes and other macroeconomic and exchange rate management difficulties (known as safeguard provisions). This language may result from the lessons learned in the Argentinian crisis arbitrations, where Argentina relied on general non-preclusion measures clauses to defend its debt restructuration. Under the SADC Model BIT safeguard provisions, such a situation would be covered with more certainty.

Lastly, article 25 provides more general exceptions to nondiscrimination provisions and expropriation and compensation disciplines. The exceptions to nondiscrimination are somewhat reminiscent of GATT article XX, inasmuch as they cover measures

> (a) to protect public morals and safety;
>> (b) to protect human, animal or plant life or health;
>> (c) for the conservation of living or non-living exhaustible natural resources; and
>> (d) to protect the environment.[129]

Measures the state considers necessary to maintain or protect international peace and security, or to protect its national security interests, are also exempted from treaty obligations. It is noteworthy that the necessity standard is cast as a subjective one (under the Model SADC, the state determines necessity), rather than the objective test that has been developed in WTO case law to interpret several GATT article XX clauses.

4 Brazil CIFAs

Brazilian CIFAs include a right to regulate national security, the environment, health, labor and other areas.[130] They also allow restrictions on transfers of profits and other payments out of the host country in the case of crises or serious difficulty affecting the balance of payments.[131] Due process and nondiscrimination safeguards remain in place should such restrictions be implemented. These types of clauses are not out of the

---

[128] *Id.* art. 8.

[129] *Id.* art. 25.

[130] Brazil–Mexico CIFA, *supra* note 27, arts. 10, 11, 12; Brazil–Colombia CIFA, *supra* note 27, arts. 10, 11, 12, 15; Brazil–Chile CIFA, *supra* note 27, arts. 12, 13, 14, 17.

[131] Brazil–Angola CIFA, *supra* note 24, art. 14.2; Brazil–Mozambique CIFA, *supra* note 25, art. 14.2; Brazil–Malawi CIFA, *supra* note 26, art. 12.4; Brazil–Mexico CIFA, *supra* note 27, art. 9.3; Brazil–Colombia CIFA, *supra* note 27, art. 9.4; Brazil–Chile CIFA, *supra* note 27, art. 11.4.

ordinary in BITs generally, but are not a standard feature in all agreements. Recent Model BITs from emerging countries show a renewed interest in including such an exception.[132]

5   South Africa

Although no provision of the Promotion of Investment Act is explicitly framed as an exception, clause 12 on the "Right to regulate" creates a framework for safe-harboring government regulation from potential indirect expropriation claims or other challenges from investors. The subject matters covered include, but are not limited to:

(a) redressing historical, social and economic inequalities and injustices;
(b) upholding the values and principles espoused in Section 195 of the Constitution;
(c) upholding the rights guaranteed in the Constitution;
(d) promoting and preserving cultural heritage and practices, indigenous knowledge and biological resources related thereto, or national heritage;
(e) fostering economic development, industrialisation and beneficiation;
(f) achieving the progressive realisation of socio-economic rights; or
(g) protecting the environment and the conservation and sustainable use of natural resources.[133]

---

[132] Bilateral Agreement for the Promotion and Protection of Investments between the Republic of Colombia and (blank), August 2007, www.italaw.com/documents/inv_mo del_bit_colombia.pdf (allowing restrictions on transfers for balance-of-payment-purposes, as do the proposed Model Text for the Indian Bilateral Investment Treaty – a change from the earlier 2003 Model – and the SADC Model BIT); 2016 Indian Model BIT, *supra* note 10, art. 6.4; SADC Model BIT, *supra* note 22. U.S. treaties normally do not have such provisions: a rare exception is found in the Treaty between the United States of America and the Democratic Socialist Republic of Sri Lanka. Treaty between the United States of America and the Democratic Socialist Republic of Sri Lanka concerning the Encouragement and Reciprocal Protection of Investment, Sri Lanka–U.S., Sept. 20, 1991. BITs signed by France often include such a provision. *See* Agreement between the Government of the Republic of France and the Government of the United Mexican States on the Reciprocal Promotion and Protection of Investments, Fr.–Mex, Nov. 12, 1998; Agreement between the Government of the Federal Republic of Ethiopia and the Government of the Republic of France for the Reciprocal Promotion and Protection of Investments, Eth.–Fr., June 25, 2003; Agreement between the Government of the Republic of France and the Government of the Republic of Uganda on the Reciprocal Promotion and Protection of Investments, Fr.–Uganda, Jan. 3, 2003. However, Australian BITs do not typically feature a balance-of-payments safeguard clause.
[133] Protection of Investment Act 22 of 2015, *supra* note 28, §12(1).

Unlike the SADC Model, this list of carve-outs is not inspired by the GATT but rather by the South African Constitution. Clause 11(2) resembles the more traditional non-preclusion measures clauses of bilateral investment treaties.[134]

Emerging economies are now quite intentional and reflective in the negotiation and drafting of exceptions clauses in BITs. Still, the range of drafting techniques and approaches reflects a global regulatory laboratory, rather than the emergence of a new gold standard or even a range of best practices.

D   Investor and Home State Obligations

Several new BITs from emerging countries include not only rights but also robust obligations for investors. Beyond fairly obvious (and likely redundant) obligations to comply with the law of the host state, new investor obligations typically cover corporate governance, anti-corruption matters and corporate social responsibility.

1   India

Perhaps the most innovative feature of the 2016 India Model BIT is chapter III on investor obligations. Such undertakings include anti-corruption obligations for the investors and their investments,[135] general legal and administrative compliance, and specific tax compliance with the law of the host state.[136] Article 12 includes a best-efforts obligation for investors to incorporate "internationally recognized standards of corporate social responsibility in their practices and internal policies . . . These principles may address issues such as labour, the environment, human rights, community relations and anti-corruption." The draft Model included an additional best-efforts provision obligating foreign investors to "strive, through their management policies and practices, to contribute to the development objectives of the Host State. In particular, Investors and their Investments should recognise the rights, traditions and customs of local communities and indigenous peoples of the Host State and

---

[134] *Id.* §12(2). ("The government or any organ of state may take measures that are necessary for the fulfilment of the Republic's obligations in regard to the maintenance, compliance or restoration of international peace and security, or the protection of the security interests, including the financial stability of the Republic.")

[135] 2016 India Model BIT, *supra* note 10, art. 11(ii).

[136] *Id.* art. 11(iii).

carry out their operations with respect and regard for such rights, traditions and customs."[137]

While many of these obligations would previously have been part of
domestic law, India's strategy elevates them to treaty obligations. This
strategy may result in creating a defense for India not to give the protections of the treaty to investors or investments in breach of such obligations. Hence, while investors are traditionally third-party beneficiaries to
BITs, the 2016 India Model BIT also makes them third-party obligors in
a much stronger sense than they might have been previously. However,
disputes regarding these provisions are excluded from investor–state
dispute settlement.[138] Two possible processes could ensue for arbitral
tribunals when India as a host state argues that the investor has breached
its chapter III obligations. First, arbitrators could stay the arbitration
pending resolution of the chapter III breaches in domestic venues, and
take judicial notice of any outcome in adjudicating any remaining chapter II claims brought by the investor. Second, the arbitrators could
dismiss the host state's arguments for lack of jurisdiction, if article 13.2
is interpreted to strip them of jurisdiction on any chapter III counter-
claim, justification or defense. It is therefore uncertain whether India
could claim that a breach of chapter III obligations by the investor
justifies its actions, or justifies a reduction in the amount of compensation that might be awarded by the tribunal.

2 SADC

The Model BIT devotes an entire part 3 to the "Rights and Obligations of
Investors and State Parties." The main topics addressed therein cover
anti-corruption measures, environmental protection, corporate governance, human rights and labor standards, and development and investor
liability.

Investors would need to complete environmental and social impact
assessments pre-establishment (art. 13) meeting the most stringent
requirements of either the host state, the home state, or the International
Finance Corporation.[139] Article 15 on "Minimum Standards for Human
Rights, Environment and Labour" uses a similar approach when it prohibits investors from managing or operating "investments in a manner
inconsistent with international environmental, labour, and human rights

---

[137] Indian Draft Model BIT, *supra* note 11, art. 12.2.
[138] 2016 India Model BIT, *supra* note 10, art. 13.2.
[139] SADC Model BIT, *supra* note 22, art. 1.

112   NEW BALANCE OF RIGHTS AND OBLIGATIONS

obligations binding on the Host State or the Home State, whichever obligations are higher."[140] The reference to the most stringent regulatory framework of the home state, the host state, or an international organization is an original device to avoid regulatory races to the bottom and the exploitation of lower environmental and labor standards by investors. At the same time, it could resolve the issue of investors puzzling whether to comply with home state laws with uncertain extraterritorial reach.[141] Such an approach could be deployed beyond impact assessments to topics including corruption, corporate governance (fiduciary duties and accounting) and data protection, for instance.

Quite uniquely among the new wave of BITs and Model BITs from developing countries, article 21 on the "Right to Pursue Development Goals" reflects a number of debates that have unfolded in recent years about potential clashes between foreign investors' expectations and developmental state policies.[142] This provision of the SADC Model BIT provides three main avenues for developmental objectives:

> The provision allows exceptions to nondiscrimination clauses in order to implement regional development goals. The now defunct article 8.2.b of the WTO's Agreement on Subsidies and Countervailing Measures also allowed an exception to disciplines for subsidies meant to foster regional development. The EU was and still is a major user of regional subsidies to promote the economy of disadvantaged or vulnerable regions. Developing countries are now seeking to follow that path, too.
>
> The provision also allows the state to impose certain requirements designed to "support the development of local entrepreneurs" and increase the local workforce capacity through requirements imposed on investors at the time of establishment. This provision is a response to the longstanding critique of the often limited benefits of foreign investment to assist the local workforce in moving up the corporate ladder and eventually help develop a more sophisticated local business community, rather than merely use the local workforce as a source of cheap, low-qualified labor.

[140] *Id.* art. 15.
[141] *See, e.g.,* Environmental Defense Fund v. Massey, 986 F.2d 528 (D.C. Cir., 1993) (holding that presumption against application of statutes extraterrritorially does not apply when the conduct occurs primarily in the United States); EEOC v. Arabian American Oil Co., 499 U.S. 244 (1991) (holding that Title VII does not apply to American employers that employ American workers overseas); Saudi Arabia v. Nelson, 507 U.S. 349 (1993) (holding that detention by the Saudi government was not "based upon a commercial activity" within the Foreign Sovereign Immunities Act).
[142] SADC Model BIT, *supra* note 22, art. 21.

Last, the provision enshrines the ability of the state to "take measures necessary to address historically based economic disparities suffered by identifiable ethnic or cultural groups due to discriminatory or oppressive measures against such groups prior to the signing of this Agreement."[143] This clause seems particularly tailored in response to post-apartheid reforms in South Africa and the investment arbitration challenges some of these policies have led to in recent years.

3 Brazil CIFAs

The new Brazilian agreements include a section on the responsibility of investors. Some versions are very detailed. For example, the Brazil–Chile agreement[144] states that the parties should encourage companies to follow policies of sustainability and corporate responsibility that will further the development of the host country, and use best efforts to comply with the OECD Guidelines for Multinationals, including respecting human rights, building local capacity and developing human capital in the host country, following best practices in corporate governance, protecting whistleblowers, and other duties. Although phrased only as best efforts commitments, these obligations could be taken into account in efforts at dispute settlements, including state-to-state arbitration. A few other CIFAs have equally detailed clauses, and others, though less specific, all include a corporate social responsibility clause.[145]

In conclusion, recent evolutions in the drafting of definitions, rights and obligations in BITs and other investment agreements involving emerging countries reflect common trends toward better control by the states of who and which assets may benefit from treaty protection. Much of this may be interpreted as a reaction to expansionary tendencies in arbitral interpretations.

III Preserving Domestic Judicial Power and Reforming Investor–State Arbitration

Investor–state arbitrations under the auspices of the International Centre for the Settlement of Investment Disputes ("ICSID") Convention or the United Nations Commission on International Trade Law ("UNCITRAL") and

---

[143] *Id.* art. 21.
[144] Chile CIFA *supra* note 27, art. 15.
[145] Brazil–Angola CIFA, *supra* note 24, art. 10; Brazil–Mozambique CIFA, *supra* note 25, art. 10; Brazil–Malawi CIFA, *supra* note 26, art. 9; Brazil–Mexico CIFA, *supra* note 27, art. 13; Brazil–Colombia CIFA, *supra* note 27, art. 13.

similar frameworks have come under fire from states (whether developed or developing), civil society and local communities. Critiques leveled at such arbitrations are both procedural and substantive. On the procedural front, the lack of clear and universally accepted codes of conduct and ethics rules for arbitrators has left the practicing world vulnerable to accusations of conflicts of interest, clientelism and other biases.[146] The cost of the process is another concern for low-income developing countries and even middle-income emerging powers.[147] Civil society advocates lament the opacity of the process and their lack of standing to participate when a foreign investor's activities have a deleterious impact on the public interest, a local community or a vulnerable ecosystem that the state is either unable or unwilling to protect.[148] BITs do not grant host states the right to request international arbitration proceedings against a foreign investor. The host state is therefore limited to seeking whatever domestic administrative and judicial remedies may be contractually available between the investor and state agencies, or as a matter of general law in that country.

In response, developing countries are pursuing a variety of tactics to bypass or reform investor–state arbitration in hopes of gaining better control over the process and substantive law. These fall mainly in three categories: limiting access to arbitration by investors and giving preeminence to domestic courts of the host state (Part A), relying on state-to-state processes for resolving investor claims (Part B), and substantive rules regarding arbitrators' competence to offer better guarantees of impartiality (C).

A   Limiting Access to Arbitration by Investors

In some cases, the backlash against BITs does not focus on a particular developmental policy but rather on the perceived intrusion on the

---

[146] See, e.g., Susan D. Franck et al., *The Diversity Challenge: Exploring the "Invisible College" of International Arbitration*, 53 COLUM. J. TRANSNAT'L L. 429, 496–97 (2015) (identifying the characteristics of the practicing bar involved in international arbitration).

[147] See, e.g., Silvia Karina Fiezzoni, *The Challenge of UNASUR Member Countries to Replace ICSID Arbitration*, 2 BEIJING L. REV. 134, 134 (2011) (discussing myriad complaints and concerns of Latin American countries with ICSID).

[148] See, e.g., TRANSFORMING THE IIA REGIME: EXITING THE UNNECESSARY, DAMAGING INVESTOR STATE DISPUTE SETTLEMENT SYSTEM (UNCTAD World Investment Forum, Feb. 20, 2014), https://worldinvestmentforum.unctad.org/wp-content/uploads/2015/05/Public-Citizen-Draft.pdf; *Civil Society Groups Say "No" to Investors Suing States in RCEP*, PUBLIC SERVICES INTERNATIONAL (Aug. 4, 2016), www.world-psi.org/en/civil-society-groups-say-no-investors-suing-states-rcep.

normal functioning of domestic institutions, including the judiciary. For instance, the vast number of BITs that India has entered into only garnered attention after a number of arbitration proceedings found not only against Indian regulatory measures, but more specifically against decisions of the Indian judiciary.[149] A number of emerging countries are therefore exploring procedural rules to limit access to ISDS.

"Fork in the road" provisions giving investors the choice to use domestic legal remedies in the host state or ISDS have been a feature of BITs for some time. In practice, investors typically prefer ISDS. Some BITs also have waiting periods after investors raise a grievance but before they can engage in litigation or arbitration, presumably to give the parties a chance to work out a settlement. More drastically, requirements to exhaust local remedies create an even greater hurdle for investors to initiate arbitration proceedings. Limiting arbitral jurisdictions to certain claims is another way to constrain the scope of international investment arbitration. These steps, and other measures taken by developing countries, are illustrated in the coming sections.

1 India Model BIT

The long and detailed chapter IV on disputes between investors and a state party reflects the government's effort both to narrow the scope of ISDS claims as well as to improve its procedures. India's reservations concerning ISDS are also clear from the fact that it is not a member of ICSID. Nonetheless, India has been a respondent in some twenty investment arbitrations since 2003. Nine of these settled (all involved the financing of the Dabhol energy project in Maharashtra), one was decided in favor of the investor, and ten were pending in 2018.[150] Indian investors were involved in three cases, one of which settled, one that had an unknown status, and one that is pending. They held arbitrations at the PCA under UNCITRAL rules[151] with a single arbitrator or three

---

[149] See Prabhash Ranjan & Deepak Raju, *Bilateral Investment Treaties and the Indian Judiciary*, 46 GEO. WASH. INT'L L. REV. 809 (2014) (offering three ways to avoid these conflicts: exclude judicial actions from the ambit of treaty-based arbitrations, exclude judicial actions from the ambit of substantive treaty protections, or require exhaustion of local remedies).

[150] India Country Case, UNCTAD INVESTMENT POLICY HUB, http://investmentpolicyhu bold.unctad.org/ISDS (Click "India").

[151] Indian Metals & Ferro Alloys Ltd. v. Republic of India, PCA Case No. 2015-40, UNCTAD INVESTMENT POLICY HUB, http://investmentpolicyhubold.unctad.org/ ISDS/Details/682; Louis Dreyfus Armateurs SAS v. The Republic of India, PCA Case No. 2014-26, UNCTAD INVESTMENT POLICY HUB, http://investmentpolicyhubold

arbitrators.[152] The 2016 Model BIT allows arbitrations under the ICSID Convention "provided that both the Parties are full members of the Convention" (which seems inapplicable since India is not a party), or the Additional Facility Rules of ICSID "provided that either Party . . . is a member of the ICSID Convention."[153]

The restrictive nature of ISDS under the 2016 India Model BIT comes from the interaction of two features: exhaustion of domestic remedies and immunity of domestic court decisions. On the one hand, the Model requires that investors must exhaust remedies available under domestic law that cover "the same measure or similar factual matters for which

.unctad.org/ISDS/Details/600; CC/Devas (Mauritius) Ltd., Devas Employees Mauritius Private Limited, and Telcom Devas Mauritius Limited v. Republic of India, PCA Case No. 2013-09, UNCTAD Investment Policy Hub, http://investmentpolicyhubold .unctad.org/ISDS/Details/484; Tenoch Holdings Limited et al. v. The Republic of India, PCA Case No. 2013-23, UNCTAD Investment Policy Hub, http://investment policyhubold.unctad.org/ISDS/Details/491.

[152] Networks and South Asia Entertainment Holdings Limited v. India, UNCTAD Investment Policy Hub, https://investmentpolicyhubold.unctad.org/ISDS/Details/ 735; Vedanta Resources plc v. India, UNCTAD Investment Policy Hub, http:// investmentpolicyhubold.unctad.org/ISDS/Details/733; Cairn Energy PLC v. India, PCA Case No. 2016-7, UNCTAD Investment Policy Hub, http://investmentpolicy hubold.unctad.org/ISDS/Details/691; Vodafone International Holdings BV v. India, PCA Case No. 2016-35, UNCTAD Investment Policy Hub, http://investmentpolicy hubold.unctad.org/ISDS/Details/581; Deutsche Telekom v. India, UNCTAD Investment Policy Hub, http://investmentpolicyhubold.unctad.org/ISDS/Details/ 550; Khaitan Holdings Mauritius Limited v. India, UNCTAD Investment Policy Hub, http://investmentpolicyhubold.unctad.org/ISDS/Details/553; White Industries Australia Limited v. The Republic of India, UNCTAD Investment Policy Hub, http://investmentpolicyhubold.unctad.org/ISDS/Details/378; ABN Amro N. V. v. Republic of India, UNCTAD Investment Policy Hub, http://investmentpolicy hubold.unctad.org/ISDS/Details/149; ANZEF Ltd. v. Republic of India, UNCTAD Investment Policy Hub, http://investmentpolicyhubold.unctad.org/ISDS/Details/ 151; BNP Paribas v. Republic of India, UNCTAD Investment Policy Hub, http:// investmentpolicyhubold.unctad.org/ISDS/Details/147; Credit Lyonnais S.A. (now Calyon S.A.) v. Republic of India, UNCTAD Investment Policy Hub, http://invest mentpolicyhubold.unctad.org/ISDS/Details/148; Credit Suisse First Boston v. Republic of India, UNCTAD Investment Policy Hub, http://investmentpolicyhubold.unctad .org/ISDS/Details/150; Erste Bank Der Oesterreichischen Sparkassen AG v. Republic of India, UNCTAD Investment Policy Hub, http://investmentpolicyhubold.unctad .org/ISDS/Details/141; Offshore Power Production C.V. et al. v. Republic of India, UNCTAD Investment Policy Hub, http://investmentpolicyhubold.unctad .org/ISDS/Details/139; Standard Chartered Bank v. Republic of India, UNCTAD Investment Policy Hub, http://investmentpolicyhubold.unctad.org/ISDS/Details/ 152; Bechtel Enterprises Holdings, Inc. and GE Structured Finance (GESF) v. The Government of India, UNCTAD Investment Policy Hub, http://investmentpolicy hubold.unctad.org/ISDS/Details/104.

[153] 2016 India Model BIT, *supra* note 10, art. 16.1.

a breach of [the] Treaty is claimed"[154] for at least five years from the date when the investor first knew of the measure[155] before proceeding with investor–state arbitration under the BIT. However, if no domestic recourse exists or no resolution was reached within the five-year period, investors may proceed to arbitration,[156] subject to another six-month negotiation period,[157] but only if less than six years have elapsed since the investor first knew or should have known of the measure.[158] On the other hand, the Model BIT states that arbitration tribunals lack the jurisdiction to "review the merits of a decision made by a judicial authority of the Parties."[159] In practice, then, it appears that investors must first vindicate their grievances in Indian courts; if they win, they will not need ISDS. If they lose, they will be precluded from resorting to ISDS on those same issues because the tribunal cannot take up an issue once decided by a court. In any case, investors have a six-month window to make a claim, after five years and six months but before six years after they first knew or should have known of the measure. Referring to similar requirements in the draft Model BIT, the Law Commission of India commented:

> This provision renders the entire BIT unworkable ... Pursuing domestic remedies would entail an interaction with the judicial authorities of the Host State, which would result in ... decisions on the merits. However ... any finding by a local Court [acts] as a jurisdictional bar in as so far as the Arbitral Tribunal is concerned. It is hard to contemplate too many scenarios where an investor would comply with the provision for exhaustion of local remedies and yet overcome the jurisdictional bar imposed by Article 14.2(2).[160]

---

[154] Id. art. 15.1.
[155] Id. art. 15.2.
[156] Id. art. 15.2.
[157] Id. art. 15.4.
[158] Id. art. 15.5(i).
[159] Id. art. 13.5.
[160] Analysis of the 2015 Draft Model Indian Bilateral Investment Treaty, Report No. 260, Law Commission of India, available at http://lawcommissionofindia.nic.in/reports/Report260.pdf. The commission accepts the provision that bars the arbitral tribunal from reviewing the merits of a judicial decision but believes tribunals should be able to determine if such a decision, taken as a final and irreversible government act, violates some provision of the treaty. The jurisdictional bar could make this impossible. The U.S. National Association of Manufacturers argues that these provisions foreclose "any ISDS cases in areas that might be covered by judicial action, including the very important area of intellectual property protection." NAT'L ASS'N OF MFRS., COMMENT ON DRAFT INDIAN MODEL BILATERAL INVESTMENT TREATY, supra note 6 at 7.

2 China

BITs involving China at times include procedural and substantive limitations or prerequisites to investor–state arbitration, but no systematic drafting strategy transpires from a review of recently negotiated BITs. A number of recent BITs include a "cooling-off" period of six months since the events giving rise to the claim before the investor may submit an arbitral claim.[161] Moreover, a notice period to the contracting party may be required declaring the investor's intent to file for a claim, and it is unclear whether it runs concurrently with the cooling-off period (see, e.g., four-month notice period and six-month period since the events giving rise to the claim in the China–Canada BIT).

With respect to forum, China signed on to ICSID in 1990 and ratified it in 1993, but restricted ICSID tribunals' jurisdiction to claims regarding compensation for expropriation. Moreover, not all BITs signed by China after its ICSID ratification refer to ICSID jurisdiction, which some commentators interpret as a continued reluctance from China to embrace ICSID proceedings.[162]

Some BITs provide for an exhaustion of certain local remedies. For instance, the China–Malta BIT requires investors to go through "the administrative review procedures according to the laws of the [PRC]" prior to submitting an arbitration claim. Similarly, Malta requires Chinese investors to exhaust local judicial or arbitral recourses prior to undertaking international investor–state arbitration.[163] While the language may be straightforward, navigating the requirements may be much more complicated in practice since it requires research and interpretation of the local law regarding which local administrative or judicial proceedings are required in each legal system. This may be all the more so the case for China, where local, regional and central administrations amount to as many layers of potential administrative proceedings.

Substantive restrictions typically either exclude certain sectors from arbitration or seek to protect the host state's prudential and regulatory authority. For instance, the China–Canada BIT provides that a contracting party may

---

[161] *See, e.g.,* Canada–China BIT, *supra* note 118, art. 21.2(b) ("at least six months have elapsed since the events giving rise to the claim").

[162] Norah Gallagher & Wenhua Shan, Chinese Investment Treaties – Policies and Practice 39 (2009).

[163] Agreement between the Government of the People's Republic of China and the Government of Malta on the Promotion and Protection of Investments, China–Malta, art. 9, Feb. 22, 2009, http://investmentpolicyhubold.unctad.org/Download/TreatyFile/3368.

respond to an arbitral claim by invoking article 33(3), which in turn may trigger a state-to-state arbitration between the BIT signatories. The investor–state proceedings are stayed while the state-to-state claim is adjudicated.[164] Article 33(3) states:

> Nothing in this Agreement shall be construed to prevent a Contracting Party from adopting or maintaining reasonable measures for prudential reasons, such as:
>
> (a) the protection of depositors, financial market participants and investors, policy-holders, policy-claimants, or persons to whom a fiduciary duty is owed by a financial institution;
> (b) the maintenance of the safety, soundness, integrity or financial responsibility of financial institutions; and
> (c) ensuring the integrity and stability of a Contracting Party's financial system.[165]

It may be that Canada was the party advocating for such a provision, though the treaty was signed in 2012, when the aftermath of the 2008 financial crisis would still have been very much at the forefront of regulators' priorities. Argentina's financial and economic crisis of the early 2000s, and the ensuing string of arbitrations that revealed the very limited safeguards to protect prudential measures, may also have been motivations behind article 33.

By contrast, some Chinese BITs are mostly free of procedural or substantive limitations to arbitration.[166] Ultimately, it is questionable how much of a recourse an investor-initiated arbitration against China would be. Relationships with government officials may be more critical to the redress of grievances. A breakdown in such relationships, by contrast, means that even if arbitration leads to a victory for the investor, it may be a hollow one. Conversely, outward investments where Chinese investors seek arbitration against a host state may play out differently depending on whether the investor has the support of the Chinese government.

---

[164] Canada–China BIT, *supra* note 118, arts. 20.2(a), 33(3).
[165] *Id.* art. 33(3).
[166] *See, e.g.*, Agreement between the Government of the People's Republic of China and the Government of the Republic of Uzbekistan on the Promotion and Protection of Investments, China–Uzb., art. 12, Apr. 19, 2011, http://investmentpolicyhubold.unctad .org/Download/TreatyFile/3357 (requiring only a six-month negotiation period for certain claims).

3   Central America

The Central American Free Trade Agreement draft treaty text included an interpretative footnote to the MFN clause explicitly rejecting the *Maffezini* approach allowing investors to import a broader dispute settlement clause from another BIT through the operation of MFN clauses:

> The Parties note the recent decision of the arbitral tribunal in Maffezini (Arg.) v. Kingdom of Spain, which found an unusually broad most-favored-nation clause in an Argentina-Spain agreement to encompass international dispute resolution procedures . . . By contrast, the Most-Favored-Nation Treatment Article of this Agreement expressly limited its scope to matters "with respect to the establishment, acquisition, expansion, management, conduct, operation and sale or other disposition of investments." The parties share the understanding and intent that this clause does not encompass international dispute resolution mechanisms . . . and therefore could not reasonably lead to a conclusion similar to that of the Maffezini case.[167]

Eventually, the footnote was abandoned and the final version of the MFN clause in the investment chapter was worded to exclude dispute settlement procedural matters instead: "Each Party shall accord to investors of another Party treatment no less favorable than that it accords, in like circumstances, to investors of any other Party or of any non-Party with respect to the establishment, acquisition, expansion, management, conduct, operation, and sale or other disposition of investments in its territory."[168]

B   *Moving Away from the Pro-Investor Bias in Arbitration*

Investor–state arbitration has fallen prey to increasingly vocal critiques regarding bias in favor of investors, due to shortcomings in the vetting mechanism for arbitrators, procedures for arbitration, and a culture of skepticism regarding the legitimacy of states' regulatory measures when they adversely affect foreign investments. These concerns have taken on all the more visibility with the European Union advocating for

---

[167] Draft US–Central America Free Trade Agreement (CAFTA), Jan. 28, 2004, reprinted in OECD, *Most-Favoured-Nation Treatment in International Investment Law*, OECD Working Papers on International Investment, 2004/02, OECD Publishing, http://dx.doi.org/10.1787/518757021651 at n. 8.

[168] The Dominican Republic–Central America–United States Free Trade Agreement, art. 10.4, Aug. 5, 2004, https://ustr.gov/trade-agreements/free-trade-agreements/cafta-dr-dominican-republic-central-america-fta/final-text [CAFTA–DR].

a permanent international investment court in lieu of ISDS.[169] The topic is therefore no longer solely a sore point for emerging countries, but a shared issue for many developed and developing countries alike. This section reflects on some proposals from emerging countries to improve the legitimacy of investor–state dispute resolution.

1 India

The 2016 India Model BIT includes detailed sections on qualifications and selection of arbitrators, and transparency of procedures. Article 18.1 lists the fields of expertise acceptable for arbitrators. Articles 18.1 and 19 specify how the arbitrators and the parties should deal with arbitrators' potential conflicts of interest. Despite their length, the provisions still leave much to interpretation and to the appreciation of the parties and the arbitrators alike. Article 19.10 does list specific circumstances in which a "justifiable doubt as to an arbitrator's independence or impartiality or freedom from conflicts of interests shall be deemed to exist." Additionally, other unlisted events or circumstances may also give rise to a "justifiable doubt" regarding an arbitrator's suitability. Most have to do with arbitrator's connections with the parties or their attorneys, for instance if the arbitrator is in the same law firm as one of the counsels. Arbitrators are required to disclose in writing any potential conflict of interest[170] and the existence of such circumstances is a ground for a challenge by a party to the dispute.[171]

The 2016 Model BIT also includes provisions on the dismissal of "frivolous claims," defined as "a claim submitted by the investor [. . .]: (a) not within the scope of the Tribunal's jurisdiction, or (b) manifestly without legal merit or unfounded as a matter of law."[172] Meritless suits brought by investors primarily to put pressure on host states have been a recurrent concern of developing host countries, particularly because of the limited resources they have at their disposal to defend claims.

---

[169] See, e.g., European Commission, *EU–Canada Trade and Investment Negotiations*, Press Release MEMO/16/4350, Dec. 13, 2016, http://europa.eu/rapid/press-release_MEMO-16-4350_en.htm ("The European Commission and the Canadian Government are working together to establish a multilateral investment court"); European Commission, *TTIP Negotiations with the UN*, Press Release IP/15/5651, Sept. 16, 2015, http://europa.eu/rapid/press-release_IP-15-5651_en.htm ("The European Commission has approved its proposal for a new and transparent system for resolving disputes between investors and states – the Investment Court System").

[170] 2016 India Model BIT, *supra* note 10, art. 19.2.
[171] *Id.* art. 19.3.
[172] *Id.* art. 21.1.

In response to another critique often leveled at the ISDS system, the Model BIT includes a transparency provision,[173] which creates a presumption that key legal documents relating to investor–state arbitrations will be made publicly available, including the notice of arbitration, written submissions by the parties, transcript of the hearings, and awards of the tribunal. This constitutes a radical departure from the traditional ISDS framework.

2   SADC

A recurring critique of traditional investor–state dispute settlement Models is that only the investor has the ability to trigger arbitration procedures. Arguably, a host state could contract with the investor for a reciprocal arbitration clause in any contract made between the state and the investor (such as concession contracts), or simply use its domestic courts in any disputes with the foreign investor. The problem with the latter is that investors increasingly tend to challenge domestic court decisions in BIT arbitrations, at times frustrating the finality of domestic court judgments. BITs and Model BITs from developing countries offer a variety of responses to this phenomenon.

The SADC Model BIT explicitly affirms the right of the host state to present counterclaims in arbitrations initiated by foreign investors.[174] In addition, the host state may initiate domestic proceedings against the investor in its home state, under the domestic law of that home state.[175] Such an avenue dovetails with other provisions in the SADC Model BIT on environmental impact assessment, and labor and human rights standards that are to be taken from the host or home state (or an international organization), whichever is the most stringent. Moreover, it avoids the issue of foreign judgment recognition if the host state were to win its case in its domestic courts but sought to enforce the judgment in the home state, presumably because the investor has assets there. Along the same lines, the ability to sue directly in the investor's home state makes recovery against the investor's local assets much more likely, as domestic attachment measures to prevent assets from fleeing the jurisdiction are much easier to obtain than so-called Mareva injunctions[176] to prevent the

---

[173] *Id.* art. 22.
[174] SADC Model BIT, *supra* note 22, art. 19.
[175] *Id.* art. 19.4.
[176] Worldwide Mareva injunctions refer to the freezing of assets outside of the court's jurisdiction. *See, e.g.,* Obégi v. Kilani, 2011 ONSC 1636 (Can.) (discussing whether the court could assume jurisdiction on the matter regarding the freezing of assets in

transfer of assets located in another jurisdiction. Despite the many potential benefits of article 19.4, a number of hurdles may frustrate its purpose. First, the home state domestic law might not provide standing for the host state to sue. Second, the host state, by initiating proceedings, would be relinquishing its sovereign immunity and may expose itself to counterclaims from the investor. Third, the trend of "reverse incorporations" for tax-shielding purposes may make it difficult to identify the home state of an investor, or may result in the home state not having any assets of the investors, if it was used merely as a nominal incorporation location.

3 UNASUR

UNASUR countries have declared their opposition to ICSID as a forum, and some members have sought to develop an alternative arbitral forum in Latin America. More radically, the Bolivarian Alternative for the Peoples of Our America (ALBA) strongly opposes the traditional ISDS system. Principle 16 of the Fundamental Principles of the Peoples' Trade Treaty (TCP) provides "[t]he exigency that foreign investment respects national laws. Unlike FTAs which impose a series of advantages and guarantees in favour of transnational companies, the TCP looks for a foreign investment that it respects the laws, reinvest the utilities and solves any controversy with the State like any national investor."[177] Bolivia and Ecuador, two member countries of ALBA and TCP, now have constitutional provisions prohibiting the respective governments from entering into treaties where the domestic judiciary would be displaced by international arbitration.[178]

Ontario). *See generally* David Capper, *Worldwide Mareva Injunctions*, 54 MODERN L. REV. 329 (1991) (examining worldwide Mareva injunction cases and obstacles posed to asset freezing).

[177] Fundamental Principles of the Peoples' Trade Treaty, BOLIVARIAN ALLIANCE FOR THE PEOPLES OF OUR AMERICA [ALBA], http://alba-tcp.org/en/contenido/governing-principles-tcp [https://perma.cc/MV4B-9BKX].

[178] Constitución de Ecuador, Sept. 2008, art. 422 (Ecuador); República de Bolivia – Constitución de 2009, Feb. 7, 2009, art. 366 (Bol.). *See also* INTERNATIONAL INVESTMENT LAW IN LATIN AMERICA / DERECHO INTERNACIONAL DE LAS LAS INVERSIONES EN AMÈRICA LATINA: PROBLEMS AND PROSPECTS / PROBLEMAS Y PERSPECTIVAS, 180–81 (Attila Tanzi et al., eds., 2016). ("It may be noted that both Bolivia and Ecuador have recently amended their own constitutions in the sense of banning international arbitration.")

C   Diplomatic Recourses and Domestic Remedies[179]

Amid heated critiques of investor–state arbitrations and proposals for alternative venues, some developing countries are opting for a return to diplomatic protection and other state-based processes for solving investment disputes. The move may seem anachronistic but reflects some emerging countries' deep disenchantment with international investment law in general. Also in part, it pertains to a broader trend of reasserting host states' control of foreign investment policy.

1   Domestic Remedies: the Examples of South Africa and Indonesia

The Protection of Investment Act enacted in 2015 by South Africa now specifically excludes investor–state arbitration, and South Africa is considering new BITs without an investor–state arbitration clause, particularly with countries where it is exporting. The legislation also calls for letting lapse current BITs that include investor–state arbitration. While the official rationale for such moves is constitutional requirements, it was only after some related legislation came under threat from investor–state arbitrations that South Africa resolutely moved away from BITs.

Moreover, the South African Development Community (SADC) took the position in its Model BIT template with commentary that the preferred option is not to include investor–state dispute settlement.[180] Negotiations are ongoing at the African Union and United Nations Economic Commission for Africa to design a Pan African Investment Code that would likely result in a text close to the features of the SADC Model. The hope is that such a text would also serve as a model for regional groupings and BITs involving African countries.

Indonesia has also denounced a slew of BITs and is drafting a new Model BIT, though it is unclear whether it plans to exclude investor–state arbitration from its new approach. Where it is able to terminate its BIT obligations, Indonesia would be mostly reverting to domestic remedies, with the applicable law including domestic rules and customary international law.

---

[179] This section draws from Sonia E. Rolland, *The Return of State Remedies in Investor–State Dispute Settlement: Trends in Developing Countries*, 49 Loy. U. Chi. L.J. 387 (2017).

[180] SADC Model BIT, *supra* note 22, art. 29.

2   Return to Diplomatic Protection? The Case of Brazil

In those countries denouncing BITs (South Africa, Indonesia and Ecuador, for instance) or declining to participate in them (Brazil), foreign investors may only rely on domestic law and institutions, and international customary law, which might be vindicated through diplomatic protection. Traditionally, diplomatic protection requires a private entity aggrieved by a foreign state to call upon the state of its nationality to seek redress on its behalf from the foreign state. The state is not obligated to provide protection. With respect to legal entities such as corporations, the International Court of Justice held in the landmark *Barcelona Traction* case[181] that the state of incorporation, rather than the state of nationality of the shareholders, would be the state in a position to offer diplomatic protection. As Noel Maurer has extensively researched in the case of Latin America,[182] pressure from U.S. investors to persuade the state to seek remedies on their behalf became severely burdensome on foreign policy, and still failed to protect U.S. investments from expropriation abroad. Ultimately, the United States and other major capital-exporting countries found that the constant demands of diplomatic protection impeded broader diplomatic strategies, and they created an avenue for investors to seek direct recourse against the host state via international arbitration.

Most Brazil CIFAs envision a state-to-state dispute settlement process that is reminiscent of traditional diplomatic protection. Such a move bucks the trend of judicialization of foreign investment law over the past century. It is therefore quite a radical response to emerging countries' demand for the protection of their policy space against norms of international economic law perceived to be at times incompatible with their development needs. In the Brazil–Mozambique and Angola contexts, this issue may be less salient because of the history of trade and investment relations between the two countries. Additionally, Brazilian investors may not be concerned about overreach by these African states, as they appear to be comfortable with this new approach to investment protection. Whether such a Model would operate equally well in other circumstances remains an open question.

---

[181] Barcelona Traction, Light and Power Company, Ltd. (Belgium v. Spain), 1970 I.C.J. 3 (Feb. 5).

[182] *See generally* NOEL MAURER, THE EMPIRE TRAP: THE RISE AND FALL OF U.S. INTERVENTION TO PROTECT AMERICAN PROPERTY OVERSEAS 1893–2013 (2013).

This section takes the Brazil–Mozambique CIFA as an illustrative benchmark because it was the first such agreement, and subsequent ones include essentially similar mechanisms. The agreement establishes a Joint Committee composed of government representatives appointed by each state. The committee is expected to meet at least once annually under an alternating presidency to discuss implementation, work toward deeper coordination and cooperation, and help resolve disputes.[183] Alongside the committee, the states are each to designate a domestic "Focal Point," which is a specific government agency tasked with offering support to investors of the other state. The Focal Point liaises with other governmental authorities domestically and with its counterpart in the other state. The Focal Point (at times also called "ombudsman" in the CIFAs), backed by the Joint Committee, also assists in the conciliatory settlement of disputes.[184] Despite the use of the term "ombudsman," this process does not designate a neutral independent person to help resolve disputes.

Anecdotal evidence suggests that the ombudsman model was initially inspired by the South Korean institution of a foreign investment ombudsman, established in 1999, which has enjoyed vast success in resolving disputes outside of formal judicial or arbitral proceedings.[185] The office of the ombudsman was created as a one-stop service to handle grievances by foreign investors in South Korea. The office of the ombudsman focuses on post-investment services for foreign investors in areas covering finance, taxation, accounting, intellectual property rights, construction and labor. The ombudsman is the head of the grievance settlement body. Grievances are resolved through the direct deployment of licensed and experienced experts to business sites, and indirectly by taking preemptive measures to prevent future grievances through systemic improvements and legal amendments. The ombudsman is commissioned by the president on a recommendation of the minister of trade, industry and energy, through the deliberation of the Foreign Investment Committee.

Since 2010, the ombudsman has been the chair of South Korea's Regulatory Reform Committee, and also sits on the Presidential Council

---

[183] Brazil–Mozambique CIFA, *supra* note 25, art. 4.
[184] *Id.* art. 15.
[185] *See, e.g.,* Kim Wan-Soon, *Foreign Direct Investment In Korea,* Korea Development Institute (2003), www.kdevelopedia.org/Resources/all/foreign-direct-investment-korea-04201201180005040.do;jsessionid=D1F37B76E210DDEF2581496B122313D4#.W9J_OhNKjsE.

on National Competitiveness (PCNC), thus ensuring that the opinions of foreign investors are heard at the highest levels of policy making within South Korea. The ombudsman is empowered to directly contact heads of ministries and government agencies for requests and recommendations. The ombudsman therefore plays a mix of alternative dispute resolution intermediary, diplomatic and political roles.

The Brazilian ombudsman/Focal Point system, however, differs substantially from the South Korean model. The role is not embodied by a person, but rather is envisioned as a committee with interministerial representation.

While the agreements establish a process to encourage settlement of disputes, only the governments of the states party to a particular CIFA may trigger these procedures. In the Mozambique agreement, a dispute must be officially initiated by the state party of the investor by filing a request to the Joint Committee. The latter then has sixty days, renewable by mutual agreement, to present relevant information and to invite representatives of the investor, as well as representatives of governmental and nongovernmental entities involved in the dispute. Following meetings as necessary to resolve the situation, the procedure may be closed by request of either state party. If the dispute has not been resolved, the state parties may then proceed to arbitration. Joint Committee actions and documents remain mostly confidential.

The early CIFAs did not provide any details concerning the nature of arbitration, other than to make clear that it was limited to state-to-state disputes. Subsequent agreements signed with Latin American countries have added substantial detail, although the agreements are rather varied. Thus, the Mexico and Colombia agreements specify that the arbitral tribunal for state-to-state disputes may determine damages and award compensation,[186] while other agreements are silent on this issue. All provide a general framework for arbitration covering the number of arbitrators, the use of World Trade Organization (WTO) rules on the conduct of arbitrators, and time limits for the arbitral proceedings. However, they vary in the procedures for the arbitration and other aspects.

Thus, although the legal conduit created by Brazil is different from diplomatic protection, the Brazilian and South Korean Models share

---

[186] Brazil–Colombia CIFA, *supra* note 27, art. 23; Brazil–Mexico CIFA, *supra* note 27, art. 19.2.

a core political element due to the governmental nature of joint commit-
tees and Focal Points.

3   Limitations of State-Centric Dispute Resolution

Moves away from investor–state arbitration, however, are fraught with
legal risks and political hurdles. This section focuses on some substantive
and procedural legal issues. On the political front, obstacles to ISDS
reform may spring from private parties as well as states. For instance,
the vested interest from beneficiaries of the current system, including
established arbitrators and practitioners, will likely generate resistance.
Joost Pauwelyn has argued that the international investment regime's
legitimacy crisis, and in particular critiques leveled at ISDS, largely
proceeds from a shift in the respective roles of the rule of law, the rule
of lawyers, and politics in procedural and substantive frameworks.[187] But
inasmuch as a retreat from ISDS is meant to rebalance public and private
interests in favor of the state, we must question whether a process giving
the state increased power would actually lead to more prominence of
public interests. If states fail to provide a consistent and legitimate legal
framework for asserting the preeminence of the public interests and
dealing with clashes between public interests and private property interests, then adjudicators, regardless of who they are and how they are
empowered or constrained, have little reason to depart from current
approaches.

With respect to South Africa and Indonesia, it must be noted that
a number of claims may survive the termination of BITs and still be
capable of being submitted to investor–state arbitration. Both
Indonesia's and South Africa's policy is to notify partners of its intent
not to renew BITs that reach the ten- or fifteen-year period for initial
validity. Survival clauses in some of these treaties may continue to
protect existing investments for a number of years after the treaty has
been terminated. This period varies from treaty to treaty. For instance,
the South African BIT with Belgium and Luxembourg extends the
coverage of the treaty for existing investments for a period of ten
years following termination of the treaty,[188] as do the BITs with

---

[187] Joost Pauwelyn, *The Rule of Law without the Rule of Lawyers? Why Investment
Arbitrators are from Mars, Trade Adjudicators from Venus*, 109 AM. J. INT'L L. 761,
763–65 (2015).

[188] Accord entre l'Union économique belgo-luxembourgeoise et la République d'Afrique du
Sud concernant l'encouragement et la protection réciproques des investissements, Belg.–
Lux.–S. Afr., art. 12(2) (Aug. 14, 1998), 2218 U.N.T.S. 3.

Denmark[189] and Spain.[190] The latter explicitly includes dispute settlement provisions within the ambit of the survival clause. The South Africa–China BIT has a ten-year survival clause. The term of the survival clause for the BIT with the Netherlands is fifteen years.[191] The BIT with Austria provides a survival clause of twenty years,[192] as do the BITs with France[193] and Switzerland.[194] With respect to these treaties, South Africa may be subject to investor–state arbitration until as late as 2034, should a dispute arise regarding an investment made before 2014 and protected by a treaty denounced in 2014 with a twenty-year survival clause. Terminated Indonesian BITs also include survival clauses: ten years for Cambodia, China, Italy, Laos, Malaysia, Norway, Romania, Slovakia, Turkey and Vietnam. The Indonesia–Netherlands BIT includes a fifteen-year survival clause. The Indonesia–France BIT is remarkable for its indefinite survival clause: article 10 provides that in the case of termination, the provisions of the treaty shall continue to apply to investments covered by the treaty and approved by the parties prior to the denunciation.[195] The possibility of disputes being brought under expired treaties using survival clauses is not merely a theoretical one. Indonesia notified

---

[189] Agreement between The Kingdom of Denmark and The Republic of South Africa concerning the Promotion and Reciprocal Protection of Investments, Den.–S. Afr., art. 16.2 (Feb. 22, 1996; terminated Aug. 30, 2014), 2547 U.N.T.S. 3.

[190] Acuerdo para la Promoción y Protección Recíproca de Inversiones entre el Rieno de España y la Repùblica de Sudáfrica, Spain–S. Afr., art. XII.3 (Sept. 30, 1998; terminated Dec. 22, 2013), 2098 U.N.T.S. 203.

[191] Agreement on Encouragement and Reciprocal Protection of Investments between the Republic of South Africa and the Kingdom of the Netherlands, Neth.–S. Afr., art. 14.3 (Sept. 5, 1995; terminated Apr. 30, 2014), 2066 U.N.T.S. 413.

[192] Abkommen Zwischen der Regierung der Republik Österreich und der Regierung der Republik Südafrika über die Förderung und den Gegenseitigen Schutz von Investitionen samt Protokoll, Austria–S. Afr., art.12.3 (Nov. 28, 1996; terminated Oct. 11, 2014).

[193] Accord entre le Gouvernement de la République Française et le Gouvernement de la République d'Afrique du Sud sur l'encouragement et la protection réciproques des investissements, Fr.–S. Afr., art. 11 (Oct. 11, 1995; terminated Aug. 30, 2014), 2055 U. N.T.S. 455.

[194] Accord entre le Conseil fédéral suisse et le Gouvernement de la République d'Afrique du Sud concernant la promotion et la protection réciproque des investissements, Switz.–S. Afr, art. 13.2 (June 27, 1995; terminated Aug. 30, 2014), 2008 U.N.T.S. 103.

[195] Accord entre l'Union économique belgo-luxembourgeoise et la République d'Afrique du Sud concernant l'encouragement et la protection réciproques des investissements, Belg.–Lux.–S. Afr., art. 10 (Aug. 14, 1998), 2218 U.N.T.S. 3: "Au cas où le présent Accord viendrait à prendre fin, ses dispositions continueront à s'appliquer aux investissements couverts par ledit Accord et agréés par la Partie contractante préalablement à la dénonciation de cet Accord."

India of its intent not to renew the BIT between those two countries and the termination took effect in April 2016; in the intervening period, Indian Metals & Ferro Alloys Limited initiated arbitration proceedings against Indonesia under the lame duck BIT in November 2015 for USD 560 million.[196]

With the issue of survival clauses now squarely in the limelight, other countries seeking to denounce BITs, such as Indonesia, should be carefully considering the limited effect of such moves with respect to existing investments. It may be argued that in practice, an investment that has gone trouble free for several years is less likely to result in a major investor–state dispute decades later. At the same time, it may be that legislators in host states, thinking themselves free of the constraints of denounced BITs and the related exposure to arbitral claims, may take regulatory actions that are in fact still likely to trigger major arbitral proceedings under the various survival clauses. Additionally, developing countries' poor tracking of the type of FDI, its origin, and its nature may make it very difficult for governments to ascertain the possible consequences of regulatory measures that could be seen as indirect expropriation under traditional BITs. That landscape may be even further complicated by investors who reincorporate and nominally recast their investment to fall within the ambit of another treaty, which might not yet have been denounced, or might offer a longer survival clause.

South Africa's and Indonesia's moves also offer important lessons in treaty drafting for those countries that are crafting new Model BITs or are currently negotiating investment agreements (bilaterally or as part of regional trade agreements). A number of options could be considered. First, survival clauses may be excluded altogether or dramatically shortened. Second, survival clauses could be neutralized by mutual agreement at the time of denunciation or termination of the treaty. This technique was deployed by the Czech Republic[197] and also by

---

[196] Randy Fabi, *Indian Metals and Ferro Alloys Miner Files $560 mln Claim against Indonesia*, REUTERS (Nov. 18, 2015), http://in.reuters.com/article/indonesia-imfa-idINKCN0T70O320151118.

[197] Luke Eric Peterson, *Czech Republic Terminates Investment Treaties in Such a Way as to Cast Doubt on Residual Legal Protection for Existing Investments*, INV. ARB. REPORTER, Feb. 1, 2011, www.iareporter.com/articles/czech-republic-terminates-investment-treaties-in-such-a-way-as-to-cast-doubt-on-residual-legal-protection-for-existing-investments/.

Indonesia and Argentina.[198] Third, survival clauses could extend to the substantive rights and obligations under the BIT, but not to the arbitration clause. It may also be prudent to exclude the MFN clause from the ambit of any survival clause in order to avoid *Maffezini*-type imports of dispute settlement provisions from other BITs.[199]

Developing countries' concerns with investor–state arbitration relate in large part to the process as it currently exists, but their critique is also leveled at substantive outcomes or the risk of certain outcomes in the arbitration awards. Inasmuch as the rationale for rejecting or limiting ISDS is to preserve host state autonomy, it might stand to reason that reverting to domestic processes and the filter of the state through diplomatic protection and quasi-diplomatic processes, such as those delineated in the Brazil CIFAs, would deliver such policy space. However, reverting to diplomatic processes and domestic remedies may not assuage all of the substantive concerns. The question of policy autonomy and host states' ability to condition foreign investments on their domestic development and regulatory priorities is affected by many sources of international investment law including BITs, trade agreements or customary international law. Doing away with investor–state arbitration will not change this framework. Letting BITs lapse – or actively denouncing them – may help sidestep some objectionable language or interpretations of BITs, but customary law will still apply in state-to-state proceedings.

Moreover, shifting to a state-to-state dispute process alone will not satisfy many concerns about transparency, accountability, and recourses for affected communities. These issues can only be addressed if the domestic law of host countries provides an adequate framework to protect such interests and the means for implementing them. In many cases, foreign investments involve a slew of contracts, agreements, letters

---

[198] Luke Eric Peterson, *Indonesia Ramps Up Termination of BITs – and Kills Survival Clause in One Such Treaty – but Faces New $600 mil. Claim from Indian Mining Investor*, Dec. 7, 2015, www.bilaterals.org/?indonesia-ramps-up-termination-of.

[199] In 2000, the tribunal in *Maffezini v. Spain* applied a BIT's most-favored nation obligation ("MFN") to procedural issues relating to jurisdiction. The award shaped subsequent treaty negotiations as well as other ICSID arbitrations. Emilio Agustín Maffezini v. Kingdom of Spain, ICSID Case No. ARB/97/7 (Jan. 25, 2000), 5 ICSID Rep. 396 (2002). More recently, RosInvestCo v. Russia, a Stockholm Chamber of Commerce arbitration, went even further by using an MFN clause to broaden the types of claims that could be brought under a BIT when another BIT signed by the host state included coverage for a wider range of claims. RosInvestCo UK Ltd. v. Russia, Arb. V079/2005, Award on Jurisdiction (Arbitration Institute of the Stockholm Chamber of Commerce 2007) www.italaw.com/sites/default/files/case-documents/ita0719.pdf.

and other documents exchanged between various host government agencies and the investor, typically out of the public eye and not available for review. Chinese investments in Africa and Latin America, for instance, are notorious for the shroud of secrecy surrounding the specifics of the deals. Local communities are typically not parties to these agreements, and their legal standing to engage in the process ex ante or to seek remedies ex post are often limited or nonexistent. Obligations on foreign investors to generate social, economic and environmental impact assessments, subject to community scrutiny and public comment, may help but ultimately fall far short of leveling the playing field between affected communities and foreign investors in places where the state is unable or unwilling to protect local interests. Domestic governance shortcomings in host states create additional hurdles to the full expression of the public interest.

In addition to concerns about the role of host developing states in improving the operation of foreign investment law, there is the possible role of investors' home states in shaping the international investment framework. Home states could hold their investors accountable for breaches of human rights, environmental obligations, and other international laws to which the home state has subscribed. Indeed, the very notion of a foreign investor suggests that the investor falls within the jurisdiction of its home state; but almost universally, few legal avenues exist to hold investors accountable for their actions when they contravene the state's international commitments. Recourses could be envisioned under penal/criminal law and tort law, particularly in monist countries where international law takes direct effect domestically, and in dualist countries where the necessary domestic adoption measures have been enacted.

IV Conclusion: Lessons from Emerging Economies

There is no single strategy for investment governance in emerging countries. Positions seem to range from China's embrace of the BITs system, at least as far as its outbound investments are concerned, to ALBA's categorical and vitriolic rejection of BITs. The debates over international investment law are ongoing and the system is in flux. Emerging economies have sent a signal that they are no longer willing to accept the system as it emerged twenty years ago. The impact of this message on ongoing bilateral, regional and multilateral negotiations remains an open question.

The debate over BITs goes beyond technical legal issues. Different views of development strategy and the role of FDI in a successful development model are at stake. At one end of the spectrum are those who want to create a fully integrated global economic space in which capital, unfettered by regulation, will seek its highest and best use. From this point of view, it makes sense to keep foreign investment free of as many restrictions as possible. There is no trade-off between promoting investment on the one hand, and regulation in the name of development strategy on the other. In this paradigm, most restrictions are seen as economically inefficient and the best strategy is to allow unfettered FDI. At the other end are those like ALBA who see FDI as part of an imperialist project that will undermine inclusive development and should be limited to the extent possible.

The approach in most emerging economies lies between these two poles. In what we might consider the consensus view, FDI is neither good nor bad a priori. Everything depends on the nature of the investment and the rules that govern it. Host countries want to maintain their ability to regulate investments so they conform to development priorities. That leads to the demand for policy autonomy and for an increased space for domestic debate regarding the articulation of socioeconomic development strategies and investment policy. It is fair to say that all countries insist on greater protection for policy space.

Countries that accept ISDS, like India and China, preserve regulatory capacity by carving out exceptions and spelling them out with great specificity. China is both the host for massive amounts of inward investment and a major overseas investor. Initially, China resisted many features of the BITs regime including ISDS. Its early Model BIT defined investment and MFN narrowly and allowed a lot of room for national regulation of FDI. But over time this has changed, and China has come to accept more elements of the system including ISDS. However, China has maintained substantial protection for its domestic policy space while seeking maximum protection for its own investors.[200] While China seeks to protect its internal regulatory capacity and no investor has made a claim against China as of 2018, Chinese investors have used ISDS against developed and developing countries. Recently, a tribunal found that regulatory actions by Peru constituted indirect appropriation

---

[200] *See* Leon Trakman, *Geopolitics, China, and Investor–State Arbitration*, in CHINA IN THE INTERNATIONAL ECONOMIC ORDER (Lisa Toohey et al., eds., 2015).

and awarded compensation to the affected Chinese investor.[201] On the one hand, China appears to be using different standards for different kinds of partners; on the other China is now revising its Model BIT. Observers think that China will evolve toward a new paradigm that will allow it to maintain its state-led and highly regulated economy at home while gaining substantial protection abroad. Trakman sees China as engaged in an effort to find a balance between Western liberal values and its demands to reinvent itself as a sophisticated planned economy. This, he thinks, may lead to a "new paradigm in international investment law that will rebalance interests in state regulation and free market protection to foreign investors."[202] Given China's economic power, that could have a major impact on the overall system.

The Brazil CIFAs reaffirm "legislative autonomy and space for public policies" but do not contain specific carve-outs. It would seem that Brazil expects to handle that by ensuring that it can maintain control of any dispute settlement process more than by specific language.

Recent developments suggest that resistance by emerging economies, as well as concerns of developed countries who are themselves facing ISDS claims by investors (including from emerging countries), may lead to major changes in the BITs regime. A recent report authored by UNCTAD proposed an Investment Policy Framework for Sustainable Development listing eleven core principles for investment policy making for sustainable development.[203] The report recommends incorporating concrete commitments to promote and facilitate investment for sustainable development: requiring investors to comply with investment-related domestic laws of the host state, including regulation regarding environmental cleanup; formulating a fair and equitable treatment clause as an exhaustive list of state obligations; limiting full protection and security provisions to physical security and protection only; and including carefully crafted exceptions to protect human rights, health, core labor standards and the environment.[204]

Similar ideas are being put forth in the context of the debates over the mega-regionals. The United States agreed to public health exceptions in the draft for ISDS in the TPP before withdrawing from the project. The

[201] Señor Tza Yap Shum v. La Republica del Perú, ICSID Case No. ARB/07/6, Laudo (Sept. 11, 2007), www.italaw.com/sites/default/files/case-documents/ita0881.pdf.
[202] Trakman, *supra* note 200.
[203] WORLD INVESTMENT REPORT 2012: TOWARDS A NEW GENERATION OF INVESTMENT POLICIES 107 (UNCTAD, ed., 2012).
[204] *Id.* at 135–41.

EU made a number of suggestions for the ISDS section of the proposed TTIP, now also shelved by the United States. For example, the EU sought to restrict the concept of fair and equitable treatment to exclude the "legitimate expectations" standard. The EU also wanted to ensure that the concept of full protection and security was limited to physical protection and security, not the protection of intangibles such as intellectual property. Finally, the EU proposed a courtlike system to replace private arbitration and create greater certainty concerning prevailing norms. To some extent, these proposals are congruent with some of the concerns from emerging countries. The Regional Comprehensive Economic Partnership (RCEP), led by China and involving the ten ASEAN members, plus Australia, India, Japan, South Korea and New Zealand,[205] will include an investment chapter. While negotiations are still ongoing, drafts of the investment chapter that have emerged so far suggest that some of the innovations being pushed by emerging economies are on the agenda and may end up in the final version of the agreement. Proposals have reportedly been put forward to include ISDS, but details are not available and a final decision on this section has not been reached.[206] One observer, noting that China has accepted ISDS in numerous BITs, believes that RCEP will include ISDS of some type.[207] Finally, even if any of these mega-regional agreements fail to come about, bilateral negotiations will likely be infused by the range of concerns and drafting experimentation of the past decade. The successor to NAFTA, the USMCA, pertains to this trend with more restrictive provisions on ISDS and limitations on the type of claims that can be made by investors, for example.

---

[205] *See generally* Australian Government, Department of Foreign Affairs and Trade, Regional Comprehensive Economic Partnership, http://dfat.gov.au/trade/agreements/rcep/Pages/regional-comprehensive-economic-partnership.aspx (describing the RCEP including interest, benefits and relevant news).

[206] A 2015 leaked draft chapter on investment does not mention ISDS. RCEP Draft Investment Text India (based on Draft Investment Text October 2015), www.bilaterals.org/IMG/pdf/rcep-draft-investment-text-india.pdf.

[207] *Id.* Heng Wang, *The RCEP and its Investment Rules: Learning from Past Chinese FTAs*, 3 CHINESE J. GLOBAL GOVERNANCE 2 (2017).

5

Emerging Economies, Developmental Strategies and Trade Standards: the Search for Alternative Space

Introduction

Chapter 3 highlighted the practices of developing countries in regard to international trade law, including playing within the WTO system, but also breaching or instrumentalizing it for their own purposes, as well as outright rejection of expanding the traditional trajectory of trade liberalization. This chapter examines whether and to what extent emerging countries may be able to engage in alternative approaches to trade regulation among themselves and in their relations to developed economies. It shows that liberal orthodoxy is in retrenchment. It documents the reservations that many emerging powers have about the neoliberal approach, and shows the conflict between some trade rules and state-led development strategies ("developmentalism"). It shows that in some areas, emerging powers are resisting liberalization pressures by ignoring certain existing rules, refusing to agree to others, and seeking to create alternative orderings with more flexible standards.[1]

However, it also shows that there is not always consensus within key countries about trade and development policy; there are differences among them on many aspects of liberalization; and there are limits to their capacity to create alternative economic spaces. While resistance from the South and rising protectionism in the North has stalled the liberalization drive, leaving trade law more open to developmentalism for now, the South has not developed the kind of strong ideological

[1] This chapter draws in part from David M. Trubek et al., *Brazil in the Shadow of TPP: Beyond the Grand Debate, Pragmatic Responses,* in MEGAREGULATION CONTESTED: GLOBAL ECONOMIC ORDERING AFTER TPP (Benedict Kingsbury et al., eds.) (forthcoming Oxford University Press).

consensus and strategic coordination that would be needed to fundamentally alter the trade regime. Countries are guided by pragmatism and divergent national interests. In this context, what might have been a historical turning point could turn into a well-rehearsed mercantilist story with slightly different winners and losers compared to the 1990s.

I   Globalization and the Potential for Export-Led Growth

Globalization may be credited for raising millions of people from poverty in emerging economies.[2] Reduction of trade barriers, coupled with new technologies in transport and communication, made it possible for many countries to adopt an export-led strategy and build strong manufacturing bases. The most recent example of this strategy is in China. Through strong government control of the economy and an ability to manipulate World Trade Organization (WTO) rules to its advantage, China became an export powerhouse, absorbing millions of workers into its manufacturing sector and raising incomes for a sizable percentage of the population. The China story, as well as those of the Asian Tigers, has led some to argue for continued and expanded liberalization so the China experience can be replicated by other countries.

Another reading views global income growth and its distribution as largely ascribable to a one-time transformation in the global economy,

---

[2] A 2012 study by Branko Milanovic confirms the commonly held belief that the biggest winners of globalization between the late 1980s and the 2008 crisis are the very rich (top 1 percent, which numerically includes those who come largely from old industrial countries and Japan, but also includes significant representation from Brazil, Russia and South Africa) and the middle class in large middle-income emerging countries (those in the 50th to 60th percentile of the global income distribution, thought to include about "200 million Chinese, 90 million Indians, and about 30 million people each from Indonesia, Brazil and Egypt"), Branko Milanovic, *Global Income Inequality by the Numbers: in History and Now*, 12–13, WORLD BANK DEVELOPMENT RESEARCH GROUP, WORKING PAPER No. 6259 (2012), http://documents.worldbank.org/curated/en/959251468176687085/pdf/wps6259 .pdf. The new evidence brought to light in Milanovic's "elephant curve" is that real incomes have also risen between 40 percent and 70 percent for those in the bottom third of the world's income distribution. He identifies two groups as the main losers: the poorest 5 percent and those in the 75th to 90th percentiles, who have seen no gain in their income or even a slight loss over the past twenty years. Geographically, the main losers are located mostly in Africa, Latin America and post-Communist countries (though the drop in percentile of income is lesser for the latter), as well as those citizens of rich countries whose incomes have stagnated. For instance, "the average Kenyan went down from the 22nd to the 12th percentile globally ... In 1988, an African with the median income of the continent had an income equal to two-thirds of the global median. In 2008, that proportion had declined to less than one-half." *Id.*, at 15.

where technological changes have played a major role, and where one country, China, accounted for a vast portion of the welfare gains. Indeed, there are reasons to doubt whether increased liberalization will lift further millions out of poverty through export-led industrialization. The first is that the conditions in China are hard to replicate: for example, where China had the ability to manage its economy and provide the right kind of incentives needed to exploit the world demand for manufactured goods, other countries may lack such capacity. Second, even well-managed countries may find that they cannot successfully compete with established players in the world market for manufacturing exports. Economist Dani Rodrik argues that the world may not need more capacity to produce manufactured goods: between old industrialized countries and established new entrants like China, all the capacity needed may exist.[3] Even if that is not the case, it may not be possible for new entrants to compete with established players from the North and South. With manufacturing productivity increasing rapidly in both the developed world and among those emerging economies that have already become major exporters, it may be hard for late entrants to produce manufactured goods at prices that are competitive with those produced – or that can be produced – in established emerging economy exporters and industries in the advanced countries. For that reason, they may find it hard to replicate China's success via trade in goods.

II   Developing Country Strategies

Despite concerns of scholars like Rodrik, developing countries continue to favor policies that would allow them to benefit from export-led growth. Their strategies fall into two broad categories: to a large extent, they accept the concept of trade liberalization, but protest continued protectionism by developed countries in key sectors such as agriculture; at the same time, they seek to foster growth and development by implementing industrial policies that often run afoul of liberal orthodoxy. These tensions could not be resolved in the Doha Round. Developed countries have been largely unwilling to dismantle their protectionist barriers even as they pressured other countries to continue to liberalize. Developing countries continue to design industrial policies in breach of

---

[3] Dani Rodrik, remarks in Mexico City (Jun. 2017). *See also,* Dani Rodrik, *Premature Deindustrialization* 1, NAT'L BUREAU OF ECON. RESEARCH, WORKING PAPER NO. 20935 (2015).

WTO disciplines, and point to similar measures taken by rich countries, particularly in the wake of the 2008 crisis.

In this chapter, we explore the tension between developing country policies and the demands of the liberal trading order to see if a robust alternative trade vision has emerged in the Global South. To that end, we employ the Trans-Pacific Partnership Agreement (TPP) and its updated version, the Comprehensive and Progressive Agreement for Trans-Pacific Partnership (CPTPP) as a heuristic device standing for a continuation of the neoliberal policies of the 1990s. The CPTPP incorporates by reference the original TPP signed in 2016 except for a dozen provisions of the latter, which are suspended until the parties decide otherwise. Hence, our analysis refers to the TPP text as still representing the latest version of the neoliberal trade agenda. Some updates to the United States – Mexico – Canada Agreement follow the same patterns as the TPP. It is a useful tool to measure the distance between that vision and the views of emerging powers that have embraced state-led development ("developmental states"). We contrast TPP-type regulation with economic and trade policies in such states, focusing particularly on Brazil, China and India. We chose these countries for several reasons: their economies are large enough, in terms of their domestic markets and their external trade, to matter to their trade partners; India and China are at strategic and transformative junctions in global supply and value chains; all three have a history and current practice of trade and development policies that span the ideological spectrum.

If WTO+ commitments in RTAs and the TPP were the high point of the United States' attempt to impose neoliberal standards on its trading partners, this moment appears to have passed, and the lull in U.S. leadership since 2016 has created a space for alternative trade projects to gain momentum. Rather than a new trade ordering, however, we find that the field is characterized by uncertainty and inconsistent statements and policies.

China is poised to play a pivotal role in these dynamics. At the 2017 Davos meeting, China declared that it wanted to "protect globalization," all the while promoting state-owned enterprises and vigorously defending subsidies as a cornerstone of its industrial policy. With U.S.- and EU-led mega-regionals stalled, and China pushing forward its Regional Comprehensive Economic Partnership (RCEP) and Belt and Road Initiative, will other emerging countries find themselves rule-makers once again in a China-led paradigm? If China is not seeking to be a hegemonic rule-maker, will other emerging countries promote trade rules that are centered more on development policies than on liberal-ization for its own sake? Will private actors seize the initiative and shape the trading order through private standards, or by using regulatory discrepancies to exploit market segmentation opportunities?

China became the world's largest-trading country in 2010, when it surpassed the United States in its value of trade with the rest of the world.[4] While China has a vast surplus with respect to trade in goods, it has a growing deficit in its balance of trade in services.[5] Mainstream economists do not see this evolution as cause for concern with respect to global economic stability, but the political fallouts of China's trade policy have taken increasingly acrimonious form around the world. Leaving aside the increasingly vituperative discourse, the political backlash against China translates into the use of a range of protectionist trade instruments where Chinese exports are – or are perceived as – a threat to local industries. These include trade remedies such as antidumping duties, countervailing duties, and safeguard tariffs as well as regulatory measures, such as security reviews of proposed Chinese investments and policy monitoring by government agencies. Developed and developing countries alike have deployed most of these instruments, and done so ostensibly within the framework of existing trade law. Such responses to shifts in patterns of global trade and industrial output may be considered to be "business as usual," and were clearly envisioned by the architects of contemporary trade law.

At the same time, WTO members have long alleged that China is not, in fact, upholding its accession commitments and not abiding by the organi-zation's trade rules. These concerns have been a staple of industry groups' discourse since China's WTO accession in 2001, and feature in many complaints lodged against China since the United States initiated the first case against it in 2004.[6] The aforementioned trade remedies and other trade policy mechanisms and the WTO dispute settlement system are increasingly viewed as insufficient to rein in trade policies considered unfair or illegal. As a result, since 2018 the United States in particular is

---

[4] Malcolm Scott & Cedric Sam, *Here's How Fast China's Economy Is Catching Up to the U.S.*, published May 12, 2016; updated May 24, 2018, www.bloomberg.com/graphics/2016-us-vs-china-economy/.

[5] Ministry of Commerce, People's Republic of China, China trade in services statistics, Jan. 20, 2018, http://english.mofcom.gov.cn/article/statistic/tradeinservices/201801/20180102706539.shtml (transportation, travel and intellectual property were the largest sectors for import of services in 2017).

[6] China – Value-Added Tax on Integrated Circuits, Request for Consultations, WT/DS309/1, Mar. 24, 2004.

taking extraordinary measures outside of the existing legal framework, allegedly to coerce China back into compliance.[7] Such measures echo the nineteenth century's infamous Opium Wars, which are a major part of Chinese nationalist identity building.[8] In terms of China's relationship to international economic law, two questions therefore arise. First, is China's trade policy legal? Second, if it is not legal, should it be? This chapter will revisit these questions, and their implications for trade law instruments with respect to a number of trade policies undertaken by China and others.

This chapter assesses the extent to which TPP-like trade regulations clash with state developmentalism, with particular respect to industrial policy, state-owned enterprises, competition, intellectual property and the digital economy. A second section explores alternative, South-led initiatives for economic integration in three regions: Asia, Africa and Latin America. A conclusion explores future prospects for heterodoxy in trade regulation.

III CPTPP-Type Provisions in Contrast to State Developmentalism

In this section we deal with certain TPP provisions as proxy for future agreements, and question what would be the real impact of TPP-type policies on emerging economies. Would they be a fundamental challenge to the core of developmental models, or are they sufficiently flexible to accommodate state-led development strategies like those followed by China, Brazil and India? To understand the significance of TPP-type policies, we look at specific provisions of the TPP and divide them into two types: (i) regime-altering and (ii) problem-creating. "Regime-

---

[7] David Lawder & Ben Blanchard, *Trump Administration Adds to China Trade Pressure with Higher Tariff Plan*, REUTERS (Aug. 1, 2018), www.reuters.com/article/us-usa-trade-china/trump-administration-adds-to-china-trade-pressure-with-higher-tariff-plan-idUSKBN1KM63U.

[8] On the Opium Wars, *see generally* STEPHEN R. PLATT, IMPERIAL TWILIGHT: THE OPIUM WAR AND THE END OF CHINA'S LAST GOLDEN AGE (2018). The Opium Wars enabled the British to force open China's economy to international trade. In a macabre irony, while the British supported opium exports to China as a preliminary to gaining an economic foothold in the country in the late eighteenth century, China is now the major exporter of synthetic opioids to the United States, amidst a public health crisis regarding opioid drug addiction and overdoses. U.S.–China Economic and Security Review Commission, *Fentanyl: China's Deadly Export to the United States*, 5–7, Feb. 1, 2017, www.uscc.gov/sites/default/files/Research/USCC%20Staff%20Report_Fentanyl-China%E2%80%99s%20Deadly%20Export%20to%20the%20United%20States020117.pdf.

altering" provisions are those that might require abandonment of one or
more core feature of a nation's developmental strategy. Provisions that
would present serious political problems, but might not affect the core
developmental model, we consider "problem-creating."

A   Regime-Altering Provisions

To understand the nature and scope of potentially regime-altering
provisions, we need to determine what is included in the "core" of the
developmental state. Both historically and today, industrial policy plays
a central role. For several examples, direct transfer subsidies and tax
breaks to particular industrial sectors or particular constituencies (e.g.,
women- or minority-owned businesses), state aid to exports in the form
of trade financing, exemptions from taxes on imports, export-processing
zones with fiscal and regulatory incentives, infrastructure development,
strategic use of government procurement, local content requirements,
and technical training are all typical instruments of states' efforts to shift
from producing raw commodities to manufacturing industrial goods
with higher value added. While a number of these features are clearly
prohibited by WTO disciplines and their counterparts in RTAs, some
are conditionally allowed. Most notably, subsidies contingent on export
performance and those conditioned on the use of local content are
prohibited. Many subsidies typically used to promote a particular sector
are tolerated, but may be subject to countermeasures by other states. By
contrast, trade disciplines on government procurement are less intrusive,
inasmuch as states can exempt themselves from stringent commitments.
State-owned enterprises are another feature of the developmental state
that is increasingly being constrained by trade disciplines. Competition
law is also a core issue, since emerging sectors are often promoted
through a single corporate entity, potentially with partial state ownership. Even when the state does not encourage monopolies, many developing countries do not have a large enough local market to make it
commercially viable for several competing businesses to thrive, particularly in industries requiring significant start-up capital and infrastructure. This section analyzes the extent to which TPP-like rules are
incompatible with such core features of the developmental state.

1   Industrial Policy Restrictions

Policies in many emerging economies that support the development of
domestic industry and limit foreign firms are a significant area where

trade policy could have regime-altering effects. Advocates of TPP-like disciplines point out that restrictions on industrial policies help developing countries steer away from costly policies that all too often fail to deliver long-term economic net benefits. The markets, as the story goes, are better at determining a country's comparative advantages than the state, particularly in the context of weak governance where policy might be dictated more by cronyism, rent-seeking and populism than by economic rationality. Responses to such critiques are equally well rehearsed: the *homo economicus* is not rational; the assumption of perfect competition underpinning trade liberalism is dispelled in practice; there is no such thing as a perfect market where arbitrage is instantaneous, cost free, and based on perfect information; comparative advantage theory falls short when considered in a dynamic context; and path dependency in practice tends to lock countries in established trade patterns even if alternative paths could be viable.

Undeniably, industrial policy programs in Asia and Latin America in the 1960s and 1970s had mixed results, and were implemented concurrently with heavy trade restrictions on imports through the use of tariffs, quotas and currency restrictions. In most cases, such programs sought to transform agrarian, rural countries into industrial urban societies. Industrial policy in the twenty-first century operates in a different social, economic and regulatory environment. Policymakers now assume a baseline of trade openness, and are demonstrating a sophisticated understanding of the need to integrate trade and investment policies. Sidestepping the old dichotomy between inward and outward development strategies, emerging countries craft industrial policy programs mindful of the entire supply and consumption chain, from optimizing sourcing of raw materials to leveraging domestic resources and know-how, exploring how to carve out a competitive niche in particular sectors, seeking to connect innovation and industrial development, attracting domestic and foreign capital, and considering where the consumer base might be located.

Meanwhile, international trade and investment regulation has grown equally complex and multifaceted, raising hurdles for policymakers. A single government measure such as a loan guarantee or subsidized interest rate might run afoul of subsidies disciplines in trade agreements, but its withdrawal might create a claim against the state under investment treaties, as foreign investors might claim that they had expectations regarding economic concessions and that the value of their investment was based on the government measure.[9]

What constitutes a fair or legitimate trade restriction in this context simply cannot be determined by economics alone, and it may not even be possible to assess whether a supposed market distortion (such as a local content requirement) has net positive or negative economic impacts, all factors taken into account. In this context, it is critical to recognize that international trade rules are, and must be, dictated by policy and governance preference, rather than by an attempt to conform to a specific economic model. Economics certainly provides some guidance as to which government interventions tend to be least efficient overall, such as export subsidies. However, the decision whether to allow the ever more creative government interventions of new industrial policies that create benefits for some actors and costs for other actors is a political one, with redistribution and value creation preferences at its core. Using illustrations from Brazil, China and India, this section assesses potential clashes between TPP-like standards and domestic industrial policy programs.

a   Brazil   The Brazilian state has played a major role in the economy throughout the current democratic period. In a major study entitled "The Unchanging Core of Brazilian State Capitalism, 1985–2015," Matthew Taylor demonstrates the embeddedness and continuity of the state-led model dating back as far the 1930s, when Brazil started on its developmentalist path.[10] Many think this model has served Brazil relatively

---

[9]   While liberalization rules are ostensibly designed to "level the playing field," the question of who is served by a particular rule is also increasingly murky. For instance, investors of country A might wish to avail themselves of the benefits of country B's industrial policy, while competing manufacturers of country A seek countervailing duties against exports from country B (including those manufactured in country B by investors of country A). If the product in question relates to renewable energy, there may also be broader spillover effects on environmental public goods.

[10]   Taylor lists several elements that make up the core policies of such state-led growth: i) *trade policy* that favors a closed economy and focuses on growth of the domestic market; ii) *tax and fiscal policy* that support a very large state; iii) *state ownership* of companies including use of minority shares; iv) *industrial policies* including tax breaks and low-cost loans from the state development bank for selected sectors; v) use of *regulation* to channel private investment; vi) *monetary and credit policy* that favors state banks and influences investment patterns; and vii) *redistributive labor and social policy*. See Mathew M. Taylor, *The Unchanging Core of Brazilian State Capitalism, 1985–2015*, SCHOOL OF INTERNATIONAL SERVICE PAPER No. 2015-8, https://ssrn.com/abstract=2674332.

well.[11] Core policies have been developed to mobilize capital, allocate it to growth sectors, nurture local industry, attract and channel foreign investment, and provide incentives for priorities like infrastructure, innovation and exports.[12] Consequently, international commitments that significantly restrain such state actions would certainly be considered as "regime-altering."

We identify three areas in which current Brazilian policy seems to be at odds with TPP-type standards so that alignment would require major changes. These are industrial policy, the role of state-owned enterprises, and the regulation of foreign direct investment.[13]

At the heart of Brazil's developmental model is industrial policy. Measures that favor priority industries include tariff protection, export subsidies, tax incentives, and domestic content requirements. For example, generally speaking, bound tariffs are still high and the government uses that space to favor its policies. Domestic auto producers have received tax breaks if the cars they produce use local content. Investors in the exploration of the Pre-Sal oil fields – large, recently discovered oil reserves – have been required to use local firms and products. Export finance has been conditioned on high levels of local content in exports.

For Brazil to align with TPP-type policies, it might have to lower or eliminate many of its tariffs and get rid of local content requirements for investment, production, and export finance. Such changes would go to the heart of the developmentalist project. Some of these policies are already under attack in the WTO. Take Brazil's Inovar-Auto Program.[14] Inovar-Auto is a global value chain-oriented industrial

---

[11] Brazil's state capitalist model has not been without flaws. Low domestic savings made growth dependent on foreign capital whose availability ebbs and flows. Sometimes the state lacked needed management capacity. There has been massive corruption. Even so, this model served Brazil well for a long time, attracting foreign investment and ushering in several periods of rapid growth. While the nature, the tools and the extent of state involvement has varied over time, the state has maintained an important role through different economic cycles and different administrations. See generally LAW AND THE NEW DEVELOPMENTAL STATE: THE BRAZILIAN EXPERIENCE IN LATIN AMERICAN CONTEXT (David M. Trubek, Helena A. Garcia, Diogo Coutinho & Alvaro Santos, eds., 2013).

[12] Taylor, supra note 10.

[13] As this book goes to press, Brazilian economic policy seems to be at an inflection point. A new administration, sworn in on Jan. 1, 2019, promises to radically alter Brazil's developmental strategy and move away from developmentalism. As no measures have yet been announced, our analysis is based on Brazilian policy as of 2018.

[14] See Act No. 12.715/2012 (2012) (regulating the Inovar-Auto Program).

policy[15] created in 2012 under the umbrella of the *Plano Brasil Maior* (Greater Brazil Plan). It lowers the Industrial Product Tax for firms that manufacture in Brazil and invest in local R&D: the reduced tax depends on the amount of local content in the cars produced, and energy efficiency targets. From an industrial policy perspective, Inovar-Auto has been praised as a successful tool to encourage foreign direct investment in Brazil's large and growing automotive market.[16]

From a trade law perspective, however, it raises several concerns and has already been attacked by the WTO. The European Union and Japan brought two cases against Inovar-Auto for alleged breaches of several WTO obligations.[17] The panel agreed with the complainants and the Appellate Body upheld these findings. First, by giving tax advantages to domestic products and imported products that meet certain local content requirements, Brazil violated GATT's national treatment obligations. Second, the local content requirement of the Brazilian measure is inconsistent with Brazil's commitments under the TRIMS agreement. Third, the Inovar-Auto Program breached most-favored nation obligations because it accorded more favorable treatment to the like products imported from Mexico and Mercosur members than to the products from the European Union and Japan. However, the Appellate Body reversed the panel findings that Brazil's tax advantages for exporting companies constituted prohibited export subsidies, in violation of the SCM Agreement. The AB partially upheld and partially reversed the panel's findings on import substitution subsidies.[18]

b China   Like Brazil, China has a vast array of provisions designed to build up the capacity of domestic industry. They include export restrictions and subsidies, technology transfer requirements, local content requirements, government procurement policies, and special technical standards that favor domestic firms. While not all of these provisions may be seen as being at the core of China's development strategy, the

---

[15] Etienne Michaud, *Driving Up Local Content of Brazilian Cars: The Inovar-Auto Program and Supply Chain Strategy*, BRAZILWORKS BRIEFING PAPER, 2015.

[16] *Id.*, at 4.

[17] *See* Panel Reports, *Brazil – Certain Measures concerning Taxation and Charges*, WT/DS472/R, WT/DS497/R (circulated Aug. 30, 2017), AB Reports, *Brazil – Certain Measures concerning Taxation and Charges*, WT/DS472/AB/R, WT/DS497/AB/R (circulated Dec. 13, 2018).

[18] The new administration is likely to move away from many of these policies but is sure to encounter resistance as developmentalism is deeply embedded in Brazilian thought and institutions.

overall agenda favoring the development of local industry over foreign interests, and the mobilization of a vast array of measures to that end, is central to the regime's approach to growth. Imposition of trade policies that would force abandonment of a major part of this array would be regime altering.

The 2016 USTR Report to Congress on China's WTO Compliance concluded:

> China continued to pursue a wide array of industrial policies in 2016 that seek to limit market access for imported goods, foreign manufacturers and foreign service suppliers, while offering substantial government guidance, resources and regulatory support to Chinese industries. The principal beneficiaries of these constantly evolving policies are state-owned enterprises, as well as other favored domestic companies attempting to move up the economic value chain.[19]

The U.S. trade representative has identified a series of industrial policies that raise issues under the WTO; we can assume that they would create similar if not more problems under a regime like TPP. They include:

- A program that conditions receipt of a subsidy on an enterprise's use of at least 60 percent Chinese-made components when manufacturing intelligent manufacturing equipment
- Special product standards for ICT products that must be used by China's financial sector, which favor local firms and restrict foreign ICT products
- Tying preference in government procurement and regulatory review of pharmaceuticals to transfer of technology to China
- Export restraints of key commodities that operate to favor local producers in value chains[20]
- Subsidies for domestic industries in general

---

[19] UNITED STATES TRADE REPRESENTATIVE, 2016 REPORT TO CONGRESS ON CHINA'S WTO COMPLIANCE (2016) at 11.

[20] UNITED STATES TRADE REPRESENTATIVE, 2016 REPORT TO CONGRESS ON CHINA'S WTO COMPLIANCE (2016) at 57. "Typically, the objective of China's border tax adjustments is to make larger quantities of primary and intermediate products in a particular sector available domestically at lower prices than the rest of the world, giving China's downstream producers of finished products using these inputs a competitive advantage over foreign downstream producers. To accomplish this objective, China discourages the export of the relevant primary and intermediate products by reducing or eliminating VAT rebates and perhaps also imposing export duties on them, resulting in increased domestic supply and lower domestic prices. China's downstream producers, in turn, benefit not only from these lower input prices but also from full VAT rebates when they export their finished products."

- Restrictions on investment requiring technology transfer, location of research facilities, export and local content requirements
- Aggressive use of trade remedies

Some of the most recent concern over industrial policy stems from China's "indigenous innovation policy."[21] This program is designed to make China a world leader in several key areas with high knowledge content. The most recent manifestation of the program, and one in which Chinese industrial policy and TPP-like standards may clash, is the "Made in China 2025" action plan, which outlines a ten-year strategy to build intelligent manufacturing capabilities, enhance innovation and upgrade ten key sectors. These sectors, many of which were previously designated as heavyweight, strategic, or strategic emerging industries, are:

(1) Energy-saving and new energy vehicles
(2) Next-generation information technology
(3) Biotechnology
(4) New materials
(5) Aerospace
(6) Ocean engineering and high-tech ships
(7) Railway
(8) Robotics
(9) Power equipment
(10) Agricultural machinery

The plan to promote indigenous production in critical areas will employ a wide variety of industrial policy tools that are likely to conflict with existing WTO standards in areas like local content rules and subsidies, and, a fortiori, will clash with CPTPP-like WTO+ rules. The "Made in China 2025" plan and the earlier Medium- and Long-Term Plan on the Development of Science & Technology promulgated in 2006 illustrate these policies,[22] including some of the following policy tools:

- Large, low-interest loans from state-owned investment funds and development banks

---

[21] *See e.g.*, UNITED STATES CHAMBER OF COMMERCE, CHINA'S DRIVE FOR INDIGENOUS INNOVATION: A WEB OF INDUSTRIAL POLICIES (2010).

[22] Official information on Made in China 2025, http://english.gov.cn/2016special/madein china2025/. For a brief overview of this plan and China's 2006 Medium- and Long-Term Plan on the Development of Science & Technology, *see e.g.*, Scott Kennedy, *Made in China 2025*, CENTER FOR STRATEGIC & INTERNATIONAL STUDIES, Jun. 1, 2015, www .csis.org/analysis/made-china-2025.

- Extensive research subsidies
- Laws requiring that government have access to all data stored in China
- Restrictions on access to high-tech markets to local firms on the grounds that ICT products must be "secure and controllable"
- Tying government preferences to the localization of technology in China
- Regulatory review and approval preferences to innovative drug manufacturers that shift their production to China
- Creation of national product standards in strategic industries that favor local firms
- Programs to acquire high-tech companies overseas and repatriate their technology including investments by SOEs and other government-related entities and subsidies for private firms[23]

While many of these practices could be challenged under WTO rules, the TPP goes even further, and would impose even greater limits on policies of this type. Commenting on Made in China 2025, U.S. trade law expert Amelia Porges noted: "Made in China involves not just equipment localization but also data localization, investment screening, regulation that forces onshore manufacturing of technology by a foreign-Chinese JV, and forced technology transfer to Chinese JV partners. The rules in TPP were designed to rule out this sort of behavior."[24]

While the United States has been critical of "Made in China 2025" for some time, opposition reached a crescendo in 2018 when the Trump administration launched an all-out trade war with China. One goal of this offensive was to force China to cut back or halt the Made in China 2025 initiative. In a clear break with the de facto truce, the United States has essentially demanded that China dismantle its system of state capitalism and remove most barriers to, and conditions on, access to the Chinese market. At the same time, it has sought to isolate China by seeking bilateral FTAs including clauses that would stop the partner country from entering an FTA with China (as it did in the 2018 USMCA revising NAFTA). Escalating this conflict from an economic dispute to a global power struggle, the Trump administration has labeled China along with Russia as "strategic competitors," noting that they " ... challenge American power, influence and interests, attempting to erode American security and prosperity. They are determined to make

---

[23] UNITED STATES CHAMBER OF COMMERCE, MADE IN CHINA 2025: GLOBAL AMBITIONS BUILT ON LOCAL PROTECTIONS 17–37, 42–64 (2017).
[24] Interview with Amelia Porges, Attorney, New York, NY (May 15, 2017).

economies less free and less fair, to grow their militaries, and to control information and data to repress their societies and expand their influence."[25]

c   India

India too makes extensive use of industrial policy tools. Its Five-Year Plans typically identify particular sectors and, at times, geographic targets for growth, industrialization, technology transfer, etc. The compatibility of such programs with WTO commitments has not gone unchallenged. The Jawaharlal Nehru National Solar Mission (JNN Solar Mission) launched in 2010 and implemented by the Ministry of New and Renewable Energy is a prime example. It aims to increase access to energy without increasing dependency on fossil fuel imports, and provide access to a healthier and more sustainable source of energy than the kerosene, coal and biomass used by India's rural and urban poor. With its assortment of local content requirements, subsidies and finance facilities, it bears the hallmarks of traditional "national champions" industrial policy. The program also has several import substitution objectives. At present, India relies significantly on imports of solar photovoltaic power equipment. Developing a globally competitive domestic industry for the solar power equipment supply chain would help reduce imports in those sectors (mostly from China). Moreover, if the target of bringing the price of solar power to parity with traditional energy sources is achieved,[26] the program also has the potential to reduce imports of fossil fuels.

However, unlike industrial support programs of decades past, the JNN Solar Mission aims to build significant research and development capacity in a high-tech sector with high value-added goods production chains. It seeks to boost fundamental research as well as applied research through collaborations between academic institutions worldwide. While it plans to use government funding and funding available under the United Nations Framework Convention on Climate Change, it also envisions start-up incubators with a venture capital approach to project selection. In the spirit of injecting some market mechanisms in a state-sponsored industrial program, the mission statement further provides that "[t]he

---

[25] National Security Strategy of the United States 2 (2017), www.whitehouse.gov/wp-con tent/uploads/2017/12/NSS-Final-12-18-2017-0905.pdf.

[26] Minister of New and Renewable Energy, Jawaharlal Nehru National Solar Mission – Towards Building SOLAR INDIA 1 (2012), https://mnre.gov.in/file-manager/UserFiles/ mission_document_JNNSM.pdf.

Mission will be technology neutral, allowing technological innovation and market conditions to determine technology winners."[27] Additionally, rather than combining the domestic program with protectionist trade positions on competing imports, the mission statement calls for "custom duties and excise duties concessions/exemptions be made available on specific capital equipment, critical materials, components and project imports"[28] in order to accelerate the development of India's downstream manufacturing capacity in the solar sector.

Like Brazil's Inovar program, the JNN Solar Mission was challenged at the WTO, under the GATT and TRIMs agreement. Specifically, the United States complained that the program included domestic content requirements in breach of GATT article III:4 and TRIMs article 2.1.[29] India presented several defenses, which failed at the panel stage as well as on appeal.[30] Of particular interest is India's contention that the measures were covered by GATT article XX(d) because they were taken pursuant to India's international law obligations under the United Nations Framework Convention on Climate Change, among other international instruments. The panel and the Appellate Body found insufficient normativity in these texts, and that they did not sufficiently translate into domestic legal requirements for India. While the United States initially requested consultations regarding the compatibility of the JNN Solar Mission with the SCM agreement, no further action was pursued on that count. India notified the Dispute Settlement Body that it "had ceased to impose any measures found inconsistent" with the AB report,[31] a point that the United States disputed in its request for authorization to retaliate.[32]

The Make in India program, launched in 2014,[33] is a broad-ranging initiative that aims on the one hand at reducing administrative and governmental impediments to doing business, and on the other hand at attracting foreign investors and companies to site production in India for

---

[27] *Id.* at 6.

[28] *Id.* at 9.

[29] Panel Report, *India – Solar Cells*, WT/DS456/R. The following third parties also joined the case: Brazil, Canada, China, the European Union, Japan, South Korea, Malaysia, Norway, the Russian Federation, Turkey, Ecuador, Saudi Arabia and Chinese Taipei.

[30] AB Report, *India – Solar Cells*, WT/DS456/AB/R.

[31] Status report regarding implementation of the DSB recommendations and rulings by India, *India – Solar Cells*, WT/DS456/17 (Dec. 14, 2017).

[32] Recourse to article 22.2 of the DSU by the United States, *India – Solar Cells*, WT/DS456/18.

[33] Make in India, www.makeinindia.com/about.

twenty-five target sectors.[34] Tailored incentives within each sector include waiving of excise fees, export support, other tax breaks at the central and state levels, waiving of import duties on raw and intermediate goods used in that sector, export-processing zone types of fiscal and regulatory frameworks, and support for setting up projects in particular geographic areas. In line with Prime Minister Modi's call for "Minimum Government, Maximum Governance," the Make in India initiative is structured to provide a legible, accessible, one-stop-shop resource for potential investors. By contrast, the ongoing complexity and uncertainties of trading with India were underscored in the WTO's most recent Trade Policy Review Report noting that "India continues to use trade policy as a means to regulate domestic supply and to address short-term objectives such as containing inflation and fluctuations in commodity prices. Thus export taxes, minimum export price, as well as adjustments to import duties, are used on an ad hoc basis through a notification by the [Directorate General of Foreign Trade]."[35] It concludes in agreement with a report drafted by India's Economic Advisory Council: "Such frequent changes to policy are disruptive and reduce predictability in India's trade policy."[36]

The viability of Make in India and other industrial promotion initiatives under the WTO or more rigorous trade agreements will largely depend on disciplines regarding local content requirement and subsidies. For instance, the TPP prohibits waivers of customs duties conditioned on a "performance requirement," including the use of domestic goods over imported goods.[37] With respect to agricultural products, the

---

[34] Automobiles (and components), aviation, biotechnology, chemicals, construction, defense, electrical machinery, electronics, food processing, IT and BPM, leather, media and entertainment, mining, oil and gas, pharmaceuticals, ports and shipping, railways, renewable energy, roads and highways, space, textiles and garments, thermal power, tourism and hospitality, and wellness.

[35] Report by the Secretariat, India – Trade Policy Review, at ¶ 2.14, WT/TPR/S/313 (Apr. 28, 2015).

[36] *Id.* at ¶ 2.15 (footnote omitted). A report prepared on sugar policy, headed by the Chairman of the Economic Advisory Council to the Prime Minister on Oct. 5, 2012, stated that "the export–import policy of the Government does not allow firms to have a long-term relation internationally and impedes the growth of the sector. The policies are unanticipated and create uncertainty for the firms. Also the short term cyclicality, which is largely a consequence of Government intervention, adversely affects the long-term strategic development of the sector."

[37] TPP art. 2.1 (defining performance requirement), art. 2.5.

TPP provides that "[n]o Party shall adopt or maintain any export subsidy on any agricultural good destined for the territory of another Party."[38]

Additionally, the status of export restrictions would likely be a critical issue for India. Dubbed by some a "regulatory deficiency" or "unintended policy space," export restrictions have soared in the wake of the food crisis of 2007–08, but also have been used on nonagricultural raw materials.[39] With the issue now squarely in the limelight, it is likely that future trade pacts will address export restrictions more explicitly than the WTO agreements. Indeed, the TPP provides that "no Party shall adopt or maintain any prohibition or restriction on ... the exportation or sale for export of any good destined for the territory of another Party, except in accordance with Article XI of GATT 1994 and its interpretative notes," which are thereby incorporated by reference. Also incorporated by reference are GATT provisions on price undertakings (whereby countries resolve dumping allegations by agreeing that the "dumped" product will not be exported at less than an agreed-upon price) and voluntary export restrictions, as well as other relevant provisions of the Antidumping Agreement and the SCM Agreement pertaining to export price restrictions. Moreover, article 2.15 of the TPP generally prohibits parties from adopting or maintaining "any duty, tax or other charge on the export of any good to the territory of another Party, unless such duty, tax or charge is adopted or maintained on that good when destined for domestic consumption." However, the TPP reaffirms the WTO framework permitting export restrictions for food security purposes.[40]

d Conclusion: Industrial Policy and Trade Agreements Industrial policy clearly remains an important feature of various development models; trade law instruments such as the TPP fail to accommodate such domestic policy choices. Recent studies have pointed to the phenomenon of "premature deindustrialization" in developing countries,[41]

---

[38] TPP art. 2.21(2).

[39] Baris Karapinar, *Export Restrictions and the WTO Law: "Regulatory Deficiency" or "Unintended Policy Space,"* WORLD TRADE INSTITUTE WORKING PAPERS May 21, 2010, www.wti.org/research/publications/80/export-restrictions-and-the-wto-law-regulatory-deficiency-or-unintended-policy-space/; Baris Karapinar, *Export Restrictions and the WTO Law: How to Reform the 'Regulatory Deficiency,'* 45 J. WORLD TRADE 1139 (2011).

[40] TPP art. 2.24.

[41] Deindustrialization describes the shift from a GDP reliant mostly on industrial output to one that is reliant mostly on service sector output. In the past, this transition has taken

which may lead some to question whether the quest for industrial policy space is a rearguard action that is unlikely to yield the socioeconomic gains its promoters hope for. While these views warrant careful consideration, industrial policy-type programs are far from passé. First, as we have shown, a number of emerging countries still aspire to industrialize, at least in certain sectors where they have a competitive advantage, where they meet a domestic demand that may not be otherwise fulfilled, or where they have a strategic interest. Second, programs similar to industrial policy are increasingly used in the service sector. To the extent that trade disciplines for services mirror those for trade in goods, the analysis largely applies mutatis mutandis. And in areas where no rules about trade in services now exist, policymakers in emerging countries that focus on trade in services would do well to study the impact of subsidies regulation on industrial policy programs and take heed of the risks they create.

2   SOEs

Rules governing SOEs in the TPP aim at ensuring a level playing field for SOEs and private firms operating in the same business, both domestically and abroad. The level of detail of the rules, along with the many exceptions and a number of broader terms open to interpretation, is unprecedented in international trade law. As a result, open questions abound regarding the scope and impact of this type of provision.

The TPP chapter on SOEs includes various procedural obligations and provides two broad types of disciplines: nondiscrimination treatment of suppliers and clients of SOEs (article 17.4), and a duty for the state parties to ensure that SOEs do not cause "adverse effects" or "injury" to the interests of another party through any assistance the government might provide to their SOEs on a noncommercial basis (articles 17.6–17.8). The latter is reminiscent of the WTO's SCM agreement. SOEs typically benefit from subsidies and other state aids. Under the TPP, these would be allowed so long as they do not create an adverse effect or injury on

---

place after a country reaches a certain income level. However, Dani Rodrik and others have observed that "premature deindustrialization" increasingly affects low- and middle-income developing countries as their manufacturing sector shrinks or is expected to shrink before the country has reached an income level typical of fully industrialized economies. *See generally* Sukti Dasgupta & Ajit Singh, *Manufacturing, Services and Premature Deindustrialization in Developing Countries: A Kaldorian Analysis*, UNU-WIDER, UNU-WIDER, UNITED NATIONS UNIVERSITY RESEARCH PAPER No. 2006/49 (2006); Dani Rodrik, *Premature Deindustrialization*, NBER WORKING PAPER No. 20935 (2015).

other parties. The issue, then, is whether SOEs can serve state developmentalism purposes given those restrictions. The TPP provides a number of exceptions, but a vast degree of uncertainty exists as to their scope and possible interpretation. For instance, it is unclear how the "public purpose" standard will be construed. It may well be that the TPP exceptions, broad as they seem, may not be sufficient for SOEs to play their developmental role. If that is the case, then it is an open question whether the state wishing to implement policies that run afoul of TPP restrictions on SOEs would be able to compensate other state parties for any adverse effect or injury caused by the nonconforming measure. Here again, the underlying ethos reflects the general compromise struck in the WTO's SCM agreement, which allows certain subsidies to be challenged when they cause an injury to another party, possibly resulting in compensation for such injury.

Unlike WTO injury-based trade remedies, however, the TPP rules on SOEs also provide remedies for foreign investors whose investments in the state of the SOE are affected. Here again, we draw on examples from China, Brazil and India to illustrate clashes between development-oriented SOEs and TPP-like trade liberalization standards.

a   **Brazil**   Given the major role that various types of SOEs play in the Brazilian economy, Brazil could face many challenges were it to try to follow the standards set by TPP-type regulation. We use the example of BNDES, the national development bank, to illustrate the issues.

TPP section 17.6 bans noncommercial assistance by government with respect to the production of goods and services if that affects the interests of another party. Noncommercial assistance (NCA) includes direct transfer of funds, below-market-rate loans, and investments that "depart from usual investment practice." Such a standard could affect the operation of BNDES. Indeed, this limitation of SOEs goes to the heart of the rationale for a development bank, which is to make up for market failure by supplying finance on terms not available in the market.

One of the largest development banks in the world, BNDES plays a crucial role in the Brazilian economy. As it competes with the private banking sector, including foreign banks operating in Brazil, its operations could fall afoul of the section to the extent that it receives noncommercial assistance. There are two sources of funding for the bank that seem to meet the test for NCA: below-market loans from the *Fundo de*

Amparo ao Trabalhador, and transfers from the treasury either directly or as below-market loans.[42]

At the same time, a competitor of BNDES might challenge its operations under standards based on those found in the SOEs chapter of TPP. Competitors of other SOEs or private firms that receive loans or investments from BNDES might complain because BNDES loans are below prevailing market rates, and its investment practices may not be deemed "usual." Similar concerns could arise from the operation of major SOEs like Petrobras, which receives subsidies and operates in many markets where it has control over prices and other terms.

b   China   The challenges for China are probably greater than for Brazil. China's state-owned sector is much larger and more central to its development strategy than is Brazil's, and its industrial policies are ubiquitous. In 2014, all SOEs accounted for 17 percent of urban employment, 22 percent of total industrial profits (with industrial production accounting for 42.7 percent of gross domestic product [GDP] in 2014), and 38 percent of China's industrial assets.[43] The U.S.–China Economic and Security Review Commission commented in 2016:

> Beijing continues to use SOEs as a tool to pursue social, industrial, and foreign policy objectives, offering direct and indirect subsidies and other incentives to influence business decisions and achieve state goals.[44]

Standards like TPP chapter 17, which curtail the role of SOEs, would have a major impact on China's development model. While Brazilian SOEs remain important in key areas like energy, Chinese SOEs are pervasive and are at the center of China's current development strategy. Indeed, as Mark Wu points out, given the complex relations between state, party and private sector, it is hard to say where to draw the line between state and market in China. For that reason, China could not comply with standards like TPP chapter 17 without abandoning major

---

[42] For an appraisal of BNDES's role and impact in Brazil, *see* SETH COLBY, SEARCHING FOR INSTITUTIONAL SOLUTIONS TO INDUSTRIAL POLICY CHALLENGES: A CASE STUDY OF THE BRAZILIAN DEVELOPMENT BANK (2013). Although the current government has taken steps to bring BNDES rates closer to market levels, they still deviate substantially (*see* Law No. 13483/2017 (Braz.)).

[43] U.S.–CHINA ECONOMIC AND SECURITY REVIEW COMMISSION, 2016 REPORT TO CONGRESS OF THE U.S–CHINA ECONOMIC AND SECURITY REVIEW COMMISSION, at p. 92.

[44] *Id.*

features of its current development strategy.[45] This should come as no surprise as many believe that TPP chapter 17 was drafted with just that end in mind.[46] One commentator observed that:

> Beijing may still be resistant to Chapter 17, as it is believed to be part of a deliberate strategy by the United States to create an international regulatory regime for SOEs specifically targeting China's use of such enterprises as tools of industrial policy and economic statecraft.[47]

The issue of TPP-like standards and SOEs has entered into the political debate in China. Scholars favoring further moves toward a market economy point to such standards, and note that adherence to them would further the reforms they desire.[48] But recent statements by President Xi Jinping and other leaders suggest that the SOEs remain at the center of government strategy.[49]

The importance of SOEs for China's development strategy will be enhanced by the development of the Belt and Road Initiative (BRI) to increase transport and communication links from China through South Asia, Africa and the Middle East to Europe. Billed as a revival of the old Silk Road, BRI is a massive project of regional infrastructure development. Given the scale of the planned infrastructure projects, Chinese SOEs are sure to play a major role in implementing BRI, thus strengthening their central role in China's political economy and creating further sources of resistance to trade standards that would limit their capacities.[50]

c **India** In India, successive and ongoing privatizations are cementing the move away from SOEs (called Central Public Sector Enterprises) as a share of the GDP. In 2012–13, SOEs contributed a gross value addition of 6 percent and a net value addition of 32 percent (profits before tax) to

---

[45] *See* Qingjiang Kong, *Emerging Rules in International Investment Instruments and China's Reform of State-Owned Enterprises*, 3 CHINESE J. GLOB. GOVERNANCE 57 (2017).

[46] Marc Wu, *The China Inc. Challenge to Global Trade Governance*, 57 HARV. INT'L L.J. 261 (2016); Jing Tao, *China and TPP: A Tale of Two Economic Orderings?*, in MEGAREGULATION CONTESTED: GLOBAL ECONOMIC ORDERING AFTER TPP (Benedict Kingsbury et al., eds., forthcoming Oxford University Press).

[47] Victor Ferguson, *Why China Won't Save the TPP*, EAST ASIA FORUM (Feb. 11, 2017), www.eastasiaforum.org/2017/02/11/why-china-wont-save-the-tpp/.

[48] Kong, *supra* note 45 at 61.

[49] Tao, *supra* note 46.

[50] *Id.*

the country's GDP.[51] As of 2015, 235 SOEs were in operation and showed a net profit of about USD 17,167 million in 2014–15 (1,03,003 Crore INR, with an exchange rate of 60 INR to 1 USD).[52] SOEs are used by India to provide jobs for socially and economically disadvantaged groups, with reserved quotas ranging from 50 to 77 percent of employees.[53] Over the past decade, the total number of SOE employees has slowly decreased, but their salaries have grown significantly, outpacing compensation for counterparts in the private sector. There were 1.2 million employees in SOEs in 2016[54] compared to a total labor market (employed and unemployed) of over 511 million.[55]

Since the Guidelines on Corporate Governance for CPSEs[56] became mandatory for all SOEs in 2010, India has been professionalizing the boards of SOEs and getting rid of loss-making SOEs (by winding up operations or selling the company). The number of SOEs is growing slightly, but the newer SOEs differ from their earlier counterparts in that they involve significant private capital, particularly foreign investment. All Indian SOEs are open to private investment, including sensitive sectors such as defense equipment, railways and aerospace.[57]

Inasmuch as the TPP chapter on SOEs applies only to entities where the state has a majority ownership stake or control, or appoints a majority of the board members, and the main disciplines do not apply to SOEs with a revenue of less than a defined threshold, the impact of such disciplines on different economies will vary greatly.[58] As an example, given the anticipated starting threshold is 200 million Special Drawing Rights (SDRs), only the top 66 Indian SOEs would be covered by the TPP chapter, assuming all other conditions were also met, out of 227 reported

[51] Ram Kumar Mishra, *Role of State-Owned Enterprises in India's Economic Development*, OECD Workshop on State-Owned Enterprises in the Development Process 24, Apr. 4, 2014, www.oecd.org/daf/ca/Workshop_SOEsDevelopmentProcess_India.pdf.
[52] Government of India, Ministry of Heavy Industries & Public Enterprises, Department of Public Enterprises, Annual Report 131 (2016).
[53] OECD, Workshop on State-Owned Enterprises in the Development Process, 27 (2014).
[54] Government of India, Ministry of Heavy Industries & Public Enterprises, Department of Public Enterprises, Public Enterprises Survey 2015–16, Volume I, Statement 14 Ranking of CPSEs in Terms of Employment in 2015–16 (2016).
[55] WORLD BANK, WORLD DEVELOPMENT STATISTICS INDIA (2016).
[56] Government of India, Ministry of Heavy Industries and Public Enterprises – Department of Public Enterprises, Office Memorandum No. 18(8)/2005-GM (2010).
[57] Not everyone believes Modi is really committed to SOE reform. *Narendra Modi Is a Fine Administrator, but Not Much of a Reformer*, THE ECONOMIST, Jun. 24, 2017.
[58] Annex 17A and Article 17.13.5. 200 million SDR.

SOEs for 2015–16.[59] In practice, some of those sixty-six SOEs might be excluded for other reasons. This suggests that, under a TPP-like standard, the state could still use SOEs to jump-start an industry, but would have to graduate it to a commercial venture when it reaches the 200 million SDR revenue mark, or at least reduce the state's share of ownership or control to less than 50 percent.

d **Conclusion: SOEs and Future Trade Agreements** Enhanced disciplines on SOEs will be difficult to undertake for a number of emerging countries, albeit to different degrees.[60] While a TPP-like framework will probably be impossible for China to implement given its current practices and policies, it would likely require, at least on paper, feasible adjustments in India that would be mostly aligned with the policy to transform SOEs into mixed public–private partnerships aiming to be competitive in relatively short time frames. The TPP also envisions exceptions and grandfathering of nonconforming measures both in the main provisions and in party-specific annexes, giving states significant flexibility to exclude existing SOEs or future activities in particular sectors.

Overall, emerging countries that use SOEs to foster or guide economic developments in particular sectors, with the ultimate goal of creating or improving the competitiveness of such sectors in an open global market, would likely be able to commit to TPP-type disciplines. By contrast, countries that use SOEs as a channel to provide broad-based economic subsidies to downstream sectors (such as SOEs in the energy sector providing energy below market rates), to provide a social safety net regardless of productivity akin to a social entitlement program, or to serve as a conduit for implementing a centrally planned economy, would require a fundamental rethinking of proposed international rules. Another area of potential tension involves subnational entities: annex 17-C of the TPP sets the framework for further negotiations to extend the chapter's disciplines to SOEs owned or controlled by "sub-central level[s] of government," which would include regional authorities, states in

---

[59] In June 2017, 200 million SDR was equivalent to 178,000 Lakhs INR. Government of India, Department of Public Enterprises, Public Enterprises Survey 2015–16, Volume I, Statement 13 Ranking of CPSEs in Terms of Net Turnover/Revenue in 2015–16 (2016).

[60] Colin Picker, *The Coherent Fragmentation of International Economic Law: Lessons from the Transpacific Partnership Agreement*, in THE TRANSPACIFIC PARTNERSHIP: A PARADIGM SHIFT IN INTERNATIONAL ECONOMIC LAW RULE-MAKING (Julien Chaisse, Henry Gao, and Chang-fa Lo eds., 2017).

federal countries, municipalities, etc. Such a prospect might be problematic for emerging countries with regional entities that have significant economic policy autonomy, including India, China, Chile, Mexico and Brazil, along with their developed counterparts such as Australia and Canada.

In contrast to the TPP text, the leaked RCEP chapter on competition does not mention state-owned enterprises,[61] and some other leaked drafts, such as the services and investment chapters, envision broad exclusions from disciplines for measures affecting government procurement, subsidies, grants and government loans, certain service sectors, and modes of delivery.[62] Such approaches would serve to protect SOEs from trade opening and market disciplines. Here again, as with industrial policy, China's divergent political economy model is clearly a medium- to long-term strategy that is unlikely to be transformed to match WTO or TPP standards. Strengthening disciplines in these agreements, increasing enforcement within or outside these regimes is increasingly less likely to force a policy change, because China now has the political power to propose alternative frameworks, such as RCEP, with leeway for participants to pursue their policies regarding SOEs.

3 Competition

Long a contested area for trade regulation, competition/antitrust policies regularly surface in trade negotiations. While the issue was largely set aside after the WTO's 1996 Ministerial Conference in Singapore, TPP chapter 16 requires countries to have national laws banning anticompetitive practices, institutions to enforce such laws, procedural obligations pertaining thereto, and that the framework not be discriminatory on the basis of nationality.

Clashes between competition law requirements and the developmental state are most likely to surface with respect to monopolies created, owned or condoned by the state. In this respect, TPP-like standards on competition policy might be seen as regime altering for China. While China does have competition laws, they are administered by the body that directs

---

[61] Chapter [#] Competition, Consolidated Draft Text (Dec. 2016), www.bilaterals.org/IMG/pdf/rcep-competition.pdf.

[62] Chapter on Trade in Services in the Regional Comprehensive Economic Partnership (RCEP), Draft as of RCEP WGTIS 9 (Aug. 2015), www.bilaterals.org/IMG/pdf/services_consolidated_text-5aug2015-2.pdf; RCEP Draft Investment Text India (based on Draft Investment Text, Oct. 2015) 3, www.bilaterals.org/IMG/pdf/rcep-draft-investment-text-india.pdf.

overall economic strategy, and they include an exception for industries under the control of the state.[63] Inasmuch as China wishes to give monopoly powers to some SOEs, such action would most likely be challengeable under standards like TPP chapter 17 (on SOEs), which also addresses state monopolies.

The issue of whether a monopoly is justified or not is a complex one, and states vary in their views of where monopolies should be allowed and where competition law should govern. The debate whether to require particular sectors to be open to competition, then, is largely a debate on the scope and nature of public services and how to best deliver them to the populations that need them. Developing countries that believe the state should provide a wide range of services may find themselves in a defensive position under international rules mandating competition, having to negotiate negative lists of sectors to be excluded from competition disciplines.

The TPP also encourages members to offer a private right of action in addition to public remedies. Perhaps most uniquely compared to the WTO framework, the TPP devotes article 16.6 to consumer protection. Consumer interests have so far been largely left out of international trade regulation, despite clear impacts on international trade and domestic economies of discriminatory consumer practices such as market segmentation. In fact, the WTO agreements scarcely mention consumer interests at all, and in the handful of instances where they do, those provisions have largely been ignored.[64] By contrast, the APEC and ASEAN have ventured into the field of consumer protection more than any other trade group.[65] Heavy on declaration of principles but light on commitments, the TPP nonetheless mandates that parties "adopt or maintain consumer protection laws or other laws or regulations that proscribe fraudulent and deceptive commercial activities" (article 16.6(3)) and calls for "cooperation and coordination" to address fraudulent and deceptive commercial practices (article 16.6(4)).[66]

---

[63] Wu, *supra* note 46.
[64] Sonia E. Rolland, *Are Consumer-Oriented Rules the New Frontier of Trade Liberalization?*, 55 HARV. INT'L L. J. 361 (2014).
[65] *See, e.g.*, ASEAN COMM. ON CONSUMER PROTECTION, CONSUMER PROTECTION IN ASEAN (2010); ASIA–PACIFIC ECON. COOPERATION (APEC), SUMMARY REPORT – ELECTRONIC COMMERCE STEERING GROUP MEETING 2002, APEC Doc. 2002/ECSG2/SUM (Aug. 17, 2002); APEC BLUEPRINT FOR ACTION ON ELECTRONIC COM., 6TH APEC ECONOMIC LEADERS' MEETING, ¶ 5, APEC Doc. 1998/AELM/DEC/3 (Nov. 17, 1998); ELECTRONIC COM. STEERING GROUP, ASIA–PACIFIC ECONOMIC COOPERATION (Jan. 26, 2014).
[66] India boasts a fairly comprehensive legal and institutional framework to police anticompetitive practices, albeit not including a private right of action: The Competition Act of

While obligations regarding competition law remain embryonic or nonexistent in most trade agreements, the TPP sets a new bar. Given that obligations are mostly procedural and that many parties to the agreement already have antitrust rules in place, they might not be as controversial as in other fora. However, China is likely to continue to resist such disciplines. Other emerging countries may prefer to forego competition disciplines in other trade agreements too, or at least to approach the area with a minimal procedural floor and a positive list of sectors subject to competition rules, rather than higher standards and negative lists as does the TPP.

The leaked competition draft chapter of the RCEP envisions a general and vague obligation to police anticompetitive activities, but article 3.5 would provide considerable leeway:

> Each Party shall apply its competition laws and regulations to all entities engaged in commercial activities. Any exclusions or exemptions from the application of each party's competition laws and regulations shall be transparent and [various bracketed versions articulating a relationship to public interest].[67]

Countries with large state-owned sectors could argue that their SOEs are not engaged in commercial activity. However, such an argument, if made by China, would undermine its case for graduating from nonmarket economy status. The undefined notion of public interest also affords space to carve out developmental programs from the ambit of the competition chapter. Moreover, the chapter is excluded from the dispute settlement mechanism, thereby limiting legal exposure for noncompliance, although there would still be economic, political and diplomatic exposure.

The tensions between China's economic growth policies and the architecture of international trade law raise concerns across the globe and across the political spectrum. To a lesser extent, industrial policies in

---

2002 (12 of 2003), amended by the Competition (Amendment) Act, 2007. On its face, the legislation generally comports with TPP-style standards. Consumer protection, on the other hand, remains a work in progress. Like the TPP, the 2002 Competition Act recognizes the impact of anticompetitive practices on consumers and explicitly encompasses as unlawful abuse of dominant position and other practices that adversely affect consumers. The Consumer Protection Act 1986 is India's main legislation, but enforcement is highly variable. Still, the existence of laws and remedies in this field is likely enough to meet, at least nominally, obligations such as those enshrined in the TPP.

[67] Chapter [#], Competition, Consolidated Draft Text (Dec. 2016), www.bilaterals.org/IMG/pdf/rcep-competition.pdf.

India and Brazil encounter similar opposition. Dani Rodrik bluntly asks, "How will the world trade regime handle a large, increasingly powerful country such as China that apparently plays globalisation by different rules?"[68] European and U.S. policymakers undertake variously coercive measures to sanction China for its noncompliance. These include skewing antidumping calculation methodologies (the infamous U.S. practice of "zeroing" and the use of nonmarket economy calculation standards) and increased tariffs. In a number of cases, these measures are themselves in breach of international trade rules, and likely to be heavily disruptive for the global economy through trade displacement and increased costs for downstream users of targeted products. Middle-income emerging countries such as Brazil and India make extensive use of trade remedies in an attempt to cushion the competitive blow to their domestic industries of Chinese-made imports. Rodrik offers a different response: it is not necessarily China that needs to change its policies, but the trade law regime that must accommodate different models of political economy. Along similar lines, Andrew Lang traces the trade regime's ability to accommodate various types of political economy – albeit with a capitalist ethos – to the GATT, and argues that the erosion of this "institutional pluralism" explains many of the current frictions.[69]

China's socioeconomic fabric has been fundamentally altered by its insertion in the global economy, which was consecrated by its joining the WTO in 2001. In that sense, the convergence toward economic liberalism, which forms the core ethos of the WTO system, has had a very real impact on China's political economy and other planned economy systems such as India. At the same time, it is also becoming abundantly clear that China and a number of other developing countries are not aiming to achieve full convergence. Even among the architects of the WTO, serious differences of perspective exist as to what such a convergence might mean, or what shade of liberal capitalism the WTO does or should commend. One only needs to consider the United States' and Europe's inability to conclude a trade agreement between themselves, with the failed TTIP.

---

[68] Dani Rodrik, *The WTO Has Become Dysfunctional*, FIN. TIMES, Aug. 5, 2018, www.ft .com/content/c2beedfe-964d-11e8-95f8-8640db9060a7.

[69] Andrew Lang, *Heterodox Market Orders in the Global Trade System*, in WORLD TRADE AND INVESTMENT LAW REIMAGINED: A PROGRESSIVE AGENDA FOR AN INCLUSIVE GLOBALIZATION (Alvaro Santos et al., eds., forthcoming Taylor & Francis, 2019).

B Problem-Creating Rules

In this section we look at other regulatory areas where TPP-type obligations could require changes in developmental policy, albeit less radically than in respect to the topics just explored. Again, we focus on the signed text of the TPP as proxy for future agreements with similar provisions. Depending on how one defines the core model, and how these provisions are interpreted, these might or might not go to the core of the developmental model. They include intellectual property and the digital economy.

1   Intellectual Property

Like the TRIPS agreement, the TPP's intellectual property (IP) chapter proceeds along three axes: first, it mandates parties to accede or ratify a list of international agreements related to IP; second, it establishes some baseline standards (national treatment and enforcement obligations, including the obligation to provide criminal penalties); and third, it enshrines some substantive obligations with respect to the traditional categories of IP (trademarks, patents, industrial designs, copyrights). It further designates some areas for cooperation. A number of these provisions have generated significant controversy in the context of the TPP, and in other international negotiations such as the failed Anti-Counterfeiting Trade Agreement.[70] These include flexibilities for public health policy, traditional knowledge associated with genetic resources, and the criminalization of certain intellectual property violations.

TPP's intellectual property chapter raises important challenges for Brazil. As a matter of negotiating strategy, TPP effectively shifts regulation of trade-related IP rights from the WTO to the mega-regional level. Whereas Brazil and other developing countries were able to block developed countries' IP agenda in the WTO, such a forum shift would mean Brazil and other developing countries could encounter standards they had no voice in establishing.[71]

In principle, the TPP seems to follow the approach defended by a group of developing countries at the WTO, set out in the Doha Declaration on Public Health, but does not spell out the flexibilities allowed by the WTO. Secondly, TPP's regulation of genetic resources

---

[70] Trans-Pacific Partnership art. 2.1, Feb. 4, 2016.

[71] The effects on IP regulation have already reached Brazil. According to interviews conducted by the authors, Mexico, one of the TPP members, approached Brazil with a TPP-like proposal in 2018.

associated with traditional knowledge is weak – essentially based on cooperation – and falls short of addressing Brazil's concerns with biopiracy. Brazil has fully internalized the Convention on Biological Diversity (CBD), which inter alia regulates access to genetic resources and traditional knowledge.[72] Most recently, Brazil passed a new law to make benefit-sharing requirements more effective and ensure that traditional knowledge holders have greater participation in decision-making processes.[73]

TPP-like standards in IP would present a major challenge for China. China has regularly been criticized for failure to meet TRIPS standards.[74] While Chinese law on the books seems consistent with TRIPS, there is concern that China does not fully enforce these provisions.[75] TPP would have created an additional level of tension, as TPP standards for IP exceed those in the WTO. If China is already falling short of WTO standards, it hardly seems that it would easily accede to the more stringent standards in TPP or similar agreements. One commentator noted:

> For example, in the pharma sector, the TPP contains extensive provisions on patent linkage, patent term restoration, and data exclusivity which go beyond the TRIPS Agreement. In addition to these substantive IP issues, there are significant challenges in non-IP area chapters that affect commercialization and utilization of IP, such as in market access for lawyers, restrictions on state owned enterprises, e-commerce, and investor–state dispute resolution.[76]

---

[72] The CBD requires prior informed consent of the party who is providing the resources, and mandates sharing the results of research and development and the benefits arising from commercial and other utilization of genetic resources with the government and with local communities that provided the traditional knowledge or biodiversity resources. *See* Convention on Biological Diversity, Jun. 4, 1993, 79 U.N.T.S. 309; Decree No. 2.519/1998 (Braz.) (ratifying the CBD in Brazil). *See also* Law No. 13.123 of May 20, 2015 (Access and Benefits Sharing of Genetic Resources and Associated Traditional Knowledge) (in force Nov. 16, 2015) (Braz.), https://wipolex.wipo.int/en/legislation/details/15741 (regulating CBD in Brazil).

[73] Brazil law already requires benefit sharing. *See* Law No. 13.123 of May 20, 2015, *supra* note 72; Decree No. 8.772 regulating Law No. 13.123 of May 20, 2015 (May 11, 2016) (Braz.), https://wipolex.wipo.int/en/legislation/details/16116 (requiring corporations to notify their use of traditional knowledge in manufacturing to a government agency newly established for this purpose).

[74] Steve Brachman, *Chinese Support of Indigenous Innovation Is Problematic for Foreign IP Owners*, IP WATCHDOG (Apr. 9, 2015), www.ipwatchdog.com/2015/04/09/chinese-indigenous-innovation-problematic-foreign-ip-owners/id=56525/.

[75] Office of the United States Trade Representative, 2017 Special 301 Report.

[76] *The TPP's IP Challenge for China*, Nov. 9, 2015, https://chinaipr.com/2015/11/09/the-tpps-ip-challenge-for-china-part-1/.

Part of the Chinese transformation from a manufacturing-dependent economy to a high-tech services-based economy has been a focus on localized innovation and technology. China has produced short-term and long-term plans to focus on indigenous innovation. In 2016, Chinese patent filings under the Patent Cooperation Treaty ranked third in volume, after the United States and Japan, accounting for over 18 percent of total applications filed. If current Chinese applications growth trends continue, the World Intellectual Property Organization expects China to overtake the United States as the largest user of the Patent Cooperation Treaty in the next two years.[77] Nonetheless, China's indigenous innovation policy includes many provisions that raise issues under both WTO and WTO+ IP standards. Indeed, given the importance of this strategy to China's long-term plans, some may fall under the rubric of "regime-altering."

In its latest 301 Report, the United States noted the expansion of indigenous innovation policies in China and elsewhere, and commented that these policies often have the effect of distorting trade by forcing U.S. companies to transfer their technology or other valuable commercial information to national entities. The report concludes:

> China's promotion of self-sufficient, indigenous innovation through poli-cies on patents and in related areas, including standards and competition law, implicates a cross-cutting set of concerns. China must ensure that present and future Information and Communications Technology ... policies (and other policies) do not disadvantage foreign IP-intensive industries by, inter alia, conditioning market access on the disclosure of IP and proprietary information, the localization of research and develop-ment, or by invoking "secure and controllable" standards, risk criteria, product reviews, or similar requirements that are disadvantageous to foreign firms. Also critical is that China eliminate discriminatory require-ments and incentives to transfer technology to, or develop technology in, China.[78]

India's main concern regarding international IP negotiations focuses on access to medicine and public health. Both domestically and internation-ally, it has actively defended the use of rights and flexibilities in this domain. Examples include the Indian Supreme Court's denial of a patent

---

[77] World Intellectual Property Organization, Press Release: Record Year for International Patent Applications in 2016; Strong Demand Also for Trademark and Industrial Design Protection, PR/2017/804 (Mar. 15, 2017).

[78] Office of the United States Trade Representative, 2017 Special 301 Report.

for Novartis' cancer drug known as Gleevec;[79] India's granting of a compulsory license on a blood thinner drug and a cancer drug both patented by Bayer, and the subsequent production and export of these drugs by Natco and Alembic, two Indian companies;[80] and India's WTO complaint against the EU regarding the seizure of generic drugs trans-shipped through Europe on the way to Brazil.[81] In this context, ambiguous language such as that contained in the TPP's chapter 18 would likely be unacceptable to India. The development of case law, and the variety of disputes at the intersection of intellectual property and public health protection over the past fifteen years, provides a wealth of lessons regarding the impact of particular IP commitments. India, Brazil, and South Africa, in particular, have gained considerable expertise in assessing the limitations of current flexibilities, which is likely to influence their negotiation strategy vis-à-vis any drive to enhance international IP protection.

Emerging powers may share convergent views on a more limited scope for intellectual property rights, and have been relatively successful at maintaining flexibilities and resisting TRIPS+ obligations. Combined with the United States withdrawing from the TPP and Australia reeling from the tobacco arbitrations, this may present an opportunity to redefine the balance of private rights and public policy in Asian and Pacific PTAs away from TRIPS+ and TPP standards in the health sector. At the same time, the United States remains a staunch advocate of strong IP rights generally and is willing to take drastic measures in their defense, as shown by the tariffs imposed against China in retaliation for what the U.S. government claims is theft of U.S. intellectual property and forced transfer of U.S. technology.[82]

[79] Novartis AG v. Union of India, AIR 2013 SC 1, App. No. 2706–2716 of 2013 (India), https://perma.cc/53RA-2LDX.
[80] Bayer Corporation v. Natco Pharma Ltd., Order No. 19/2013 (Intellectual Property Appellate Board, Chennai) (Cited at Jan. 24, 2016), www.ipabindia.in/Pdfs/Order-19-2013.pdf
[81] Request for Consultations by India, *European Union and a Member State – Seizure of Generic Drugs in Transit*, WTO Doc. WT/DS/408/1 (May 11, 2010). *See also* Request for Consultations, *European Union and a Member State – Seizure of Generic Drugs in Transit*, WTO Doc. WT/DS/409/1 (May 12, 2010) (related complaint by Brazil). Although the case has not proceeded beyond the consultations stage as of 2019, India regularly threatens to take matters further.
[82] *See, e.g.,* Office of the United States Trade Representative, *USTR Finalizes Tariffs on $200 Billion of Chinese Imports in Response to China's Unfair Trade Practices*, Press Release, Sept. 18, 2018, https://ustr.gov/about-us/policy-offices/press-office/press-releases/2018/september/ustr-finalizes-tariffs-200.

2 Digital Economy

Trade regulation of electronic commerce is a relatively new area, but the digital economy constitutes a growing sector in some emerging countries. Standards included in the TPP and some fifty other trade agreements address topics listed in this section. [83] While the impact on the developmental state may be minimal at present, inasmuch as economic policies supporting this sector are embryonic, the trade law amounts to a baseline that impacts future policies. The Mercado Común del Sur (Mercosur), comprised of Argentina, Brazil, Paraguay, Uruguay and Venezuela, was amongst the first regional trade groupings to consider frameworks for cross-border e-commerce.[84] E-commerce expenditures have grown by up to 30 percent year-on-year in Latin America over the past ten years. Similarly, APEC created numerous initiatives under the aegis of the Electronic Commerce Steering Group. Of particular note is the APEC Data Privacy Pathfinder, which was established by ministers in 2007 to achieve accountable cross-border flow of personal information within the APEC region.[85]

Of the 129 trade agreements notified at the WTO from 1995 to May 2016, forty-seven include some provisions on electronic commerce. A number of e-commerce provisions are regular fixtures in PTAs and the TPP as outlined shortly. These include provisions on customs duties, nondiscrimination, personal data protection and privacy, consumer protection, electronic signatures and future cooperation. At the December 2017 WTO ministerial meeting in Buenos Aires, some seventy members pledged to work toward electronic commerce rules. The group includes Brazil, Canada, the EU, Japan, Russia and South Korea, but excludes China, India and Indonesia.

The chapter of the TPP on electronic commerce presents several challenges to Brazil's evolving regulatory framework on computer data, the Internet, and web systems.[86] Basically, Brazilian law gives precedence

---

[83] This section is adapted in part from Sonia E. Rolland, *Consumer Protection Issues in Cross-Border E-Commerce*, in RESEARCH HANDBOOK ON ELECTRONIC COMMERCE LAW 365 (John A. Rothchild, ed., 2016).

[84] The "Digital Mercosur" initiative commissioned a study in 2013 on the structure necessary for the MERCOSUR countries to trade in the digital economy.

[85] *See* Asia–Pacific Economic Cooperation, *APEC Data Privacy Pathfinder*, APEC Doc. 2007/CSOM/019 (Sept. 2, 2007).

[86] Brazil has a general rule on the Internet, Law No. 12.965 of Apr. 23, 2014 (Establishment of Principles, Guarantees, Rights and obligations for the use of the Internet in Brazil) (in force Jun. 23, 2014) (Braz.), https://wipolex.wipo.int/en/legislation/details/15514. Other details on web services are still to be regulated by the Congress.

to network neutrality, privacy, data retention, the social function of the web, and transfer of knowledge, and imposes responsibility on users and service providers.

Brazil is considering its first agreements on electronic commerce and is negotiating agreements with Mexico and Peru, who have proposed TPP-influenced provisions.[87] We anticipate three major inconsistencies between proposed TPP-like texts and Brazilian policies: Brazil may have trouble with the concept of "digital product," with the effect of TPP-type standards on its current consumer protection code and privacy laws, and with provisions on location of computing facilities.[88]

A unique feature of India's approach to the digital economy is to integrate public functions and private transactions. The Aadhaar project, launched in 2009, seeks to create an official identity for individuals based on fingerprints and retina scans (in lieu of paper government identification and records), which would in turn be linked to the delivery of social benefits, and pave the way for increasing the prevalence of formal banking and payments via direct transfers, rather than through paper currency (another government initiative called the Unified Payment Interface).[89] As of 2016, over a billion people were enrolled in the Aadhaar identification scheme. In this context, issues such as privacy, data protection, internet access and digital signatures will be of prime concern to India in considering further trade commitments.

China's digital economy has already begun to outpace other countries, as China is now home to the largest user base of internet and mobile phone users.[90] China's position as leading manufacturer of mobile

---

[87] According to interviews conducted by the authors with Brazilian officials, the text of the e-commerce agreement proposed by Mexico and Peru is very similar, if not identical, to the e-commerce chapter of the TPP. Brazil and Peru already signed an agreement on Apr. 29, 2016. See *Acordo de Ampliação Econômico-Comercial entre Brasil e Peru*, Apr. 29, 2016. www.mdic.gov.br/convenios/9-assuntos/categ-comercio-exterior/1508-acordo-de-ampliacao-economico-comercial-brasil-peru-ainda-sem-vigencia and Legislative Decree No. 42 of 2017 that ratifies the Brazil–Peru agreement but is on hold.

[88] According to interviews with Brazilian officials, although there is an exception in the TPP to the general rule on transfer of information (art 14.11.3), it does not meet Brazil's needs. Law No. 12.965, *supra* note 86, is still more protective. Besides, Brazilian officials see no point in such provisions other than the United States' strategy to block Russia's approach, so they declared that Brazil would not be ready to accept such provision. Trubek et al., *Brazil in the Shadow of TPP: Beyond the Grand Debate, Pragmatic Responses, supra* note 1.

[89] AADHAAR (Targeted Delivery of Financial and Other Subsidies, Benefits and Services) Act, 2016 (Mar. 26, 2016) (India), https://uidai.gov.in/legal-framework/acts.html.

[90] Zheng Yangpeng & Meng Jing, *Rapidly Growing Digital Economy Set to Give China 415m Jobs, Account for Nearly Half of GDP*, SOUTH CHINA MORNING POST, Jan. 10, 2017,

devices and other technology has placed it in a unique position to deploy technological systems.[91] New reports suggest that China will add hundreds of millions of jobs by 2035 as the digital economy becomes the largest share of GDP in the country.[92] According to a commentator,

> [t]he state's agenda to expand the cyber business section, and the fact that private cyber giants control powerful Web 2.0 business models and have gained considerable political influence, have parlayed into a cyber-business-friendly legal and regulatory approach – through local or departmental loopholes . . . Unable to sever this conduit to global capital, the state is altering its own investment policy at the expense of its own security mandate.[93]

China changed its regulations as a fast-growing number of digital businesses began to operate across borders. These include an April 2016 set of regulations requiring e-commerce platforms and postal services to collect indirect taxes from online businesses. Regulations also provide a framework for expediting customs clearance.[94] This reform, called the Internet Plus Policy, is part of the government's thirteenth five-year plan for 2020. Spurred by the global economic crisis of 2008, China's economic rethinking has turned the country into a digital global powerhouse.[95] In a signal that the global infrastructure is ripe for Chinese leadership, China chaired the G20 Digital Economy Taskforce in 2016.

China has amassed a vast e-payment market, currently more than fifty times larger than U.S. counterparts.[96] Companies such as Alibaba have already begun harvesting large shares of the market, domestically in China and beyond. Chinese companies are beginning to support other companies' infrastructure around the world, and with hundreds of millions of Chinese nationals traveling abroad each year, globalized payment systems are flourishing. China has emerged as a leader in digital trade and

---

www.scmp.com/tech/article/2060895/rapidly-growing-digital-economy-set-give-china-415m-jobs-account-nearly-half.

[91] John Thornbill, *China's Digital Economy Is a Global Trailblazer*, Fin. Times, Mar. 20, 2017, www.ft.com/content/86cbda82-0d55-11e7-b030-768954394623).

[92] Yangpeng & Jing, *supra* note 90.

[93] Yu Hong, *Pivot to Internet Plus: Molding China's Digital Economy for Economic Restructuring?*, 11 Int'l J. of Com. 1486, 1499 (2017).

[94] KPMG, *China Tax in the Digital Age* (2016), https://assets.kpmg/content/dam/kpmg/pdf/2016/07/china-tax-in-the-digital-age-1.pdf.

[95] Hong, *supra* note 93 at 1487.

[96] John Thornbill, *China's Digital Economy Is a Global Trailblazer*, Fin. Times, Mar. 20, 2017, www.ft.com/content/86cbda82-0d55-11e7-b030-768954394623.

will continue to control large parts of the market in the future.[97] If China continues to invest in expanding the reach of its digital economy beyond borders, it may well be poised to become a rule-maker in this area. However, Chinese government restrictions on capital movement and currency conversion are currently limiting Chinese investors' capacity to expand their stake in the global digital economy and underlying technical innovations.

Despite the challenges outlined previously, the field is relatively open when it comes to regulating the digital economy, giving an opportunity for emerging countries active in this domain to be rule-makers rather than rule-takers. Some subject matters, such as cryptocurrencies and blockchains, are even more alien to current international rules, but certainly raise cross-border challenges. In fact, there are indications that China is an early mover in the financing[98] and regulation of blockchain projects.[99]

C Conclusion: What Cost for State Developmentalism?

The division between "regime-altering" and "problem-creating" disciplines signals some of the most salient intersections between recent trade regulation efforts and developmentalism, but like most classifications, it should not be read in absolute terms. For instance, we placed competition disciplines in the regime-altering category because some fundamental features of competition law, particularly anti-monopoly rules, run directly counter to some core elements of state developmentalism. That is not to say that any and all aspects of competition law present such a clash. Likewise, intellectual property raises some serious challenges to many emerging countries' developmental policies, especially in the areas of public health, traditional knowledge, and the patenting of biologics, but many other features, including the protection of intellectual and artistic works, are not incompatible with developmental policies. Moreover, the expansion of the trade agenda to domains such as labor, environmental protection, and anticorruption measures intersects with important aspects of development that we have not included in this

---

[97] KPMG, *China Tax, supra* note 94.

[98] Kevin C. Desouza, Chen Ye & Xiaofeng Wang, *Is China Leading the Blockchain Innovation Race?*, Jul. 19, 2018, www.brookings.edu/blog/techtank/2018/07/19/is-china-leading-the-blockchain-innovation-race/.

[99] Zhang Jie, *National Standard for Blockchain Expected Next Year*, May 10, 2018, www.chinadaily.com.cn/a/201805/10/WS5af3dd1aa3105cdcf651d1ff.html.

analysis. In other words, we recognize that our two categories are fluid and we certainly do not claim that the topics we explore are exclusive of other fields of regulation germane to trade and development.

The tensions discussed here may be somewhat mitigated by strategic noncompliance and by nonenforcement, whether because enforcement mechanisms are weak or unavailable, or because of tacit standstill positions by trade partners concerned about being challenged for similar policies. Chapter 3 explored the range of tactics that developing members and others have deployed to modulate the rules, whether by using official flexibilities or by breaking or circumventing commitments. Noncompliance, whether within or outside of the legal framework, carries economic, political and diplomatic costs. The number of WTO disputes and the retaliation granted as a result are quantifiable measures of such costs. Political backlash and countermeasures, such as the hundreds of billions of U.S. dollars in tariffs imposed against Chinese products in 2018 by the Trump administration, are also a direct cost of maintaining trade policies seen as outside the heterodox framework. Stalled or failed trade negotiations are another type of cost.

It would be a fallacy, however, solely to consider multilateral enforcement measures. Rather, the cost of noncompliance is often and increasingly displaced from the international arena to the domestic realm. Antidumping and countervailing duties, redirection of public aid to development, and a host of retaliatory economic or political measures are deployed against programs that are at least ostensibly developmental in their purpose.

Conversely, measures taken by developed and developing countries to counter other countries' state developmentalism generate costs for those imposing the measures too. Economists have long decried trade remedies as economically inefficient. These measures and other types of retaliatory tariffs inevitably impose a cost on domestic consumers of imported intermediate and final goods, thereby putting downward pressure on their purchasing power. Such measures also typically fail to address the redistributive costs of globalization in favor of those most affected by it. In some instances, they are thinly veiled populist measures to cater to specific voting constituencies, with little relationship to the alleged economic harm done by the foreign trade policy.

Having explored the legal issues raised by state developmentalism, and some of the political and economic costs that countermeasures generate, we must ask what the rules are designed to achieve. The mainstream understanding of WTO- and TPP-style liberalism is that it must promote and preserve a level playing field, such that economic development of one country is not pursued at the expense of others. The Marrakesh Agreement's preamble calls for sustainable development. Meanwhile, policymakers in emerging countries, and some economists, argue that such goals must not be interpreted to prohibit the use of development instruments that the old industrial powers extensively benefited from in the earlier days of their growth.[100] Old industrial powers' inability to fully deliver on their social contract commitment to compensation for the "losers" of globalization further exacerbates the debate about global distributional issues and the social justice values embedded in, or lacking from, existing global trade rules.

IV Forum Shifting: Emerging Powers' Drive to Create Regional Economic Integration Spaces

The United States originally used the TPP to push an essentially neoliberal agenda onto to a variety of countries with political economy models as diverse as Chile and Vietnam, and to counterbalance China's growing economic influence. Populism in the United States then disrupted this trajectory, and it is unclear whether the United States will return to this agenda, will turn to protectionism, or some combination of the two that is likely to undermine its credibility on the international scene. Faced with Western-led mega-regionals, some emerging economies have sought to create new alliances that would allow them to grow economically without facing some of the constraints on development strategy mega-regionals might demand. Meanwhile, China is proposing an alternative framework for economic collaboration in Asia that brings with it deep geopolitical implications.

A Toward a China-Led Asian Integration? ASEAN, RCEP, BRI

ASEAN has evolved from a political forum for consultations and discussions on the region's economic integration to formalizing legal agreements within the organization and in relation to third parties.[101] This activity relates not only to economic matters but also to issues of

---

[100] See, e.g., HA-JOON CHANG, KICKING AWAY THE LADDER – DEVELOPMENT STRATEGY IN HISTORICAL PERSPECTIVE (2002).

[101] Zhang Zhiyong, Economic Integration in East Asia: The Path of Law, 4 PEKING U. J. LEGAL STUD., 262, 272–4 (2013).

geopolitical interest, such as the ASEAN Convention on Counter Terrorism,[102] cross-border legal cooperation,[103] and a myriad of other topics amounting to a network of some eighty treaties. Its 2015 statement of policy identifies its guiding principles as follows: "[r]egional integration and connectivity are to be accelerated through facilitating the movement of skilled persons, capital and goods, lowering barriers to trade and strengthening the institutional mechanisms of ASEAN. There are four pillars to the AEC: 1) Single Market and Production Base; 2) Competitive Economic Region; 3) Equitable Economic Development; and 4) ASEAN's Integration into the Global Economy."[104] In practice, this overarching framework translates into much more than an MFN clause, decreased tariffs, and other hallmarks of WTO-style economic liberalization. Rather, the ASEAN seeks to enable trade integration in the region by supporting energy and transportation projects, fostering mutual recognition of qualifications, encouraging members to institute domestic competition rules, facilitating administrative procedures relating to trade, moving toward freedom of movement of persons, facilitating capital flows, and many more factors underpinning trade and development. Asymmetric provisions recognizing the differential capacities of its poorer members, particularly Cambodia, Lao PDR, Myanmar and Vietnam, are also a feature of ASEAN trade agreements.[105]

Externally, the ASEAN has concluded more traditional FTAs with China, Japan, the Republic of (South) Korea, Australia, New Zealand and India individually. It is now turning these established relationships into a possible single agreement with the RCEP. The ASEAN bills the RCEP as an "ASEAN-led agreement,"[106] which was originally the case, though it later evolved into a Chinese-led endeavor. The 2015 statement of policy for the ASEAN Economic Community presents RCEP as

---

[102] ASEAN Convention on Counter Terrorism, Jan. 13, 2007.

[103] Treaty on Mutual Assistance in Criminal Matters, Nov. 29, 2004; ASEAN Convention Against Trafficking in Persons, Especially Women and Children, Mar. 8, 2017.

[104] Ass'n. of Southeast Asian Nations [ASEAN], *Thinking Globally, Prospering Regionally – ASEAN Economic Community 2015* (Mar. 3–4, 2015), http://asean.org/storage/2016/06/ 4.-March-2015-Thinking-Globally-Prospering-Regionally-%E2%80%93-The-AEC-2015-Messaging-for-Our-Future-2nd-Reprint.pdf.

[105] *See, e.g., Framework Agreement on Comprehensive Economic Cooperation Among the Governments of the Member Countries of the Association of Southeast Asian Nations and the Republic of Korea,* arts. 2 (2)(c), 3.2 (4) (Dec. 13, 2005), http://asean.org/?static_post= framework-agreement-on-comprehensive-economic-cooperation-among-the-govern ments-of-the-member-countries-of-the-association-of-southeast-asian-nations-and-the-republic-of-korea-kuala-lumpur-13-december.

[106] ASEAN, *Thinking Globally, Prospering Regionally, supra* note 104 at 14.

"expected to deliver tangible benefits to businesses through potential improvements in market access, trade facilitation, regulatory reform and more liberal rules of origin."[107]

Challenges to the TPP spurred interest in RCEP. While negotiations for RCEP started in 2012 and moved slowly for some time, they picked up in the wake of the imminent signing of TPP and have accelerated further since the U.S. withdrawal. With the demise of TPP, China has taken a more assertive role, calling for swift completion of the pact. Some observers thought negotiations might be concluded in 2017 and the final terms announced by the fiftieth anniversary of ASEAN, but this did not come to pass and no imminent conclusion of RCEP seems likely as of early 2019.[108]

RCEP involves sixteen countries: the ten members of ASEAN plus China, India, Korea, Australia, Japan and New Zealand. Total GDP equals 30 percent of global GDP. Total trade of the bloc is USD 9.5 trillion. Interregional trade represents 44.6 percent of members' total trade. RCEP is still a work in progress, and it is unclear whether sub-stantively it will take up the baton from the TPP, or look more like ASEAN FTAs. Negotiations are ongoing in the areas of trade in goods, trade in services, investment, rules of origin, intellectual property rights, competition and e-commerce. Unlike the TPP, they do not cover labor, the environment or state-owned enterprises.[109]

Negotiations remain confidential as of 2019. Leaked material gives some idea of directions, but it will be some time before final arrangements are known. However, the broad lines of the emerging agreement are visible. Oxford Analytica notes:

> Although the RCEP is expected to cover a range of areas and issues almost as wide as the TPP, the degree of liberalisation will be significantly lower and the number of exceptions and permitted safeguards greater.[110]

---

[107] ASEAN, *Thinking Globally, Prospering Regionally, supra* note 104. (The document does not mention the TPP negotiations, which were well underway in 2015 and involved four ASEAN members and three of the ASEAN+6 partners).

[108] Compare *RCEP: Looking Ahead to 2017*, Dec. 14, 2016, www.asiantradecentre.org/talkingtrade//rcep-looking-ahead-to-2017 and www.pressreader.com/philippines/man ila-bulletin/20161107/282106341205312 with Shefali Rekhi, *Will RCEP Be a Reality by the End of 2017?*, STRAIGHT TIMES, Apr. 23, 2017, www.straitstimes.com/asia/se-asia/will-rcep-be-a-reality-by-the-end-of-2017.

[109] Benjamin Charlton, *RCEP Will Step into Gap as Trump Pulls Out of TPP*, OXFORD ANALYTICA, Jan. 23, 2017, https://dailybrief.oxan.com/Analysis/DB217448/RCEP-will-step-into-gap-as-Trump-pulls-out-of-TPP.

[110] *Id.*

An Australian report concludes:

> Importantly, RCEP offers a radically different vision for how the regional trade should evolve. Where the TPP offered an Asia–Pacific model based on the principle of 'open regionalism', RCEP instead adopts a closed approach to membership arrangements that are more Indo–Pacific in form. Its approach to liberalization is significantly lower, prioritizing tariff reductions rather than the development of new trade law in areas such as investment, environment and services. RCEP is also a decidedly China-led process, and potentially heralds an era in which China emerges as a meaningful counterweight to U.S. economic leadership in the region.[111]

The RCEP negotiations suggest that it will have fewer WTO+ provisions than TPP. State-owned enterprises are excluded from the negotiations, so it will not contain anything like TPP chapter 17 and is unlikely to include the same level of restrictions on industrial policy and competition. Nor does it seem to include restrictions on government procurement. There will be a section on intellectual property, but its scope is unclear: it seems unlikely that China and India will agree to some of TPP-style IP rules.[112] Unlike TPP, RCEP will include provisions for special and differential treatment for less-developed countries, and for economic and technical cooperation.

While, as the Australian report suggests, RCEP has been conceived as a closed Indo–Asian regional agreement, the demise of TPP has led some to suggest that it might be expanded to incorporate TPP member states like Peru and Chile, with which China already has PTAs.[113]

While RCEP appears to be China's main effort at building regional space in Asia, another aspect of China's efforts at creating an Asian economic space is the Belt and Road Initiative (BRI). This massive infrastructure program involves building roads, railroads, ports and other facilities to create better linkages between China and countries in South, Southeast and Central Asia and beyond, thus increasing access for Chinese goods to their markets and for their exports to China. China is

---

[111] Perth USAsia Centre, *The Regional Comprehensive Economic Partnership: An Indo–Pacific Approach to the Regional Trade Architecture?*, INDO–PACIFIC INSIGHT SERIES 2, Jan. 2017, http://perthusasia.edu.au/getattachment/Our-Work/Indo-Pacific-Insight-Series-Vol-2-The-RCEP-An-I/PUAC-Indo-Pacific-Insight-Series-Volume2-JeffWilson.pdf.aspx?lan.

[112] *See, e.g.*, Kajal Bhardwaj & Shiba Phurailatpam, *RCEP and Health: This Kind of 'Progress' is Not What India and the World Need*, BILATERALS.ORG (Feb. 28, 2017), www.bilaterals.org/?rcep-and-health-this-kind-of).

[113] Perth USAsia Centre, *The Regional Comprehensive Economic Partnership*, *supra* note 111.

also creating new courts to deal with commercial disputes arising in the context of outward investments under the aegis of the Belt and Road Initiative. Although such courts are touted as international tribunals, they are constituted within the Chinese court system, will be staffed by Chinese judges, and apply Chinese law. The main international components are a Committee of International Experts to assist the courts, and the ability to conduct at least some of the proceedings in English.[114] It is impossible to predict just how these initiatives will play out. China has shown flexibility with respect to the demands of trade partners. A key policy objective has been for China to obtain recognition from its partners as a market economy – and it is willing to pay for it in trade concessions.[115]

B   Prospects for Regional Integration in Latin America

Both Brazil and China seek to avoid trading rules that would significantly affect development strategy. But their situations are very different. While both play important economic roles in their respective regions, China is much more important to the economy of its Asian partners than Brazil is to most countries in Latin America. While both rely on SOEs and practice vigorous industrial policy, China's commitment to state-led growth is much firmer than Brazil's. Elites in both countries have oscillated between market-oriented reform and support for state activism. While in China the pendulum seems to have swung to the state-led side,[116] in Brazil the opposite seems to be true. In the wake of a severe recession that some think was partially caused by ill-conceived forms of state activism, and a corruption scandal involving Brazil's most important SOE, support for state activism is declining.[117]

---

[114] Matthew Erie, *The China International Commercial Court: Prospects for Dispute Resolution for the Belt and Road Initiative*, ASIL INSIGHTS Vol. 22, Issue 11, Aug. 31, 2018, www.asil.org/insights/volume/22/issue/11/china-international-commercial-court-prospects-dispute-resolution-belt.

[115] China's ultimate goal is for its status as a nonmarket economy to be lifted for purposes of trade remedies applied in the context of WTO rules and other WTO obligations. China's protocol of accession indicated a December 2015 deadline for revisiting nonmarket economy status, with the expectation that the status would phase out at that time. While that goal has not yet been reached, in large part due to U.S. and EU resistance, China is taking a firmer stand in challenging its status in WTO disputes. Request Consultations by China, *EU – Price Comparison Methodologies*, WT/DS516/1; Request for Consultations by China, *US – Price Comparison Methodologies*, WT/DS515/1.

[116] Tao, *supra* note 46.

[117] Andre Singer, *The Failure of the Developmentalist Experiment in Three Acts*, 11 CRITICAL POL'Y STUDIES 358 (2017).

For these reasons, Brazil's response to the multiregional challenge is more complex and opportunistic. Like China, Brazil seeks to create a more integrated economic space in its region. But Brazil has not tried to create a single mega-regional like RCEP. Rather, its efforts in the region so far have taken the form of bilateral initiatives with the four countries of the Pacific Alliance (Mexico, Colombia, Peru and Chile) and efforts to strengthen Mercosur (Argentina, Paraguay and Uruguay).[118]

1   The Pacific Alliance

The Pacific Alliance is a new integration process in the region. Brazil has commercial ties with all of the Pacific Alliance countries. These countries are an important part of Brazil's export market, and Brazil has sought to expand its relations with them in part to forestall Chinese penetration in these markets. Take Mexico as an example. Between 2004 and 2014, Brazil–Mexico trade flows increased by 93.7 percent.[119] In 2015, during President Rousseff's visit to Mexico, both countries decided to accelerate trade negotiation leading to new agreements[120] that involved tariff preferences in approximately 800 items. Brazil and Mexico agreed to start ambitious bilateral negotiations in July 2016, involving areas such as tariff reductions in agricultural and manufactured products, services, government procurement, and sanitary and phytosanitary measures.[121] A similar approach was adopted in relation to Colombia, Chile and Peru.

New bilateral agreements are being negotiated and signed, and trade flows have increased significantly in recent years. Since the Pacific Alliance countries all have PTAs with the United States and three are part of TPP, these countries have sought to include some TPP-like standards in bilateral negotiations. It appears that Brazil has approached these demands pragmatically, accepting at least some TPP-like standards in order to expand market access.

---

[118] Venezuela was removed in 2016 due to the political crisis.
[119] Ministry of Foreign Relations, *Estados Unidos Mexicanos*, www.itamaraty.gov.br/pt-BR/ficha-pais/6453-estados-unidos-mexicanos.
[120] Ministry of Foreign Relations, *Brazil–Mexico Decision, in 2015, to Deepen the Agreement of Economic Complementation n. 53* (2015), www.itamaraty.gov.br/pt-BR/notas-a-imprensa/12766-negociacao-brasil-mexico-paraampliacao-e-aprofundamento-do-ace-53-troca-de-listas-de-pedidos-reciprocos.
[121] Ministry of Foreign Relations, *Estados Unidos Mexicanos*, www.itamaraty.gov.br/pt-BR/ficha-pais/6453-estados-unidos-mexicanos.

2 Mercosur

The U.S. election and the decision to withdraw from TPP have had repercussions in Latin America as well as Asia. There are three pillars to developments in Mercosur. These are: further integration among the four Mercosur members, creating closer ties between Mercosur and the Pacific Alliance, and trying to jump-start stalled EU–Mercosur negotiations.

When the Presidents of Brazil and Argentina met in February 2017, they pledged to explore ways to deepen integration within Mercosur and explore closer relations with the Pacific Alliance. At the same time, the two countries have explored ways to jump-start negotiations with the EU that have been going on since the 1990s. In 2010, the EU and Mercosur negotiated a broad trade agenda, including trade in industrial and agricultural goods, trade in services, government procurement, intellectual property, trade facilitation and technical barriers to trade.[122] The first exchange of offers between Mercosur and the EU took place in May 2016. Subsequent negotiations have gone very well, despite a missed completion target date of September 2018. While a few issues remain and successful completion of a trade deal faces resistance on both sides,[123] there are real prospects that an agreement will be reached imminently.

---

[122] Council of the European Union, IV EU–Mercosur Summit, 'Joint Communiqué' (May 17, 2010) 9870/10 Presse 129.

[123] Assis Moreira, *UE e Mercosul Impõem Condições para Abrir Mercados*, VALOR ECONÔMICO, Jun. 10, 2016, www.valor.com.br/brasil/4595933/ue-e-mercosul-impoem-condicoes-para-abrir-mercados. *See also* European Comm'n, *Report from the XXIXth Round of Negotiations of the Trade Part of the Association Agreement between European Union and Mercosur*, Brasilia (Oct. 2–6, 2017), http://trade.ec.europa.eu/doclib/docs/2017/october/tradoc_156336.pdf; European Comm'n, *Report from the XXXth Round of Negotiations of the Trade Part of the Association Agreement between the European Union and Mercosur*, Brasilia (Nov. 6–10, 2017), http://trade.ec.europa.eu/doclib/docs/2017/november/tradoc_156408.pdf; European Comm'n, *Report from the XXXIth Round of Negotiations of the Trade Part of the Association Agreement between the European Union and Mercosur*, Brussels (Nov. 29, 2017), http://trade.ec.europa.eu/doclib/docs/2018/january/tradoc_156529.pdf; European Comm'n, *Report from the XXXIIth Round of Negotiations of the Trade Part of the Association Agreement between the European Union and Mercosur*, Asuncion (Feb. 21, 2018), http://trade.ec.europa.eu/doclib/docs/2018/march/tradoc_156641.pdf; European Comm'n, *Report from the XXXIIIth Round of Negotiations of the Trade Part of the Association Agreement between the European Union and Mercosur*, Montevideo (Jun. 4, 2018), http://trade.ec.europa.eu/doclib/docs/2018/june/tradoc_156963.pdf.

C   (Re)-Building an African Integration?

Just as the TPP spurred discussions about alternative economic spaces in Asia, the EU's proposed Economic Partnership Agreements (EPAs) performed a similar function in Africa. The push for further market openings in Africa via EPAs, combined with the rise in price of staple foods in the mid 2000s and the financial crash of 2008, created many incentives for African leaders to question the continued reliance on Europe as a core trade and investment partner. In the process, the EU's attempt to loosely leverage existing African trade groups reignited interest in COMESA and ECOWAS. Indeed, these groupings established several decades ago had been undermined by weak institutions and political upheaval or unrest in many of their member states. SADC had been somewhat more successful in developing trade relations among its members. The African Union had played an increasingly prominent role in peacekeeping operations in the continent, and sought to expand its activities and influence to economic matters. Meanwhile, China's thirst for land and extractive resources, the seemingly more flexible conditions of its development financing, and the willingness of its investors to engage in infrastructure projects created opportunities to expand and diversify Africa's trade patterns both externally and internally.

This section first examines the relationship between the EU's EPAs and Africa's regional groupings, and then turns to current continent-wide integration efforts under the auspices of the African Union. With the value of nonreciprocal preferences steadily eroding over the past decades, the expiration of Cotonou Agreement trade preferences in 2007, the expiration of many of the preferences in the EU's generalized system of preferences (GSP) in 2014, and the *India–GSP* case confirming the unlawfulness of certain conditional preferences, the EU moved to replace its traditional preference programs with EPAs purportedly covered by GATT article XXIV (and GATS article V for agreements including trade in services) on free trade agreements. The EU ultimately seeks to develop regional economic partnership agreements leveraging existing economic integration processes in Africa, including ECOWAS, COMESA, SADC and EAC. However, the strategy largely stalled after "stepping-stone" EPAs and EPAs with individual countries failed to lead to regional agreements encompassing all countries in each grouping.[124]

---

[124] As of 2018, "stepping-stone agreements" have been signed with Côte d'Ivoire (2008) and Ghana (2016). An EPA with ECOWAS was initialed in 2014, but has not been signed; Cameroon is the only signatory of the EU–Central Africa EPA (2009). Mauritius,

As of early 2019, Kenya is the only African state to have ratified an EPA after it lost its preferential access to EU markets in 2014.[125]

While the EU and the World Bank[126] tout EPAs as holding promise for development and sustainability in Africa, criticism has mounted from other quarters, with NGOs, think tanks and policymakers in Africa calling for a halt of the process. While preferential agreements under the aegis of the Enabling Clause aimed to provide access for products from the beneficiary countries to EU markets, EPAs opened African markets to EU goods and services. Parties may negotiate up to 20 percent exclusions, which many African countries have used to keep subsidized EU agricultural commodities competing with their domestic production out of their markets.

Some commentators argue that EPAs also undermine Africa's economic integration efforts, jeopardize African producers' access to other preferential programs such as AGOA, and threaten the development of trade relations with Africa's new economic partners in Asia and the Americas.[127] Indeed, the EU attempted to redraw the map of Africa's

Seychelles, Zimbabwe and Madagascar signed and are provisionally applying (2012) an EPA originally destined to cover all nineteen COMESA members. Alongside, the EU also negotiated an EPA with the East African Community, signed only by Kenya and Rwanda (2016); both countries are also COMESA members. Some members of SADC are included in a SADC EPA (Botswana, Lesotho, Mozambique, Namibia, South Africa and Swaziland, with a future option to join for Angola), while others are involved in the Central Africa EPA and the Eastern and Southern Africa EPA (the Democratic Republic of the Congo, Madagascar, Malawi, Mauritius, Zambia and Zimbabwe). *See generally* European Comm'n, Overview of Economic Partnership Agreements, http://trade.ec .europa.eu/doclib/docs/2009/september/tradoc_144912.pdf.

[125] A series of EU regulations excluded, then reinstated, some beneficiary countries with respect to various preference programs in moves that put pressure on target countries to enter into EPAs. *See, e.g.,* Comm'n Regulation No 978/2012, 2012 O.J. (L 303/1) (EU) and repealing Council Regulation (EC) No 732/2008, OJEU L 303/1 (Oct. 31, 2012); Commission Regulation No 1421/2013, 2013 O.J. (L 355/1) (EU) amending Annexes I, II and IV to Regulation (EU) No 978/2012 of the European Parliament and of the Council applying a scheme of generalized tariff preference, OJEU L 355/1 (Dec. 31, 2013); Commission Regulation (EU) No 1016/2014, 2014 O.J. (L 283/23) (EU) amending Annexes II to Regulation (EU) No 978/2012 of the European Parliament and of the Council applying a scheme of generalized tariff preferences, OJEU L 283/23 (Sept. 27, 2014); Commission Regulation (EU) 2015/1979, 1979 O.J. (L 289/3) (EU) amending Annexes II, III and IV to Regulation (EU) No 978/2012 of the European Parliament and of the Council applying a scheme of generalized tariff preferences, OJEU l 289/3 (Nov. 5, 2015). Additional rules cover the qualification of particular products for preferential EU access.

[126] WORLD BANK, AFRICA: ECONOMIC PARTNERSHIP AGREEMENTS BETWEEN AFRICA AND THE EUROPEAN UNION, WHAT TO DO NOW? SUMMARY REPORT (2008).

[127] Stephen McDonald, Stephen Lande & Dennis Matanda, *Why Economic Partnership Agreements Undermine Africa's Regional Integration*, www.wilsoncenter.org/sites/

regional groupings by reallocating countries between different negotiating groups. Economic projections as to the respective benefits of EPAs with the EU and increased integration within African trading groups, such as the common external tariff approved by ECOWAS in 2013, suggest marginal and uncertain benefits.[128] South Africa Minister of Trade Dr. Rob Davies warned against engaging in EPAs in a manner that jeopardizes intra-African trade integration:

> Our overriding concern remains that conclusion of the separate EPAs among different groupings of countries in Africa that do not correspond to existing regional arrangements will undermine Africa's wider integration efforts. If left unaddressed, such an outcome will haunt Africa's integration project for years to come.
>
> Different groups of countries in Africa are negotiating separate EPAs with different tariff phase down commitments, both in terms of products and time frames, different exclusions lists, different rules of origin, and all this will complicate intra-regional trade as new controls will be required at our borders. Different legal provisions (such as, for example, the MFN clause or export taxes) in the different EPAs will also complicate processes to forge common policy positions in the unfolding integration agenda in Africa.[129]

In 2010, the African Union began planning a comprehensive approach to development for the continent, which became official in 2011 with the launch of the African Platform for Development Effectiveness (APDev). This initiative involves fifty member states and international organizations including the African Union, COMESA, SADC, ECOWAS, the Arab Maghreb Union, the Economic Community of Central African States, the East African Community (EAC) and the Community of Sahel–Saharan States. In addition, APDev partners range from NGOs, civil society networks and foundations, and the private sector, to the

---

default/files/EPA%20Article.pdf (May 3, 2013); Aniekan Iboro Ukpe, *Will EPAs Foster the Integration of Africa into World Trade?* 54 J. AFR. L. 212 (2010); F. A. Ismail, *Advancing Regional Integration in Africa through the Continental Free Trade Area (CFTA)*, 10 LAW & DEV. REV. 119 (2017).

[128] *See, e.g.*, Jean-Michel Marchat & Erik von Uexkull, *Republic of Senegal: An Assessment of the Short Term Impact of the ECOWAS–CET and EU–EPA in Senegal*, WORLD BANK REPORT No. ACS18578 (Oct. 27, 2016), http://documents.worldbank.org/curated/en/209801480496403751/pdf/ACS18578-WP-OUO-9-Senegal-EPA-and-CET-Analysis-has-been-approved-P151885.pdf; Antoine Coste & Erik von Uexkull, *Benefits of the ECOWAS CET and EPA Will Outweigh Costs in Nigeria, but Competitiveness Is the Real Issue*, WORLD BANK AFRICA TRADE POLICY NOTES No. 43 (Jan. 2015).

[129] Rob Davies, *The SADC EPA and Beyond, in Economic Partnership Agreements and Beyond*, 3 GREAT INSIGHTS NO. 9 (Oct./Nov. 2014) 10–11 at 11.

African Development Bank, development agencies in Europe, the World Bank and the UNDP.[130] The New Partnership for Africa's Development (NEPAD) acts as a coordinating and implementation-planning agency to turn the African Union's Agenda 2063 into reality.

On a closer horizon, members of the African Union launched a plan for an African Continental Free Trade Area (AfCFTA). Negotiations to create a single market for goods and services, with free movement of "business persons and investments," were launched in 2015[131] and the final text was adopted in March 2018.[132] The objectives are to liberalize, harmonize and coordinate trade policies across the fifty-four member states representing a population of more than one billion (U.S. billion) and a GDP of over USD 3.4 trillion. Ultimately, the AfCFTA is meant to replace the network of smaller regional RTAs, and to provide a stepping-stone for a customs union encompassing all members. Alongside such negotiations, member states adopted in 2012 an Action Plan on Boosting Intra-Africa Trade along seven axes: trade policy, trade facilitation, productive capacity, trade-related infrastructure, trade finance, trade information and factor market integration. This initiative aims to double intra-African trade by 2022.

Pan-African economic integration efforts are proliferating at many different levels, making it difficult to estimate whether the African Union and its member states will have the political strength and governance capacity to achieve such multifaceted policies. That said, common threads across initiatives suggest that a consensus does exist on the purposes of trade integration efforts: industrial and infrastructure development are consistently framed as core building blocks of developmental policy; trade liberalization is directly linked to enabling economies of scale and creating competitive, higher value-added chains of production; economic integration is a tool to achieve durable socioeconomic development.

Inasmuch as EU and U.S. policies such as the EPAs and the AGOA are mostly focused on market access, they fall well short of the developmental

---

[130] Africa Platform for Development Effectiveness, www.africa-platform.org/partners.
[131] Launch of the Continental Free Trade Area Negotiations (Assembly/AU/Dec.569 (XXV)) AUDECISIONS 9 (Africa Union), www.saflii.org/au/AUDECISIONS/2015/9 .html.
[132] Agreement Establishing the African Continental Free Trade Area, Kigali Draft Text, Mar. 2018, www.tralac.org/documents/resources/african-union/1870-agreement-estab lishing-the-afcfta-kigali-draft-text-march-2018-1/file.html.

objectives of African trade policy. By contrast, China's engagement with infrastructure projects such as building roads, bridges, seaports and railways to facilitate transit of goods within the continent and toward export transit points is better aligned with priorities expressed by the African Union. All three powerful trade partners (EU, United States, China), however, are primarily interested in selling their manufactured products in Africa and gaining access to its natural resources. In this context, Africa's industrialization will remain a matter for domestic leaders to achieve while resisting the sirens of short-term rent-seeking from exports of mineral resources and other raw commodities.

V Conclusion

International trade law is evolving in a multitude of directions at present. The relative political and economic retrenchment of old industrial powers in the aftermath of the 2008 crisis, combined with the emergence of investment flows from the South to the North, created a space for emerging powers to change trend patterns on the ground. The convergence – or perhaps conflagration – of trade and investment law offers an opportunity to revisit assumptions underlying dominant trade liberalization pathways. While it is too speculative to muse about leadership and new hegemons for the twenty-first century, we may more modestly argue that some aspects of trade regulation are sufficiently in flux that they are ripe for a policy takeover. Secondarily, we might attempt to discern what forms such policy shifts might take, and which countries, if any, might have the clout to effectuate them.

Identifying certain disciplines as regime-altering provisions assumes that developing countries would be forced into a rule-taker position or be left out of new agreements. However, with the U.S. withdrawal from the TPP, and the TTIP and Doha Round faltering, we may in fact be witnessing a retrenchment from these disciplines. Regime-altering constraints then could be simply sidestepped by emerging countries for which they are not acceptable, particularly in the absence of a strong pressure from established powers. With China resisting limits on SOEs, virtually all developing countries engaging in a new wave of industrial policy programs, and Brazil, South Africa and India vocally asserting their policy preferences regarding intellectual property, the ever-expanding trade negotiation agenda on these matters may well shrink back for the coming years. Perhaps most importantly, the WTO's momentum toward mainstreaming members' political economy models into a narrow band of tolerance has reached a halt. Does this mean that the hope among U.S. and European political elites that China (and others who bend or break the rules) should and can be brought into the fold increasingly is a rearguard action, because global economic trends and China's rising diplomatic power militate the dawn of a new era of institutional pluralism in trade law? Or will the Trump administration's trade war against China succeed, thus breathing new life into the effort to force convergence and unrestricted openness on emerging economies?

While no emerging country has threatened to withdraw from the WTO, they may well be successful in ensuring that those trade disciplines are a ceiling, rather than a floor, thereby rolling back the trend of WTO+ commitments in future PTAs. New trade and investment agreements will supplant some existing PTAs, creating opportunities for renegotiation. Moreover, PTAs typically include softer dispute settlement processes than the WTO, and even then, such mechanisms have not been used thus far. Hence, breaches of WTO+ obligations are not challenged in practice. Whether this trend is a lasting one, or a by-product of the informal standstill agreement not to challenge the range of protectionist measures enacted in many countries after the 2008 crisis, remains to be seen. If the relative decrease in the number of new disputes filed at the WTO is any indication, we may be witnessing a relaxing of compliance and enforcement that is a soft way to abate the impact of WTO and WTO+ disciplines, particularly against the backdrop of stalled multilateral negotiations. Inasmuch as the United States and the EU are not at present leading participants in the making of multilateral trade law, and interests align between emerging powers and developed economies such as Australia, there may be an opportunity for the consensus to shift away from TPP-type disciplines, or to develop and interpret standards in a way that is more congruent with state developmental objectives. However, unilateral rulemaking by the United States threatens such an effort.

Problem-creating disciplines create space for regulatory diversification as emerging countries undertake to define the rules of the game in PTAs where they have a dominant voice. The RCEP, ASEAN partner agreements, pan-African initiatives, and Brazilian negotiations with Mexico and others will likely spur diverse approaches to trade regulation that put development at the core of the agreement, with commitments framed in relation to this objective. For instance, a number of South–South RTAs devote significant attention to infrastructure development among the parties, particularly with respect to transportation and energy.

Additionally, in domains where international trade rules are budding, emerging powers have the opportunity to become rule-makers. Whether they will succeed in setting global standards, however, is an open question. The digital economy is a case in point. Given the weakness of commitments on e-commerce in trade agreements, and the vested interest in emerging countries that have a vast market and the technological capacity, there may be an opportunity for the latter to be the first movers in terms of rulemaking. Unlike in the domain of intellectual property, though, Brazil, China and India have vastly different objectives and methods regarding digital regulation. India, South Africa and Brazil aim for openness and accessibility as the means to empower their populations to participate more effectively in the local and global economy, as well as the political and social life of the country. China, by contrast, wishes to continue to control access and exchange of digital information and products by its people in an extension of brick-and-mortar censorship. Perspectives on privacy and personal data protection also vary greatly among these countries. While there are areas of relative regulatory vacuum where emerging powers could take the lead, divergences in policy objectives may come in the way of building a strong international consensus.

Competing interests between emerging powers further contribute to a situation fraught with uncertainties. Brazil is seeking to enhance its relations with the Pacific Alliance in order to protect its markets in those countries from Asian competition. As it does this, it is encountering pressure from the other side to adhere to some TPP type of provisions that these countries have incorporated in their trade law framework. India is wary of Chinese geopolitical influence regionally. It shares with China a desire to move its economy toward ever higher value-added production and exports. In the meantime, it largely failed to stem the flood of cheap Chinese imports that threatens its industry. Despite China being Brazil's most important trading partner, and the increase of Chinese investments in Brazil in 2017–18, a trade agreement with China remains unlikely. China has never pushed for that, and Brazilian industry will continue to pressure its government to reject negotiating trade agreements with China for fear of increased competition.

6

Emerging Economies and the Future of the Global Trade and Investment Regime

Il n'y aura pas de grand soir.

After the fall of the Soviet Union and the opening of China, a new world economic order emerged. It was built on four pillars: the WTO, a network of bilateral investment treaties, policies of the international financial institutions, and regional and bilateral free trade agreements (FTAs). This order stressed the importance of free markets and open economies, and imposed restrictions on many forms of state intervention in the economy. It facilitated the growth of global trade and enabled an increasing flow of capital across borders.

Emerging economies chafed at some of the limitations imposed by this regime. But, on aggregate, they benefited from it. The BRICS and other countries developed new export sectors fueled in part by FDI, and expanded their exports to developed and developing markets. This in turn gave a stimulus to domestic markets, which grew rapidly. As they became industrial powerhouses, leading emerging economies began to catch up with the older industrialized nations. As they grew, their share of the world economy increased to the point where it now constitutes almost 60 percent of world GDP. While millions were lifted out of poverty, not all benefited from this economic transformation within emerging countries. The increased economic wealth also did not necessarily accrue to all developing countries, nor did it necessarily translate into equitable redistribution policies, or into social, health, educational and other empowerment opportunities for the segments of the population that were vulnerable or that did not benefit directly from economic gains.

Although many countries benefited from the new environment, China stands out. Enjoying growth rates without precedent in world history, in a short time China has created the largest economy in the world (when

187

adjusting for purchasing power parity)[1] or second-largest economy at official exchange rates. It has eclipsed the other BRICS: the IMF estimated that in 2018 Chinese GDP would be larger than that of the other four BRICS combined.[2] As a result it emerged as a unique challenger to U.S. economic dominance, and the influence on global governance that came with it.

International economic law has played a crucial role in this development. The order has frequently been described as "rule-based." Various bodies of legal rules have cemented this new, relatively open capitalist economic order. The rules of the WTO helped developing countries open their economies, and facilitated access to developed country markets. BITs added some security for FDI, although it is hard to find conclusive evidence that it had a causal effect on capital flows. These legal regimes were buttressed by FTAs.

As this book has shown, there are many indications that this world order is undergoing a fundamental transformation both in terms of who the influential players are and the governance norms and structure they seek to pursue. By way of conclusion, this chapter first summarizes these transformations (Section I) and offers a mapping of their current repercussions in international economic relations (Section II). This chapter then argues that overcoming the current disintegration of international economic relations would require a pluralist world order. Sections III and IV outline the normative parameters of what such an order could comprise.

I   Emerging Powers Pushing the Boundaries of IEL

The resulting order has brought benefits to emerging economies, but also imposed restrictions, as the effort to use law to create an open global free market economy clashed with domestic developmental strategies and political economy preferences. This volume has shown how emerging economies have used international economic law to take advantage of the benefits while trying to limit the effect of the restrictions. Emerging countries built the legal capacity needed to deal with the rule-based

---

[1] World Bank, International Comparison Program database, https://data.worldbank.org /indicator/ny.gdp.mktp.pp.cd?end=2017&start=1990&view=chart. In 2017, China's GDP in PPP was USD 23,300,782 million while the U.S. GDP amounted to USD 19,390,604 million.

[2] International Monetary Fund, *GDP Based on PPP* (Apr. 2018 Economic Outlook), www .imf.org/external/datamapper/PPPSH@WEO/OEMDC/ADVEC/WEOWORLD.

order and won many victories in the WTO. They found ways around some of the more onerous restrictions and blocked efforts to impose new ones. Particularly noteworthy are victories in dispute settlement, the use of flexibilities such as trade remedies, and the successful resistance against the expansion of free trade disciplines.

At the WTO, emerging countries have prevailed in a number of disputes against developed members whose policies restricted their access to markets. Developing members also successfully challenged each other's trade restrictions. They have maintained industrial policies in the face of neoliberal restrictions. Sometimes they have used exceptions and flexibilities to continue heterodox policies. Even when such measures have been successfully challenged in the WTO and countries have been required to end them, they have been able to maintain the policies for some time because the dispute process allows developing countries to temporarily adopt policies that contravene the rules. The system, in practice, allows members to breach obligations for some time until the complainants can retaliate. By then, the objectionable program may have served its useful life. Developing countries also have been able to mount an effective resistance to the expansion of the trade liberalization agenda at the WTO. From the rollback on the so-called Singapore issues, to the reckoning at the Seattle Ministerial Meeting, and the Doha Work Programme, emerging countries have asserted their voices to exclude from the negotiations or circumscribe items they disfavor, and include topics of interest to them.

Meanwhile, emerging powers have also sought alternative trade arrangements outside of the multilateral system, and outside of FTAs led by the old powers. The Asia–Pacific region is the most prominent example, with several vast regional agreements in force (CPTPP) or in the making (RCEP, BRI). Africa is also pursuing ambitious initiatives for improved regional integration, whether by sector (mining, transportation) or for trade and investment generally. While some of the regulatory principles are the same as in traditional trade and investment agreements, the topical coverage of these new schemes is more in line with emerging country priorities and capacities.

Similar changes impend in the investment regime. While emerging economies have resisted aspects of the global investment protection system, most have accepted many of its values, and some continue to sign investment agreements albeit with fewer protections for investors. Some countries, particularly South Africa, Indonesia, and India, have pushed back against traditional BITs; Brazil pursued a different approach altogether. States opposing the system, most notably Brazil, were able to refrain from entering into BITs while continuing to access global capital markets for investment. Even countries such as India, South Africa, Indonesia and Ecuador, which more recently retrenched from their participation in BITs, do not appear to have suffered significant capital outflow in response.

The embedded neoliberal "order," if we want to call it such, also facilitated an era of remarkable growth in the world economy and ushered in an unprecedented level of economic interdependence. It enabled the rise of global value chains (GVCs), thereby changing the nature of trade. While the traditional exchanges of raw materials and finished products continued, more and more products were created and assembled in several countries, tying economies ever more closely together. Emerging economies gained from being embedded in these GVCs and were major beneficiaries of the new interdependence.

For a while, these compromises and strategies in the conflict between neoliberal policies and developing country resistance resulted in something of an equilibrium. Maintained by the international trade and investment law system, the system offered benefits to developing countries, although the rules still tilted toward the interests of advanced economies; even when developing countries secured hard-won concessions, they sometimes turned out to be pyrrhic victories. While the system seemed to be working at least temporarily, it was, in many ways, an agreement to disagree based in part on de jure and de facto derogations, strategic noncompliance and effective resistance to new rules. The post-2008 period, however, threw this uneasy truce into crisis.

II   The Crisis of the World Order and the Fate of Embedded Liberalism

The fragile equilibrium is now in danger of unraveling. Four developments have challenged the status quo. First are the economic problems experienced by advanced economies after 2008. A decade later, the adverse effects of that crisis are still being felt. In most developed countries, wages have continued to stagnate, jobs became more precarious, income disparities grew more aggravated, and recovery was slow. This has led to a second development: the rise of populism and the scapegoating of trade. Populists have pointed to trade as a major cause of the changes that have led to popular dissatisfaction. While the real causes of distress are more complex, trade has played a role, and this scapegoating has fueled desires for protectionism. Third is the ascendance of China and the consolidation of its state capitalist development strategy. With China in the process of overtaking the United States as the world's largest economy, it is harder to see it as a "developing" country deserving of special treatment. And as the current Chinese administration has doubled down on state capitalism as a development strategy, it is equally hard to think it will gradually evolve into a "normal" market economy. Finally, the role of the United States has changed radically. Once the guarantor of the rules-based global order, the United States now has appeared to reject the rule-based system, withdrawing from some treaties, threatening to cancel others, and announcing unilateral moves that are in direct violation of WTO law. While the United States has threatened many countries with tariffs and other restrictions, it has launched an all-out trade war with China.

What does all this mean for world order, and for the role of emerging economies? Will international economic law become more fragmented, and its capacity to knit together different economies weakened? Will the wave of pressures for de-globalization undermine the economic interdependence emerging economies have benefitted from? The answers lie in the way the world responds to the crisis of this world order.[3]

A The End of U.S. Hegemony

The 2008 financial crisis spurred protectionist reactions from most regions, but has not radically turned the tide of economic interdependence. Much to the contrary, global economic integration continued apace after 2008. The international institutional and regulatory framework, however, is very much in turmoil. This could bring about the end of the truce and lead to economic disintegration. Is there some way to avoid massive de-globalization? While some may yearn for the restoration of U.S. hegemony, or seek another hegemon, we do not see either outcome as likely for the near future. Rather than being a transitory phase toward a new hegemonic system, we think we are witnessing the emergence of an era of pluralism in the face of economic interdependency.

While the United States (in tandem with Western Europe) largely played the role of a normative hegemon for international economic law

---

[3] See also Gideon Rose, The Fourth Founding – The United States and the Liberal Order, 98 FOREIGN AFF. 1 (2019); David Singh Grewal, Three Theses on the Current Crisis of International Liberalism, 25 IND. J. GLOBAL LEGAL STUD. 595 (2018).

after the end of the Cold War, it seems no longer able or willing to occupy that space. Yet there is no other actor or series of actors in a position to pick up the baton. China seeks regional influence, but lacks the experience, deep capital markets, soft power, and legitimacy needed. Perhaps most importantly, China appears to expand its influence through instruments other than formal international law. The Belt and Road Initiative is a paramount example in that respect. It is a set of domestic policies and economic instruments, supported by domestic Chinese institutions and law, but devoid of multilateral or bilateral agreements with target countries. The EU has a number of assets, but is internally divided and in a very fragile state right now. To be sure, private actors continue to expand their roles as rule-makers, but their ability to establish and enforce global rules remains dependent on states and the international machinery they agree on, such as investor–state investment arbitration.

Systems that facilitated interdependence up to now have relied on a hegemon, whether it was the United Kingdom in the gold standard era or the United States since Bretton Woods. But is there a way to maintain interdependence without a hegemon? Conceptually, there are three alternatives to a global economy guided by a hegemon: autarky, anarchy and pluralism. We look briefly at the first two in order to set the stage for the analysis of the third.

B   Autarky as an Alternative to Hegemonic International Economic Governance

By "autarky," we mean a global governance system that allows and facilitates the withdrawal of some or all parts of an economy from the flux of global economic interdependence. Political economy models of import substitution and infant industry protection were a form of autarky, at least in their initial phase. Latin America and India experimented with both, and global institutions tolerated these moves. Sectoral self-sufficiency policies are also autarkic in this sense and have been a feature of most economies during most of the twentieth century.[4] Agricultural policies driven by food security concerns in India and elsewhere are equally meant to insulate countries from changes in conditions on the world markets.

---

[4] France's nuclear energy policy since the 1960s was very much driven by a desire for autonomy; U.S. energy policy in response to the 1970s oil shocks and in the early twenty-first century, with the exploitation of shale gas, tar sand, and offshore oil drilling in the Gulf of Mexico, strived for energy autonomy.

For those countries that were unable to achieve autonomy through autarky in at least some of their economic sectors, attempts to control interdependence took the form of commodity agreements. Most aimed to create economic stability and control for developing countries reliant on undiversified exports of raw commodities. While dependence on exports seems inconsistent with the notion of autarky strictly defined, commodity agreements may be understood as a second-best order of preference where strict autarky is not possible. States participating in the commodity price control scheme are collectivizing their autonomy in order to counter or even control external economic fluctuations. Commodity agreements typically include a reserve fund mechanism to further support participating members' ability to control their economic fate, thanks to the collective management of their main exports.

Import substitution strategies, commodity agreements, and sectoral self-sufficiency all have a poor track record of achieving their proponents' goal of growth with autonomy. Import substitution has given way to targeted industrial policy programs that often promote sectors aiming at global competitiveness; even OPEC, the most successful commodity control scheme, is challenged by hydrocarbon producers that are not members; sectoral self-sufficiency has been replaced by sectoral security through diversification of sources. Autarky from world markets and international economic flows, no matter what form it took, appears largely to be a failed experiment.

While many of the autarkic policies of the post-World War II era originated in the developing world, one could view elements of the Trump trade agenda as autarkic. What else to call the dubious claim that national security demands high tariffs on imported automobiles because a large auto industry is essential to national defense? Nonetheless, we think it unlikely that major moves of an autarkic nature will ensue. Given the failed experiences of import substitution policies and commodity agreements, coupled with the high degree of economic interdependence today, it is improbable that real efforts of this nature will take hold in the near future.

C Anarchy as an Alternative to Hegemonic International Economic Governance

Another form of world order radically different than hegemony is the choice not to engage in multilateral regulation, and leave individual countries free to manage their economic and social needs with limited external legal constraints. In this model, which we label "anarchy," domestic regulation and private corporate economic calculus provide the constraints.

The question is: What effect would such an approach have on economic interdependence? In theory, it should be possible to maintain current levels of interdependence without resorting to an international regime led by a hegemon. Countries could see the benefits of an open economy and steer away from protectionism and "beggar-thy-neighbor" policies. But history suggests it is unlikely, at least for trade.

To some extent, the unchecked colonial conquest and exploitation, and events like the Opium Wars of the 1800s, reflected an era of anarchism in international economic relations. Today, some may argue that, inasmuch as the multilateral regime has proved oppressive and limiting to developing countries' policy choices, a less integrated model may not be so bad. But the curtailment of multilateral institutional power does not necessarily mean that small developing countries would gain more autonomy. In particular, how much autonomy a small country will truly have may be limited by its place in global trade flows and the influence of multinational corporations.

The interwar period of the 1920s and 1930s also may be characterized as anarchic. In that period the gold standard had collapsed. With no global regulation, states pursued unilateralist trade policies characterized by high tariffs and beggar-thy-neighbor strategies. The League of Nations encouraged open and just economic relations between nations, but never created an institutional framework to support interdependence. It called on countries to enter into agreements for freedom of communications and commerce, but few did.[5] The result was a series of trade policies that aggravated the effects of the Depression and helped push Germany and Japan toward war. The experience of the 1930s serves as a reminder of the

---

[5] The Covenant of the League of Nations made a vague reference to international economic relations in its preamble to "promote international co-operation ... by the prescription of open, just and honourable relations between nations." Article 23 calls upon members to "endeavour to secure and maintain fair and humane conditions of labour for men, women, and children, both in their own countries and in all countries to which their commercial and industrial relations extend, and for that purpose will establish and maintain the necessary international organisations," but no such organization existed. It also provides that members "will make provision to secure and maintain freedom of communications and of transit and equitable treatment for the commerce of all Members of the League." Treaties of Friendship, Commerce and Navigation concluded by the United States since its independence and by a few other states (including Germany) in the 1920s and 1930s are the main achievements of this entreaty.

perils of "anarchy," and there is little formal support for moves of this kind today. Yet, threats from the United States to withdraw from the WTO, and flaunting of the rules by major players (particularly the United States and China), all edge toward this model of anarchy, de jure or de facto.

While there is a need for international-level governance to avoid trade wars and beggar-thy-neighbor policies, is the same true for flows of international investment? A case can be made that investment differs from trade, and might not suffer as much from a lack of international-level governance. For example, proponents of global regulation of investment warn of a race to the bottom as states compete for investment by lowering standards for labor, health, education and the environment, and suggest that global regulation is needed to head off such efforts. However, there is evidence that suggests global regulation may not be necessary in this situation. Thus, Brazil is not a party to any investment treaty and has attracted substantial foreign capital without employing deregulation or lowering of standards, and South Africa, which has recently been moving away from BITs, does not appear to be "compensating" an assumed lost advantage by engaging in a regulatory race to the bottom. The desire to maintain access to global financial markets may deter the kind of behavior BITs were meant to protect against.

States may not need international regulation to avoid a race to the bottom in the investment regulatory realm. But can international regulation itself lead to lower standards as investors demand protection from regulation? That is the argument of those who oppose BITs. While there isn't much evidence that BITs have led to the dismantling of existing systems of social protection, there is legitimate concern about regulatory chill, where states refrain from engaging in legitimate regulation because an agreement is in place that might be interpreted to prevent the enactment of the contemplated regulation.[6] Chapter 3 offered many illustrations for the regulatory chill phenomenon.

If international regulation may not be needed to halt a race to the bottom, and existing international agreements may deter needed social and environmental protection measures, then perhaps leaving the regulation of investment to the domestic law of the host country may not be

---

[6] Creeping or unforeseen encroachments on domestic regulatory autonomy are very much a part of the contemporary debate about investment agreements, and are deeply concerning, though empirical studies on the exact scope and nature of race to the bottom or regulatory chill are still limited. *See, e.g.,* JONATHAN BONNITCHA ET AL., THE POLITICAL ECONOMY OF THE INVESTMENT TREATY REGIME 238–44 (2017).

such a bad idea. Developments discussed in Chapters 3 and 4 suggest that the case for international governance of investment law is much weaker than it might be in trade law. Brazil, Indonesia, South Africa, Ecuador, and to a lesser extent India, are engaged in a range of reforms that squarely question whether supranational ordering is necessary or desirable when it comes to foreign investment. The fact that neither Brazil nor South Africa have witnessed a flight of investment in the wake of their lack of participation or withdrawal, respectively, from international processes, suggests that investors are likewise undaunted by the prospect of operating in a regulatory framework that is domestic rather than international.

China's model of outward investment and foreign aid may, however, offer a cautionary tale illustrating the risks of anarchy in the investment field. Although China has signed a number of bilateral investment treaties with countries where it is engaging in outward FDI, it relies on processes outside of these traditional frameworks for the protection and promotion of its investments. The Chinese state's participation in outward investment ventures gives a political flavor and a unique type of government backing to investors that largely outstrip any benefits that could accrue from the treaties. The many conditions imposed on recipient countries, such as the use of Chinese materials and labor in the building of infrastructure projects, are contractually agreed with each investment deal outside of any international framework. Similarly, loans from China are also heavily conditioned, entirely separately from any multilateral framework or guidelines developed by the World Bank, the IMF or international investment law. Such conditions, when they involve the use of Chinese inputs, significantly decrease the benefits of foreign investment for the local economy. Increasingly, reports of Chinese firms disregarding local labor and environmental law has led to social protests from local workers and communities. When investment conditions involve the use of host state assets as collateral in case of default on loans, they can result in significant strategic losses for the host country, as Sri Lanka recently discovered when it lost control of a port to China for ninety-nine years.[7]

While, as we argued, pulling back from the existing international investment framework may not have the deleterious economic, social, environmental and developmental consequences that are often suggested, the real threats may lie elsewhere. In the new forms of investment

---

[7] Maria Abi-Habib, *How China Got Sri Lanka to Cough Up a Port*, N.Y. Times, Jun. 25, 2018, www.nytimes.com/2018/06/25/world/asia/china-sri-lanka-port.html; Kai Schultz, *Sri Lanka, Struggling with Debt, Hands a Major Port to China*, N.Y. Times, Dec. 12, 2017, www.nytimes.com/2017/12/12/world/asia/sri-lanka-china-port.html.

and foreign aid deployed by China, the existing international law frameworks appear to be of little import, and indeed, it is unclear whether they
would be fully suited to mitigating the new risks that are emerging.

Moreover, in an anarchic international investment world, the regulatory autonomy of host countries will be pitted against the power of
international financial flows, which remains in the hands of private actors
and is largely unchecked and uncontrolled. The experience of the 2008
financial collapse would be magnified as international financial flows
continue to grow in a world largely devoid of an effective governance
system to manage them. This in turn creates different kinds of social,
economic and political vulnerabilities domestically.

III Pluralism as the New Normal

If hegemony right now is elusive and anarchy and autarky are unattrac-
tive, is there an alternative governance regime for trade and investment
that can preserve interdependence while better meeting the needs of
emerging economies? That is the challenge facing international economic law today. This section offers the paradigm of pluralism as
a foundational principle for a future world order.

A regime that reflects global economic integration but seeks to better serve
its most disempowered constituents should maintain some basic rules for
global trade while allowing greater flexibility for emerging economies to
follow development strategies of their choice. Such a regime would be
"pluralist" in several senses. First, it would be normatively pluralist, understood as lacking a single normative order governing international economic
relations. At every level of effective regulation, it would be sensitive to
different normative and strategic views, and it would not seek to impose
a "one size fits all" approach to economic ordering, nor enshrine
a mainstream, orthodox approach to economic relations. Second, it would
be institutionally pluralist, looking to regional groupings and plurilateral
agreements among consenting states to bear more of the burden of transnational regulation while also making room for private ordering. Thirdly, it
would be pluralist in the sense used by Francis Snyder to refer to a situation
where there are overlapping layers of governance, and mechanisms must
exist to avoid conflicts among these levels.[8]

---

[8] Francis Snyder, The EU, the WTO and China: Legal Pluralism and
International Trade Regulation (2010).

There are various indications that point toward the emergence of such a regime. The first is the exploitation of de jure and de facto flexibilities in the neoliberal order described in Section I of this chapter. This can be seen as de facto implementation of pluralism. The second is the spread of multiregional agreements, including CPTTP and RCEP, as well as less consolidated regional groups such as those developing in Latin America and Africa. Third are the plurilateral agreements that have been negotiated under the auspices of the WTO, such as the Trade Facilitation Agreement (now in force) and the Environmental Goods Agreement, or on its sidelines, such as the proposed Trade in Services Agreement.

How might these developments be built upon for a new regime to emerge? First, a new regime must meet the core needs of the emerging economies for access and flexibility. It is important to maintain access to the developed markets that have helped spur export-led growth. And, they want freedom of policy choice. They want room to experiment with development policies, and they need to be able to craft policies that will prove acceptable to their populations. They will seek a regime that guarantees both access and flexibility. Second, the regime must offer developed countries reasonable access to emerging markets and protect them against destabilizing trade shocks. That means that emerging economies will have to accept some restrictions on their ability to protect domestic industry, while developed countries must be able to limit trade shocks and provide support for those displaced.

Taking into account current trends in international economic relations, together with the range of innovations and repositioning we have explored throughout this book, we see two paradigms for pluralism, which are not mutually exclusive, and in practice are likely to coexist. First, a comprehensive "regional" type of pluralism offers a clublike economic integration model where parties subscribe to broad-ranging and deep trade and investment disciplines, but the structure has no universal membership aspiration. The RCEP and CPTPP illustrate this approach. Second, a topical pluralism comprises agreements on specific issues or areas of economic relations, where the integration ambition is shallow, in that the subject matter of the agreement is defined narrowly and specifically, but the membership aspires to be as open and numerous as possible. Plurilateral agreements within the WTO and instruments such as TiSA illustrate this approach. This section explores the nature, features and implications of each of these two paradigms for international economic relations, with particular reference to emerging economies.

A "Regional" Pluralism

This model of economic relations aims to regulate deeply on a range of subject matters, but eschews any aspiration to universal membership. In fact, it is understood that members may participate in a variety of trade or investment agreements outside of the group. There is no exclusive dispute settlement mechanism. Such groupings reflect the traditionally horizontal and decentralized nature of public international law. In that respect, they contrast with the WTO, which posits itself as a "first amongst others" forum requiring any outside commitments by its members to be "WTO-compatible," that is, subordinated to WTO rules and standards. Whether particular regional groupings become preferred negotiation forums may be determined by politics, but is not built into the system as a legal objective or feature.

1 Normative Nature

As Andrew Lang has pointed out, much of international economic law takes as its standard a particular model of a market economy, and its rules are designed to ensure that such a model will eventually prevail everywhere. State intervention is circumscribed in the name of providing a "level playing field" for private economic actors. This approach has been rejected by many emerging economies: they wish to preserve policy space to experiment with different economic strategies and avoid being pushed into policies that could cause domestic unrest. Our study has shown the many points at which market-oriented rules in international economic law clash with those wishes. Achieving full normative pluralism would involve a willingness to accept different forms of economic ordering rather than use international economic law as a straightjacket. The "embedded neoliberalism truce" can be seen as de facto recognition of such pluralism. But emerging economies not only want to preserve that situation. Ideally, many would like to transform it into new de jure rules that were more accepting of different forms of economic organization.

"Regional" pluralism offers opportunities for different groups to enshrine different understandings of economic governance and developmental concerns. Existing regional trade agreements already offer a range of approaches to the trade and development nexus. For instance, self-reliance is at the core of several African trade groups, particularly when dealing with industrial policy provisions.[9] African trade pacts also often

---

[9] See, e.g., art. 99(a) Treaty Establishing the Common Market for Eastern and Southern Africa (COMESA) (Kampala, Nov. 5, 1993; 2314 UNTS 265) (objectives of cooperation in

emphasize equitable development – the notion that economic benefits
expected from liberalization require a distributional policy, as between
the members of the groups, but also among domestic constituencies,
which entails establishing or improving domestic governance.[10]
Agreements involving ASEAN members and some Caribbean trade
agreements are mindful of intragroup economic disparities and the
need for asymmetric commitments to address developmental and economic gaps between members.[11]

industrial development include the promotion of "self-sustained and balanced growth");
art. 79 Treaty for the Establishment of the East African Community (EAC Treaty)
(Arusha, Nov. 30, 1999; 2144 UNTS 255) (members shall take steps in industrial development to "promote self-sustaining and balanced growth"); art. 26.2(a) Treaty of the
Economic Community of West African States (ECOWAS) (Cotonou, Jul. 24, 1993; 2373
UNTS 233) (to promote industrial developments, members shall "foster self-sustained
and self-reliant development"); art. 5.1(d) Treaty of the Southern African Development
Community, as Amended (SADC) (Windhoek, Aug. 17, 1992; 32 ILM 116) (objectives
include promoting "self-sustaining development on the basis of collective self-reliance,
and the interdependence of Member States"); Preamble, Charter of the South Asian
Association for Regional Cooperation (SAARC Charter) (Dhaka, Dec. 8, 1985) (noting
that cooperation "would contribute significantly to national and collective self-reliance").

[10] Art. 6(d) COMESA; art. 5.2 EAC (objectives include "accelerated, harmonious and
balanced development and sustained expansion of economic activities, the benefit of
which shall be equitably shared"); art. 7.1(f) EAC (principles include the "equitable
distribution of benefits" of operation); Preamble, ECOWAS ("Accepting the need to
share the benefits of economic cooperation and integration among Member States in
a just and equitable manner . . . "); art. 2(b) SACU (objectives include creating "effective,
transparent and democratic institutions which will ensure equitable trade benefits to
Member States"); art. 2(g) SACU (objectives include facilitating "the equitable sharing of
revenue arising from customs, excise and additional duties levied by Member States");
Preamble, Cartagena Agreement (community will "lead to the balanced, harmonious, and
shared economic development of their countries"); art. 1 Cartagena Agreement (objectives are to "promote the balanced and harmonious development of the Member
Countries under equitable conditions"); art. 60(f) Cartagena Agreement (objectives of
industrial development include "equitable distribution of benefits"); art. 3.1(b) SAARC
Charter ("ensuring equitable benefits to all Contracting States, taking into account their
respective levels and pattern of economic development").

[11] Preamble, CARICOM; see also Preamble, SACU ("Mindful of the different levels of
economic development of the Member States and the need for their integration into
the global economy"); Preamble, Agreement Establishing the ASEAN–Australia–New
Zealand Free Trade Area (Chaam, Phetchaburi, Feb. 27, 2009) ("Considering the different
levels of development among ASEAN Member States and between ASEAN Member
States, Australia and New Zealand and the need for flexibility, including special and
differential treatment"); Preamble, South Pacific Regional Trade and Economic
Cooperation Agreement (Tarawa, Jul. 14, 1981; 1240 UNTS 66) ("Mindful of the differing
economic potential of Forum Island countries and the special development problems of
the Smaller Island countries"); art. 144 COMESA; art. 1 Cartagena Agreement (the
agreement also seeks "to reduce existing differences in levels of development");

Whether the RCEP and CPTPP will offer much by way of diverse and innovative normative approaches remains to be seen. Despite its name change to "Comprehensive and Progressive Agreement," the CPTPP does not offer a significant normative shift from its earlier incarnation as the TPP. The CPTPP suspended twenty-two provisions from the original TPP, most notably with respect to intellectual property. These clauses had been favored by the United States but were controversial with a number of other parties. The choice to suspend the application of these provisions rather than eliminate them altogether suggests that the parties are more concerned with making it easier to potentially reintegrate the United States into the agreement than to rethink the scope and nature of the commitments between the actual parties.

More germane to our normative pluralism argument is the future coexistence of the APEC, the CPTPP and the RCEP. Seven of the eleven CPTPP members are also in negotiations for the RCEP. Conversely, seven of the sixteen RCEP negotiating parties are members of the CPTPP. All members of the CPTPP are also APEC members, as are all RCEP negotiating parties except for India, Laos, Cambodia and Myanmar. All ASEAN members are parties to either the CPTPP or the RCEP, and the organization has concluded a number of free trade agreements with other participants of RCEP and CPTPP.

Beyond membership, the overlap of topical coverage of these groupings is also striking, in addition to the endorsement of general nondiscrimination rules such as most-favored-nation clauses and national treatment clauses. Table 2 provides an overview of the subject matters covered by the ASEAN, CPTPP and RCEP.

The vast topical overlap among these deep economic integration schemes could suggest a lack of normative diversity. At the same time, if members saw fit to engage in the regulation of the same topic in different fora, it may also be indicative that the ways in which each

Preamble, CARICOM ("the persistence of disadvantage, however arising, may impact adversely on the economic and social cohesion in the Community"); art. 1.6 ASEAN Charter (purposes include narrowing the development gap within ASEAN); preamble ¶ 9 and art. 1(d) Framework Agreement on Comprehensive Economic Cooperation among the Governments of the Republic of Korea and the Member Countries of the Association of Southeast Asian Nations (ASEAN–Korea) (Jeju-do, Jun. 2, 2009); preamble ¶¶ 2 and 7, arts. 1(d) and 2(d)–(e) Framework Agreement on Comprehensive Economic Cooperation between ASEAN and the People's Republic of China (ASEAN–China) (Phnom Penh, Nov. 4, 2002); preamble ¶ 6 Framework Agreement on Comprehensive Economic Cooperation between the Republic of India and the ASEAN (ASEAN–India) (Bali, Oct. 8, 2003).

Table 1 State members participating in more than one of the APEC, ASEAN, CPTPP and RCEP negotiations as of June 2018. + denotes free trade agreements with non-ASEAN countries.

	Australia	Brunei	Cambodia	Canada	Chile	China	Hong Kong	India	Indonesia	Japan	Laos	Malaysia	Mexico	Myanmar	New Zealand	Peru	Philippines	Singapore	South Korea	Thailand	Vietnam
APEC	x	x		x	x	x	x		x	x	x	x	x		x	x	x	x	x	x	x
ASEAN	+	x	x			+			x	+	x	x		x	+		x	x	+	x	x
CPTPP	x	x		x	x					x		x	x		x	x		x			x
RCEP	x	x	x			x		x	x	x	x	x		x	x		x	x	x	x	x

Table 2 Subject matters included in the ASEAN, CPTPP and RCEP.

	Trade in goods	Rules of origin	Trade facilitation	Trade remedies	SPS	TBT	Investment	Trade in services	E-commerce	Competition	IP	SOEs	Small and medium enterprises	Environment	Labor	Government procurement	Technical cooperation	Movement of natural persons
ASEAN*	×	×	×		×	×	×	×	×		×			×				
CPTPP	×	×	×	×	×	×	×	×	×	×	×	×	×	×	×	×	×	×
RCEP**	×	×	×	×	×	×	×	×	×	×	×		×	×		×	×	×

* The ASEAN combines a network of free trade agreements with nonmembers and agreements among members. The ASEAN also covers a myriad of other topics, ranging from mutual recognition of professional certifications to energy cooperation, standardization in a range of technical areas, the protection of particular environmental resources, and more.

** The contents of the RCEP are not public. Data in the table is garnered from the Joint Leaders' Statement on the Negotiations for the Regional Comprehensive Economic Partnership (Nov. 14, 2017), available at http://asean.org/storage/2017/11/RCEP-Summit_Leaders-Joint-Statement-FINAL1.pdf), and from leaked drafts posted at www.bilaterals.org/rcep-leaks and www.keionline.org/rcep.

topic is addressed, and in which subject matters relate to each other, differ across platforms. The ASEAN and APEC certainly illustrate the point. Although their respective members are engaged in economic and regulatory integration on the many subject matters also addressed by the CPTPP and the RCEP, they do so in very different ways. Rather than having a single comprehensive agreement with complex schedules of commitments by individual members, they have accumulated, over the years, dozens of topical instruments, mostly self-contained. In contrast, the CPTPP proceeds on the basis of a single common core agreement addressing all the topics at stake in the negotiations, with individual state commitments modulated in a series of side instruments and annexes. For instance, the CPTPP's main agreement, the TPP, is complemented by no less than twenty-five side instruments including different sets of parties. Additionally, 103 country-specific annexes and a few more common annexes also form a part of the agreement. Such procedurally different methods reflect different substantive approaches to economic regulation. This may help to explain why there is apparently no appetite for consolidating these various groupings into a single pan-Asian pact.

While the CPTTP seems to embody elements of the one-size-fits-all approach resisted by many emerging countries, observers believe that the RCEP, when it is finalized, will be more accepting of diverse economic models and strategies. For example, CPTTP includes restrictions on SOEs and WTO+ IP rules, while RCEP will have neither. We can therefore think of the RCEP as a regional pact that incorporates elements of normative pluralism.

2   Institutional Features

There may have been a time when one could imagine the WTO evolving into an exclusive, unitary and comprehensive site for global regulation of trade and related matters, with supportive institutions. But that is not how things have materialized. Inability to agree on many issues stalled new rulemaking in the WTO; the dispute settlement system, long the institutional crown jewel of the organization, is threatened logistically (due to insufficient resources to deal with the high volume and complexity of cases) and politically. The emergence of deep "regional" agreements devoid of strong governing institutions and dispute resolution mechanisms stands in sharp contrast to the multilateral economic governance project.

There is no necessary relationship between the normative features of regional pluralism and its institutional features, but they can come together, and the deeper integration project inherent in regional plural-ism would naturally lend itself to the creation of supportive institutions. In practice, we observe somewhat looser levels of institutional integration in regional pluralism than at the WTO. Dispute settlement processes perhaps provide the most salient illustration. A core feature of the WTO is its mandatory and exclusive dispute settlement system: members must use it, to the exclusion of any other dispute resolution forum. The WTO offered different types of dispute settlement, including a quasi-adjudicatory system with the panels and the Appellate Body, a single-step arbitration, mediation, good offices, and diplomatic negotiations, but if negotiations fail, members favor the quasi-adjudicatory process virtually exclusively. The CPTPP is more flexible, and not exclusive. Most notably, it allows complaining parties to choose which forum they wish to use to resolve disputes arising under the CPTPP and another trade agreement.[12] This a direct challenge to the exclusivity and mandatory rules of the WTO, but it may be seen as a response to the *Mexico – Taxes on Soft Drinks*[13] dispute, where a dispute arising under NAFTA even-tually spilled over into the WTO system but the WTO panel and AB refused to take into account the NAFTA elements of the dispute. The ASEAN and APEC agreements are typically devoid of adjudicatory or arbitration options for dispute settlement.

B Topical Pluralism

Another type of pluralism eschews deep multifaceted economic governance in favor of ad hoc, stand-alone agreements on specific issues or topics. Plurilateral agreements at the WTO and on its sidelines illustrate this approach. For instance, the Agreement on Government Procurement is separate from the single undertaking and deals with a specific subject matter. WTO members are free to subscribe to it or not, and have a great degree of latitude in defining which domestic entities might be covered by the agreement.[14] Participation in one agreement is not generally conditional upon participation in other agreements, and withdrawal is therefore less complex too. Although the Agreement on Government Procurement is

---

[12] Art. 28.4. ("If a dispute regarding any matter arises under this Agreement and under another international trade agreement to which the disputing Parties are party, including the WTO Agreement, the complaining Party may select the forum in which to settle the dispute.")

[13] AB Report, *Mexico – Taxes on Soft Drinks*, DS308/AB/R.

[14] Agreement on Government Procurement, art. XXIV.

conditional on WTO membership, parties may withdraw at any time with sixty days' notice without losing their WTO membership. Topical pluralism, then, is fluid over time because it would be easier for countries to extirpate themselves from an agreement that no longer suits their needs, unlike participation in a deep integration "regional" agreement.

As a rulemaking enterprise, topical pluralism offers flexibility. Amendments to such agreements or renegotiations are likely easier to undertake in a limited time frame, which makes this type of regulation nimbler and more apt to respond to changes of political, economic, technical or technological circumstances. Here again, the Agreement on Government Procurement offers an illustration of topical pluralism in action. It was originally developed as part of the 1979 Tokyo Round of trade negotiations and entered into force among its state parties in 1981. It became the Agreement on Government Procurement (GPA) 1994 at the time of the conclusion of the WTO, and underwent a broad revision between 1997 and 2012 when the Protocol of Amendment was finalized. It entered into force just two years later in 2014 and currently includes forty-seven parties (including the EU, which represents twenty-eight member states),[15] with a further ten members in the process of acceding, and another twenty-one having observer status. The Trade Facilitation Agreement, although ostensibly within the framework of the single undertaking at the WTO, operates in practice much like a plurilateral agreement. Negotiations on the Trade in Services Agreement between twenty-three WTO members also pertain to topical pluralism.

Because topical pluralism results in agreements or institutions that are limited in scope and have no universal membership ambition, it may be more responsive to technological innovation. For instance, it is reasonable to contemplate future stand-alone deals on block chains or cryptocurrencies, even as negotiations on the GATS are stalled, and the CPTPP and RCEP balance a host of issues relating to membership and issue-area coverage.

In some cases, regulatory projects that we could recognize as manifestations of topical pluralism fail. The Anti-Counterfeiting Trade Agreement (ACTA) provides a case in point. Like TiSA, it was meant as an effort to bypass the logjammed WTO negotiations, and to respond to the threat caused by a global intellectual property piracy economy

---

[15] The United Kingdom is expected to remain a party to the agreement after exiting the EU. Tom Miles, *WTO Agrees in Principle to Keep Britain in Procurement Deal*, REUTERS, Nov. 27, 2018, https://uk.reuters.com/article/uk-britain-eu-wto/wto-agrees-in-principle-to-keep-britain-in-procurement-deal-envoy-idUKKCN1NW1WN.

reportedly worth at least USD 500 billion annually[16] and often connected to organized crime, money laundering and terrorism financing.[17] However, scrutiny by civil society, and concerns over both the process and the substance of the agreement led to its effective abandonment, after Japan was the only state to ratify and the EU Parliament declined to consent to ratification in 2012. Here, the expression of pluralism resulted in a rejection of a topical regulation.

Topical pluralism may appear to be normatively light because it is not expressly or implicitly premised on the implementation of a global ordering imbued by a given theory of political economy. However, the fact that ACTA was set aside suggests that the topical approach may give a better chance to the expression and implementation of normative preferences, especially those not adequately represented by state authorities. By contrast, WTO+ disciplines have proliferated in deeper "regional" agreements, largely steamrolling opposition by the same constituencies that successfully resisted ACTA.

Hence, the normative subtext of topical pluralism must be read both in the regulatory output that is created and the potential output that is cast aside.

For emerging countries, topical pluralism offers opportunities for what we could call project-based developmentalism. Agreements or institutions meant to achieve a particular developmental objective or project, without seeking an all-encompassing economic integration, are well suited to this paradigm. The increasingly blurred lines between public aid to development, development finance, and foreign direct investment pertain to this type of development governance. Infrastructure projects in Africa, Latin America and Asia involve a mix of public and private agreements, often implemented by a corresponding mix of government actors, private entities or government-sponsored semiprivate actors, in the case of SOEs. The Belt and Road Initiative is perhaps the most prominent example of such project-based developmentalism. It ostensibly aims at developing infrastructure in the participating countries. It is not governed by a trade or investment agreement, but leverages a number of trade and investment instruments along with domestic regulation. It is implemented through government contracts as well as private contracts. Disputes might be heard in domestic courts in China that will be created

---

[16] OECD/EUIPO, Trade in Counterfeit and Pirated Goods: Mapping the Economic Impact (2016), https://doi.org/10.1787/9789264252653-en.

[17] See, e.g., Daniel C. K. Chow, Organized Crime, Local Protectionism, and the Trade in Counterfeit Goods in China, 14 CHINA ECON. REV. 473 (2003).

specifically to adjudicate such international commercial and investment projects.

C Economic Interdependence in a Plural World Order

What happens to interdependence in a world of pluralism? In the final analysis, this will depend on whether a concept of normative pluralism can be developed that is acceptable to the North and South, and whether topical pluralism proves a viable alternative or complement to deep economic integration. This means a notion of legitimate diversity that allows adequate developed-country access to developing markets, as well as developed-country capacity to limit import shocks. It also will depend on the success of mechanisms to deal with conflicts arising from overlapping and conflicting public law jurisdictions and private law arrangements.

IV Emerging Economies, Pluralism and the Future of International Economic Law

What is the future of international economic law? It seemed to promise that we could subject the whole world economy to a single system of rules and institutions that would nudge all countries toward a capitalist market economy and ensure free flows of trade and investment across all borders. While never fully successful, international economic law has made substantial progress toward that goal. But recent developments challenge that progress and may cast doubt on the core idea itself.

The embedded neoliberalism truce itself was evidence of the limits of the international economic law project; some equilibrium was achieved only by allowing de jure and de facto derogations from international economic rules and halting further progress in the completion of the liberalization project. The emergence of pluralism in all its senses is a further challenge: normative pluralism narrows the bite of any system of rules, as they must be flexible enough to accommodate fundamental diversity. Regional pluralism means there will be no single source of norms and no uniform system of disputes settlement; topical pluralism takes fragmentation even further.

These fragmenting processes overlap with two other developments that further undermine the bases for a uniform and comprehensive system of global rules for trade and investment. These are the resurgence of state-led capitalism, and increasing concerns for national security. The international economic law vision grew up in an era in which many believed that the world was on a trajectory toward universal free market capitalism. To be sure, China, Russia and to a lesser degree the other BRICS countries had strong state sectors, but it was thought they would gradually wither away. We now know that is not going to happen. Led by China, many emerging economies are doubling down on state-led growth strategies. At the same time, concerns about the relationship between trade, investment and national security are becoming more salient in the North and South. For example, China believes that its Made in China 2025 industrial policy is not just a way to increase GDP; it is also essential to its national security, while the United States and other developed countries feel that Chinese and other trade and investment policies hamper their security.

International economic law must take account of all these challenges. But to do so, it must face another challenge. Born in the era of U.S. hegemony, this legal field was heavily influenced by the dominant economic theories of the times. Scholars have pointed out that assumptions of neoliberal economics have been incorporated in international economic law doctrine under the guise of a "depoliticization" of economic policy. As we move into an era of normative pluralism and increasing concern for the political significance of trade and investment, critical international economic law scholars have called for a new approach to the field.[18] Such scholarly moves are aligned with a growing body of state practice among developing and developed countries. Calls for policy space in investment and trade law alike, and assertions by states of a range of political priorities, are transforming the discourse about international economic law in many emerging countries, as we have extensively discussed in Chapter 2. Beyond discourse, these countries are also challenging the preeminence and assumptions of neoliberal economics in their use of legal flexibility mechanisms or by creating de facto flexibilities. Chapter 3 examined some developing countries' use of flexibilities at the WTO and under BITs, as well as strategic breaches of trade law and outright rejection of investment law when the flexibilities prove insufficient to achieve their political economy objectives.

---

[18] Nicolas Perrone & David Schneiderman, *A Critique of International Economic Law: Depoliticization, Inequality, Precarity*, in RESEARCH HANDBOOK ON CRITICAL LEGAL THEORY (Emilios Christodoulidis et al., eds.) (forthcoming Edward Elgar Publishing).

The need to rethink international economic law is a major undertaking and will require input from a host of stakeholders. Emerging economies will play an important role and have already started to offer ideas. Our study suggests two that stand out – abandoning separate international and domestic regulatory spheres, and equalizing trade and non-trade concerns.

A   Abandon the Idea of Separate International and Domestic Spheres for Regulation

International economic law, like many other areas of international law, presumes the separation of domestic and international regulatory universes. In practice, rules on sanitary and phytosanitary measures, non-tariff barriers, intellectual property, and myriad others including broad disciplines such as national treatment, blur the international/domestic boundary and reach well within the state. Failing to account for this porous nature of the domestic and the international realms results in political tensions and legal conflicts, as debates about policy space have shown. Illustrations of these tensions can be found in Brexit, Australia's high-profile debates about foreign investment and tobacco regulation, and India's and South Africa's battles regarding international intellectual property rules and access to medicines. The increasingly fictitious underpinnings of international economic law as an international phenomenon, separate from domestic regulation, fail to serve states' public policy needs and priorities, and create vast opportunities for private commercial actors to bypass or manipulate states' public policies.[19] We need to acknowledge and account for this post-Westphalian world as part of rethinking the basis of international economic regulation.

B   Eliminate the Presumption That Trade Trumps Non-Trade Concerns

As it became clear in the late 1990s that conceiving of trade law as a self-contained regulatory domain separate from the rest of international law

[19] Multinational corporations have become very adept at exploiting this porosity to essentially curate legal universes of their own composed by cherry-picking benefits from BITs, taxation treaties, rules of origins, and judicial and arbitral fora. They do so by promoting creative interpretations of MFN clauses, by flipping incorporation of parent and subsidiary entities, and by strategically channeling revenues, liabilities, profits and assets through jurisdictions of their choosing, among other strategies. Dispute resolution is perhaps the most paradigmatic domain where the reconfiguration of the roles and activities of public and private actors has largely overtaken the binary international/domestic framework.

was untenable, we witnessed the emergence of a sort of buffer zone called "non-trade issues": those topics pertaining to public international law that rubbed against "purely" trade matters (though it is still a guess what the latter might be). Non-trade issues encompass labor, environment, public health, education, governance and corruption, social welfare policies and more. While recognizing the inevitable intersection between trade and non-trade issues was a critical first step, legal tools to manage the relationship are minimal and blunt. In the WTO context, article XX and XXI of the GATT and their counterparts in the GATS, article 2 of the TBT agreement, and similar provisions enshrine some level of recognition that topics outside of the trade realm may overlap with trade topics. But they have been interpreted to subordinate the non-trade issues to what are perceived as trade obligations. The trade obligation is the rule, and the non-trade concerns might at times be interpreted to be acceptable exceptions. Similar dynamics are at play with respect to international investment regulation. Voices from emerging economies and elsewhere have called for an end to this practice. This effort to equalize trade and non-trade concerns can be seen in calls for more policy space, and in recent efforts to outline a "right to regulate" as a way to legitimize the call for policy space and make it enforceable.[20]

C   Looking Ahead

Emerging economies face a new political, intellectual and institutional terrain as we move toward the third decade of the twenty-first century. We have documented the unraveling of the neoliberal consensus and the decline of universalist ambitions. This could be an opportunity for the emerging economies to play a more important role in the crafting of a new version of international economic law. But any such effort will exist

[20] Policy space, in its early to mid-2000s incarnation, means creating more flexibility in international trade law for states to implement their domestic regulatory choices. As a result, it was often associated with calls for more special and differential treatment, and for a more effective "operationalization" of special and differential treatment. At the same time, some negotiators and scholars were advocating instead for going beyond special and differential treatment and mainstreaming development, as a way to create more policy space. Over the following decade, the demand for policy space morphed into a call for a right to regulate. Finding a legal foundation for the amorphous notion of policy space is meant to both legitimize the project and give it enforceability. However, some argue that the move to promote a right to regulate only serves to legitimize the existing system and perpetuate the marginalization of policy and political elements in international economic law to the detriment of the most vulnerable participants.

in the shadow of the conflict between China and the United States. The United States is using a trade war to maintain global power and restore the market-driven vision of the world economy. Is this a last gasp of neoliberalism and U.S. hegemony in international economic law, or will it lead to a revival of neoliberalism? Only time will tell.

BIBLIOGRAPHY

Books, Articles, White Papers, Conference Papers & Manuscripts

José E. Alvarez, *Contemporary International Law: An "Empire of Law" or the "Law of the Empire"?*, 24 AM. U. INT'L L. REV. 811 (2009).

José E. Alvarez, *The Return of the State*, 20 MINN. J INT'L L. 223 (2011).

José E. Alvarez & Kathryn Khamsi, *The Argentine Crisis and Foreign Investors – A Glimpse in the Heart of the Investment Regime*, 2008–09 YEARBOOK INTL INVEST L. & POL'Y. 379.

Débora Bithiah de Azevedo, *Os acordos para a promoção e a proteção recíproca de investimentos assinados pelo Brasil*, Study for the Câmara dos Deputados (May 2001), available at www2.camara.leg.br/a-camara/documentos-e-pesquisa/estudos-e-notas-tecnicas/arquivos-pdf/pdf/102080.pdf.

Christina Binder et al., eds., INTERNATIONAL INVESTMENT LAW FOR THE 21ST CENTURY: ESSAYS IN HONOUR OF CHRISTOPH SCHREUER (2009).

JONATHAN BONNITCHA ET AL., THE POLITICAL ECONOMY OF THE INVESTMENT TREATY REGIME. (2017).

Edith Brown Weiss, *The Evolution of International Water Law*, in COLLECTED COURSE OF THE HAGUE ACAD. INT'L L. 308 (2009).

William W. Burke-White, *The Argentine Financial Crisis: State Liability under BITs and the Legitimacy of the ICSID System*, 3 ASIAN J. WTO & INTL HEALTH L. & POL'Y 199 (2008).

William W. Burke-White & Andreas von Staden, *Investment Protection in Extraordinary Times: The Interpretation and Application of Non-Precluded Measures Provisions in Bilateral Investment Treaties*, 48 VA J. INT'L L. 307 (2007).

Daniela Campello & Leany Lemos, *The Non-ratification of Bilateral Investment Treaties in Brazil: A Story of Conflict in a Land of Cooperation*, 22 REV. INTL POL. ECON. 1055 (2015).

David Capper, *Worldwide Mareva Injunctions*, 54 MODERN L. REV. 329 (1991).

Thomas E. Carbonneau & Mary H. Mourra, eds., LATIN AMERICAN INVESTMENT TREATY ARBITRATION: THE CONTROVERSIES AND CONFLICTS (2008).

Julien Chaisse et al., *The Three-Pronged Strategy of India's Preferential Trade Policy*, 26 CONN. J. INT'L L. 415 (2011).

Julien Chaisse et al., eds., THE TRANSPACIFIC PARTNERSHIP: A PARADIGM SHIFT IN INTERNATIONAL ECONOMIC LAW RULE-MAKING (2017).

HA-JOON CHANG, KICKING AWAY THE LADDER—DEVELOPMENT STRATEGY IN HISTORICAL PERSPECTIVE (2002).

B. S. Chimni, *Mapping Indian Foreign Economic Policy*, 47 INT'L STUDIES 163 (2010).

Daniel C. K. Chow, *Organized Crime, Local Protectionism, and the Trade in Counterfeit Goods in China*, 14 CHINA ECON. REV. 473 (2003).

SETH COLBY, SEARCHING FOR INSTITUTIONAL SOLUTIONS TO INDUSTRIAL POLICY CHALLENGES: A CASE STUDY OF THE BRAZILIAN DEVELOPMENT BANK (2013).

Cai Congyan, *China–US BIT Negotiations and the Future of Investment Treaty Regime: A Grand Bilateral Bargain with Multilateral Implications*, 12 J. INT'L ECON. L. 457 (2009).

Antoine Coste & Erik von Uexkull, *Benefits of the ECOWAS CET and EPA Will Outweigh Costs in Nigeria, but Competitiveness Is the Real Issue*, WORLD BANK AFRICA TRADE POLICY NOTES No. 43 (Jan. 2015).

Sukti Dasgupta & Ajit Singh, *Manufacturing, Services and Premature Deindustrialization in Developing Countries: A Kaldorian Analysis*, UNU-WIDER, UNITED NATIONS UNIVERSITY RESEARCH PAPER No. 2006/49 (2006).

Diane A. Desierto, *Necessity and Supplementary Means of Interpretation for Non-Precluded Measures in Bilateral Investment Treaties*, 31 U. PA. J. INT'L. L. 827 (2010).

DIANE DESIERTO, PUBLIC POLICY IN INTERNATIONAL ECONOMIC LAW: THE ICESCR IN TRADE, FINANCE, AND INVESTMENT (2015).

Pierre-Marie Dupuy et al., eds., HUMAN RIGHTS IN INTERNATIONAL INVESTMENT LAW AND ARBITRATION (2009).

Howard Erichson, *The Chevron–Ecuador Dispute, Forum Non Conveniens, and the Problem of Ex Ante Inadequacy*, 1 STAN. J. COMPLEX. LITIG. 417 (2013).

Shadan Farasat, *India's Quest for Regional Trade Agreements: Challenges Ahead*, 42 J. WORLD TRADE 433 (2008).

Silvia Karina Fiezzoni, *The Challenge of UNASUR Member Countries to Replace ICSID Arbitration*, 2 BEIJING L. REV. 134 (2011).

Susan D. Franck et al., *The Diversity Challenge: Exploring the "Invisible College" of International Arbitration*, 53 COLUM. J. TRANSNAT'L L. 429 (2015).

Kevin P. Gallagher & Melissa B. L. Birch, *Do Investment Agreements Attract Investment? Evidence from Latin America*, 7 J. WORLD INV. & TRADE 961 (2006).

NORAH GALLAGHER & WENHUA SHAN, CHINESE INVESTMENT TREATIES: POLICIES AND PRACTICE (2009).

David Singh Grewal, *Three Theses on the Current Crisis of International Liberalism*, 25 IND. J. GLOBAL LEGAL STUD. 595 (2018).

Grant Hanessian & Kabir Duggal, *The 2015 India Model BIT: Is This the Change the World Wishes to See?*, 29 ICSID REV. 3 (2015).

SEBASTIAN HEILMANN & LEA SHIH, THE RISE OF INDUSTRIAL POLICY IN CHINA (2013).

Yu Hong, *Pivot to Internet Plus: Molding China's Digital Economy for Economic Restructuring?*, 11 INT'L J. OF COM. 1486 (2017).

International Centre for Trade and Sustainable Development, *Crafting a Framework on Investment Facilitation* (2018), www.ictsd.org/sites/default/files/research/crafting_a_framework_on_investment_facilitation-ictsd-policy_brief.pdf.

F. A. Ismail, *Advancing Regional Integration in Africa through the Continental Free Trade Area (CFTA)*, 10 LAW & DEV. REV. 119 (2017).

Faizel Ismail & Brendan Vickers, *Reflections on a New Democratic South Africa's Role in the Multilateral Trading System*, in TRADE, POVERTY, DEVELOPMENT: GETTING BEYOND THE WTO'S DOHA DEADLOCK (James Scott & Rorden Wilkinson, eds., 2012).

Pravin Jadhav, *Determinants of Foreign Direct Investment in BRICS Economies: Analysis of Economic, Institutional and Political Factor*, 37 PROCEDIA–SOC. & BEHAV. SCI. 1 (2012).

Baris Karapinar, *Export Restrictions and the WTO Law: How to Reform the "Regulatory Deficiency,"* 45 J. WORLD TRADE 1139 (2011).

Baris Karapinar, *Export Restrictions and the WTO Law: "Regulatory Deficiency" or "Unintended Policy Space,"* WORLD TRADE INSTITUTE WORKING PAPERS May 21, 2010, www.wti.org/research/publications/80/export-restrictions-and-the-wto-law-regulatory-deficiency-or-unintended-policy-space/.

Benedict Kingsbury et al., eds., MEGAREGULATION CONTESTED: GLOBAL ECONOMIC ORDERING AFTER TPP (forthcoming, Oxford University Press).

Qingjiang Kong, *Emerging Rules in International Investment Instruments and China's Reform of State-Owned Enterprises*, 3 CHINESE J. GLOB. GOVERNANCE 57 (2017).

Jürgen Kurtz, *Adjudging the Exceptional at International Investment Law: Security, Public Order and Financial Crisis*, 59 INT'L & COMP. L. Q. 325 (2010).

Jean-Michel Marchat & Erik von Uexkull, *Republic of Senegal: An Assessment of the Short Term Impact of the ECOWAS–CET and EU–EPA in Senegal*, WORLD BANK REPORT No. ACS18578 (Oct. 27, 2016), http://documents.worldbank.org/curated/en/209801480496403751/pdf/ACS18578-WP-OUO-9-Senegal-EPA-and-CET-Analysis-has-been-approved-P151885.pdf.

Julie Maupin, *MFN-based Jurisdiction in Investor–State Arbitration: Is There any Hope for a Consistent Approach?*, 14 J. INT'L ECON. L. 157 (2011).

NOEL MAURER, THE EMPIRE TRAP: THE RISE AND FALL OF U.S. INTERVENTION TO PROTECT AMERICAN PROPERTY OVERSEAS 1893–2013 (2013).

Makane Moïse Mbengue and Mohamed H. Negm, *An African View on the CETA Investment Chapter*, in FOREIGN INVESTMENT UNDER THE COMPREHENSIVE ECONOMIC AND TRADE AGREEMENT (CETA) (Makane Moïse Mbengue and Stefanie Schacherer, eds., 2019).

Makane Moïse Mbengue and Stefanie Schacherer, *The "Africanisation" of International Investment Law: The Pan-African Investment Code and the Reform of the International Investment Regime*, 18 J. WORLD INVESTMENT & TRADE 414 (2017).

Branko Milanovic, *Global Income Inequality by the Numbers: in History and Now*, WORLD BANK DEVELOPMENT RESEARCH GROUP, WORKING PAPER No. 6259 (2012), http://documents.worldbank.org/curated/en/959251468176687085/pdf/wps6259.pdf.

Ram Kumar Mishra, *Role of State-Owned Enterprises in India's Economic Development*, OECD Workshop on State-Owned Enterprises in the Development Process, April 4, 2014, www.oecd.org/daf/ca/Workshop_SOEsDevelopmentProcess_India.pdf.

Thandika Mkandawire, ed., AFRICAN INTELLECTUALS. RETHINKING POLITICS, LANGUAGE, GENDER AND DEVELOPMENT (2005).

Michael Moser, ed., DISPUTE RESOLUTION IN CHINA (2012).

Mohammad Mossallam, *Process Matters: South Africa's Experience Exiting its BITs*, GLOBAL ECON. GOVERNANCE PROGRAMME WORKING PAPER 2015/97 (Jan. 2015), http://dx.doi.org/10.2139/ssrn.2562417.

Peter Muchlinski et al. eds., OXFORD HANDBOOK OF INTERNATIONAL INVESTMENT LAW (2008).

Nat'l Ass'n Of Mfrs., *Comment on Draft Indian Model Bilateral Investment Treaty* (2015), www.nam.org/Issues/Trade/ISDS/NAM-Comments-on-Draft-India-Model-Bilateral-Investment-Treaty-Joint-US-EU-Business.pdf.

Eric Neumayer & Laura Spess, *Do Bilateral Investment Treaties Increase Foreign Direct Investment to Developing Countries?*, 33 WORLD DEV. 1567 (2005).

OECD, Draft US–Central America Free Trade Agreement (CAFTA), Jan. 28, 2004, reprinted in *OECD, Most-Favoured-Nation Treatment in International Investment Law*, OECD WORKING PAPERS ON INTERNATIONAL INVESTMENT, 2004/02, OECD Publishing, http://dx.doi.org/10.1787/518757021651.

OECD, *Fair and Equitable Treatment Standard in International Investment Law*, OECD WORKING PAPERS ON INTERNATIONAL INVESTMENT 2004/03, https://doi.org/10.1787/18151957.

OECD, SOEs in India's Economic Development in State-Owned Enterprises in the Development Process (2015).

Uche Eweluka Ofodile, *Africa–China Bilateral Investment Treaties: A Critique*, 35 Mich. J. Int'l L. 131 (2013).

Joost Pauwelyn, *The Rule of Law without the Rule of Lawyers? Why Investment Arbitrators are from Mars, Trade Adjudicators from Venus*, 109 Am. J. Int'l L. 761 (2015).

Nicolas Perrone & David Schneiderman, *A Critique of International Economic Law: Depoliticization, Inequality, Precarity*, in Research Handbook on Critical Legal Theory (Emilios Christodoulidis et al., eds.) (forthcoming, Edward Elgar Publishing).

Stephen R. Platt, Imperial Twilight: The Opium War and the End of China's Last Golden Age (2018).

Prabhash Ranjan, *India and Bilateral Investment Treaties – A Changing Landscape*, 29 ICSID Rev. 419 (2014).

Prabhash Ranjan & Pushkar Anand, *The 2016 Indian Model Bilateral Investment Treaty: A Critical Deconstruction*, 38 Nw. J. Int'l L. & Bus. 1 (2017).

Prabhash Ranjan & Deepak Raju, *Bilateral Investment Treaties and the Indian Judiciary*, 46 Geo. Wash. Int'l L. Rev. 809 (2014).

Paolo de Renzio et al., *Brazil and South–South Cooperation: How to Respond to Current Challenges*, BRICS Pol'y Ctr. Centro de Estudos e Pesquisas, BPC Policy Brief Vol. 3 No. 55, May 2013.

Dani Rodrik, *Premature Deindustrialization*, Nat'l Bureau of Econ. Research, Working Paper No. 20935 (2015).

Sonia E. Rolland, *Are Consumer-Oriented Rules the New Frontier of Trade Liberalization?*, 55 Harv. Int'l L. J. 361 (2014).

Sonia E. Rolland, *The Return of State Remedies in Investor–State Dispute Settlement: Trends in Developing Countries*, 49 Loyola U. Chi. L. J. 387 (2017).

Sonia E. Rolland & David M. Trubek, *Legal Innovation in Investment Law: Rhetoric and Practice in the South*, 39 U. Penn. J. Intl L. 355 (2017).

Gideon Rose, *The Fourth Founding – The United States and the Liberal Order*, 98 Foreign Aff. 1 (2019).

Susan Rose-Ackerman & Jennifer Tobin, *Foreign Direct Investment and the Business Environment in Developing Countries: The Impact of Bilateral Investment Treaties*, Yale Law School Center for Law, Economics and Public Policy, Research Paper No. 293 (2005), https://papers .ssrn.com/sol3/papers.cfm?abstract_id=557121.

John A. Rothchild ed., Research Handbook on Electronic Commerce Law (2016).

Alvaro Santos et al., eds., World Trade and Investment Law Reimagined: A Progressive Agenda for an Inclusive Globalization (forthcoming, Taylor & Francis 2019)

Karl Sauvant & Michael D. Nolan, *China's Outward Foreign Direct Investment and International Investment Law*, 18 J. INT'L ECON. L. 893 (2015).

Karl P. Sauvant and Lisa E. Sachs, eds., THE EFFECT OF TREATIES ON FOREIGN DIRECT INVESTMENT: BILATERAL INVESTMENT TREATIES, DOUBLE TAXATION TREATIES, AND INVESTMENT FLOWS (2009).

John Savage & Elodie Dulac, *Chinese Investment Treaties and the Dispute Resolution Opportunities Offered by Most-Favoured Nation Provisions*, 2008 STOCKHOLM INT'L ARB. REV. No. 3.

Olivier De Schutter, ed., TRANSNATIONAL CORPORATIONS AND HUMAN RIGHTS (2006).

James Scott & Rorden Wilkinson, eds., TRADE, POVERTY, DEVELOPMENT: GETTING BEYOND THE WTO'S DOHA DEADLOCK (2012).

Wenhua Shan, *Umbrella Clauses and Investment Contracts under Chinese BITs: Are the Latter Covered by the Former?*, 11 J. WORLD INV. & TRADE 135 (2010).

Andre Singer, *The Failure of the Developmentalist Experiment in Three Acts*, 11 CRITICAL POL'Y STUDIES 358 (2017).

FRANCIS SNYDER, THE EU, THE WTO AND CHINA: LEGAL PLURALISM AND INTERNATIONAL TRADE REGULATION (2010).

M. SORNARAJAH, RESISTANCE AND CHANGE IN THE INTERNATIONAL LAW ON FOREIGN INVESTMENT (2015).

Joseph E. Stiglitz et al., eds., THE INDUSTRIAL POLICY REVOLUTION II: AFRICA IN THE 21ST CENTURY (2013).

Jing Tao, *China and TPP: A Tale of Two Economic Orderings?*, in REGULATION CONTESTED: GLOBAL ECONOMIC ORDERING AFTER TPP (Benedict Kingsbury et al., eds.) (forthcoming, Oxford University Press 2019).

Mathew M. Taylor, *The Unchanging Core of Brazilian State Capitalism, 1985–2015*, SCHOOL OF INTERNATIONAL SERVICE PAPER No. 2015–8, https://ssrn.com /abstract=2674332.

Kyla Tienhaara, *Once BITten, Twice Shy?*, 30 POL'Y & SOC. 185 (2017).

Jennifer L. Tobin & Marc L. Busch, *A BIT Is Better Than a Lot: Bilateral Investment Treaties and Preferential Trade Agreements*, 62 WORLD POLITICS 1 (2010).

Lisa Toohey et al., eds., CHINA IN THE INTERNATIONAL ECONOMIC ORDER (2015).

David M. Trubek et al., eds., LAW AND THE NEW DEVELOPMENTAL STATE: THE BRAZILIAN EXPERIENCE IN LATIN AMERICAN CONTEXT (2013).

IOANA TUDOR, THE FAIR AND EQUITABLE TREATMENT STANDARD IN THE INTERNATIONAL LAW OF FOREIGN INVESTMENT (2008).

Aniekan Iboro Ukpe, *Will EPAs Foster the Integration of Africa into World Trade?* 54 J. AFR. L. 212 (2010).

UNCTAD, GLOBAL INVESTMENT TREND MONITOR (2005).

UNCTAD, TRANSFORMING THE IIA REGIME: EXITING THE UNNECESSARY, DAMAGING INVESTOR–STATE DISPUTE SETTLEMENT SYSTEM (2014), https://worldinvestmentforum.unctad.org/wp-content/uploads/2015/05/Public-Citizen-Draft.pdf.

UNCTAD, WORLD INVESTMENT REPORT 2012: TOWARDS A NEW GENERATION OF INVESTMENT POLICIES (2012).

United States Chamber of Commerce, *China's Drive for Indigenous Innovation: A Web of Industrial Policies* (2010).

United States Chamber of Commerce, *Made in China 2025: Global Ambitions Built on Local Protections* (2017).

VALENTINA VADI, CULTURAL HERITAGE IN INTERNATIONAL INVESTMENT LAW AND ARBITRATION (2014).

Colette M. A. van der Ven, *Trade, Development and Industrial Policy in Africa: The Case for a Pragmatic Approach to Optimizing Policy Coherence between Industrial Policy and the WTO Policy Space*, 10 L. & DEV. REV. 29 (2017).

Heng Wang, *The RCEP and Its Investment Rules: Learning from Past Chinese FTAs*, 3 CHINESE J. GLOBAL GOVERNANCE 2 (2017).

Kim Wan-Soon, *Foreign Direct Investment In Korea*, KOREA DEVELOPMENT INSTITUTE (2003), www.kdevelopedia.org/Resources/all/foreign-direct-investment-korea–04201201180005040.do;jsessionid=D1F37B76E210DDEF2581496B122313D4#.W9 J_OhNKjsE.

Marc Wu, *The China Inc. Challenge to Global Trade Governance*, 57 HARV. INT'L L.J. 261 (2016).

Katia Yannaca-Small, *Essential Security Interests under International Investment Law*, in INTERNATIONAL INVESTMENT PERSPECTIVES: FREEDOM OF INVESTMENT IN A CHANGING WORLD (OECD, ed., 2007).

Zhang Zhiyong, *Economic Integration in East Asia: The Path of Law*, 4 PEKING U. J. LEGAL STUD. 262 (2013).

News Sources, Press Releases, Magazines & Blog Posts

Maria Abi-Habib, *How China Got Sri Lanka to Cough Up a Port*, N.Y. TIMES, June 25, 2018, www.nytimes.com/2018/06/25/world/asia/china-sri-lanka-port.html.

African Union, *Pan-African Investment Code: African Independent Legal Experts Kicks Off in Djibouti*, Press Release No. 292/2014, Oct. 30, 2014.

Celso Amorim, *Guinada à direita do Itamaraty*, FOLHA DE SAO PAULO, May 22, 2016, www1.folha.uol.com.br/mundo/2016/05/1773728-guinada-a-direita-no-itamaraty.shtml.

Kajal Bhardwaj & Shiba Phurailatpam, *RCEP and Health: This Kind of "Progress" Is Not What India and the World Need*, Bilaterals.org (Feb. 28, 2017), www.bilaterals.org/?rcep-and-health-this-kind-of).

Antony Boadle, *Brazil Right-Winger Would Follow Trump's Lead on Foreign Policy*, REUTERS, Oct. 16, 2018, https://www.reuters.com/article/us-brazil-election-diplomacy/brazil-right-winger-would-follow-trumps-lead-on-foreign-policy -idUSKCN1MQ2HR.

Bolivian Water Dispute Settled; Bechtel Forgoes Compensation, INV. TREATY NEWS, Jan. 20, 2006, www.iisd.org/investment/itn.

Steve Brachman, *Chinese Support of Indigenous Innovation Is Problematic for Foreign IP Owners*, IP WATCHDOG, (Apr. 9, 2015), www.ipwatchdog.com /2015/04/09/chinese-indigenous-innovation-problematic-foreign-ip-owners/id=56525/.

Benjamin Charlton, *RCEP Will Step Into Gap as Trump Pulls Out of TPP*, OXFORD ANALYTICA, Jan. 23, 2017, https://dailybrief.oxan.com/Analysis/DB217448/ RCEP-will-step-into-gap-as-Trump-pulls-out-of-TPP.

China Tax in the Digital Age (2016), https://assets.kpmg/content/dam/kpmg/pdf/ 2016/07/china-tax-in-the-digital-age-1.pdf.

Civil Society Groups Say "No" to Investors Suing States in RCEP, PUBLIC SERVICES INTERNATIONAL (Aug. 4, 2016), www.world-psi.org/en/civil-society-groups-say-no- investors-suing-states-rcep.

Rob Davies, *The SADC EPA and Beyond, in Economic Partnership Agreements and Beyond*, 3 GREAT INSIGHTS NO. 9 (Oct/Nov 2014) 10.

Junior Davis, *Unlocking Africa's Potential for a Growing Services Sector*, AFR. POL'Y REV., May 16, 2016, http://africapolicyreview.com/unlocking-africas-potential-for-a-growing-services-sector/.

Kevin C. Desouza et al., *Is China Leading the Blockchain Innovation Race?*, July 19, 2018, www.brookings.edu/blog/techtank/2018/07/19/is-china-leading-the-blockchain-innovation-race/.

DMD Advocates, *Why India's Draft Model Bilateral Investment Treaty Is a Bit of a Misnomer*, LEGALLY INDIA (May 11, 2015), www.legallyindia.com/views/ entry/why-india-s-draft-model-bilateral-investment-treaty-is-a-bit-of -a-misnomer.

Matthew Erie, *The China International Commercial Court: Prospects for Dispute Resolution for the Belt and Road Initiative*, ASIL INSIGHTS Vol. 22, Issue 11, Aug. 31, 2018, www.asil.org/insights/volume/22/issue/11/ china-international-commercial-court-prospects-dispute-resolution-belt.

European Commission, *A Future Multilateral Investment Court*, Press Release MEMO/16/4350, Dec. 13, 2016, http://europa.eu/rapid/press-release _MEMO-16-4350_en.htm.

European Commission, *Commission Proposes New Investment Court System for TTIP and other EU Trade and Investment Negotiations*, Press Release IP/15/ 5651, Sept. 19, 2015, http://europa.eu/rapid/press-release_IP-15-5651_en .htm.

Randy Fabi, *Indian Metals and Ferro Alloys Miner Files $560 mln Claim Against Indonesia*, REUTERS, Nov. 18, 2015, http://in.reuters.com/article/indonesia-imfa- idINKCN0T70O320151118.

Victor Ferguson, *Why China Won't Save the TPP*, EAST ASIA FORUM, Feb. 11 2017, www.eastasiaforum.org/2017/02/11/why-china-wont-save-the-tpp/.

William Finnegan, *Leasing the Rain: The World Is Running Out of Fresh Water, and the Fight to Control It Has Begun*, NEW YORKER 43, April 8, 2002.

India and US Reach WTO Breakthrough Over Food, BBC NEWS, Nov. 13, 2014, www.bbc.com/news/business-30033130.

International Court of Justice, Press Release, Aug. 7, 2014, www.icj-cij.org/files/press-releases/4/18354.pdf.

Zhang Jie, *National Standard for Blockchain Expected Next Year*, May 10, 2018, www.chinadaily.com.cn/a/201805/10/WS5af3dd1aa3105cdcf651d1ff.html.

Scott Kennedy, *Made in China 2025*, CENTER FOR STRATEGIC & INTERNATIONAL STUDIES, June 1, 2015, www.csis.org/analysis/made-china-2025.

Jonathan Lang, *Bilateral Investment Treaties – a Shield or a Sword?*, Dec. 13, 2013, www.bowman.co.za/FileBrowser/ArticleDocuments/South-African-Government-Canceling-Bilateral-Investment-Treaties.pdf.

David Lawder & Ben Blanchard, *Trump Administration Adds to China Trade Pressure with Higher Tariff Plan*, REUTERS (Aug. 1, 2018), www.reuters.com/article/us-usa-trade-china/trump-administration-adds-to-china-trade-pressure-with-higher-tariff-plan-idUSKBN1KM63U.

James McBride & Andrew Chatsky, *Is "Made in China 2025" a Threat to Global Trade?*, COUNCIL ON FOREIGN RELATIONS, Aug. 2, 2018, www.cfr.org/backgrounder/made-china-2025-threat-global-trade.

Stephen McDonald et al., *Why Economic Partnership Agreements Undermine Africa's Regional Integration*, May 3, 2013, www.wilsoncenter.org/sites/default/files/EPA%20Article.pdf.

Etienne Michaud, *Driving Up Local Content of Brazilian Cars: The Inovar-Auto Program and Supply Chain Strategy*, BRAZILWORKS BRIEFING PAPER, 2015.

Tom Miles, *WTO Agrees in Principle to Keep Britain in Procurement Deal*, REUTERS, Nov. 27, 2018, https://uk.reuters.com/article/uk-britain-eu-wto/wto-agrees-in-principle-to-keep-britain-in-procurement-deal-envoy-idUKKCN1NW1WN.

Assis Moreira, *UE e Mercosul Impõem Condições para Abrir Mercados*, VALOR ECONÂMICO, June 10, 2016, www.valor.com.br/brasil/4595933/ue-e-merco sul-impoem-condicoes-para-abrir-mercados.

Narendra Modi Is a Fine Administrator, but Not Much of a Reformer, THE ECONOMIST, June 24, 2017.

Aloysio Nunes, *Mercosur: más comercio, menos barreras,* EL CRONISTA, October 25, 2017, www.itamaraty.gov.br/pt-BR/discursos-artigos-e-entrevistas-categoria/ministro-das-relacoes-exteriores-artigos/17694-mercosul-mais-comercio-menos-barreiras-el-cronista-argentina-25-10-2017-espanhol.

Office of the United States Trade Representative, *USTR Finalizes Tariffs on $200 Billion of Chinese Imports in Response to China's Unfair Trade Practices,* Press Release, Sept. 18, 2018, https://ustr.gov/about-us/policy-offices/press-office/press-releases/2018/september/ustr-finalizes-tar iffs-200.

Inaê Siqueira de Oliveira, *Corporate Restructuring and Abuse of Rights: PCA Tribunal Deems Philip Morris's Claims Against Australia's Tobacco Plain Packaging Rules Inadmissible,* INV. TREATY NEWS, Aug. 10, 2016, https://iisd.org/itn/es/2016/08/10/philip-morris-asia-limited-v-the-commonwealth-of-australia-pca-case-no-2012-12/.

Perth USAsia Centre, *The Regional Comprehensive Economic Partnership: An Indo–Pacific Approach to the Regional Trade Architecture?,* INDO-PACIFIC INSIGHT SERIES, Jan. 2017, http://perthusasia.edu.au/getattachment/Our-Work/Indo-Pacific-Insight-Series-Vol-2-The-RCEP-An-I/PUAC-Indo-Pacific-Insight-Series-Volume2-JeffWilson.pdf.aspx?lan.

Luke Eric Peterson, *Czech Republic Terminates Investment Treaties in Such a Way as to Cast Doubt on Residual Legal Protection for Existing Investments,* INV. ARB. REPORTER, Feb. 1, 2011, www.iareporter.com/articles/czech-republic-terminates-   investment-treaties-in-such-a-way-as-to-cast-doubt-on-residual-legal-protection-for-existing- investments/.

Luke Eric Peterson, *Indonesia Ramps Up Termination of BITs – and Kills Survival Clause in One Such Treaty – but Faces New $600 mil. Claim from Indian Mining Investor* (Dec. 7, 2015), www.bilaterals.org/?indonesia-ramps-up-termination-of.

RCEP: Looking Ahead to 2017, Dec. 14, 2016, www.asiantradecentre.org/talking trade//rcep-looking-ahead-to-2017.

Shefali Rekhi, *Will RCEP Be a Reality by the End of 2017?,* STRAIGHT TIMES, Apr. 23, 2017, www.straitstimes.com/asia/se-asia/will-rcep-be-a-reality-by-the-end-of-2017.

The Retreat of the Global Company, THE ECONOMIST, Jan. 28, 2017, www.economist.com/news/briefing/21715653-biggest-business-idea-past-three-decades-deep-trouble-retreat-global.

Dani Rodrik, *The WTO Has Become Dysfunctional,* FIN. TIMES, Aug. 5, 2018, www.ft.com/content/c2beedfe-964d-11e8-95f8-8640db9060a7.

Kai Schultz, *Sri Lanka, Struggling with Debt, Hands a Major Port to China,* N.Y. TIMES, Dec. 12, 2017, www.nytimes.com/2017/12/12/world/asia/sri-lanka-china-port.html.

Malcolm Scott & Cedric Sam, *Here's How Fast China's Economy Is Catching Up to the U.S.*, May 12, 2016; updated May 24, 2018, www.bloomberg.com/gra phics/2016-us-vs-china-economy/.

Attila Tanzi et al., eds., INTERNATIONAL INVESTMENT LAW IN LATIN AMERICA / DERECHO INTERNACIONAL DE LAS LAS INVERSIONES EN AMÈRICA LATINA: PROBLEMS AND PROSPECTS / PROBLEMAS Y PERSPECTIVAS (2016).

John Thornbill, *China's Digital Economy Is a Global Trailblazer*, FIN. TIMES, March 20, 2017, www.ft.com/content/86cbda82-0d55-11e7-b030-768954394623).

The TPP's IP Challenge for China, Nov. 9, 2015, https://chinaipr.com/2015/11/09/the-tpps-ip-challenge-for-china-part-1/.

Zheng Yangpeng & Meng Jing, *Rapidly Growing Digital Economy Set to Give China 415m Jobs, Account for Nearly Half of GDP*, SOUTH CHINA MORNING POST, Jan. 10, 2017, www.scmp.com/tech/article/2060895/rapidly-growing-digital-economy-set-give-china-415m-jobs-account-nearly-half.

Li Yuan, *Why Made in China 2025 Will Succeed, Despite Trump*, N.Y. TIMES, July 4, 2018, www.nytimes.com/2018/07/04/technology/made-in-china-2025-dongguan.html.

Government Sources

Bolivia

Constitución Política del Estado [Constitution] (2009).

Brazil

Act No. 12.715/2012 (2012).
Act No. 13123/2011 (2012).
Constituição Federal [C.F.] [Constitution] (1988).
Decree No. 8772/2016 (2016).
Legislative Decree No. 42 of 2017.
Marco Civil da Internet, Act No. 12965/2014.
Ministry of Foreign Relations, *Brazil–Mexico Decision, in 2015, to Deepen the Agreement of Economic Complementation n. 53* (2015), www.itamaraty.gov.br/pt-BR/notas-a-imprensa/12766-negociacao-brasil-mexico-paraampliacao-e-aprofun damento-do-ace-53-troca-de-listas-de-pedidos-reciprocos.
Ministry of Foreign Relations, *Estados Unidos Mexicanos*, www.itamaraty.gov.br /pt-BR/ficha-pais/6453-estados-unidos-mexicanos.

Speech by Minister José Serra on the occasion of the ceremony in which he took office as Minister of Foreign Affairs, Brasília, May 18, 2016, www .itamaraty.gov.br/en/speeches-articles-and-interviews/minister-of-foreign-affairs-speeches/14044-speech-by-minister-jose-serra-on-the-occasion-of-the-ceremony-in-which-he-took-office-as-minister-of-foreign-affairs-brasilia-may -18–2016

China

Ministry of Commerce, People's Republic of China, China trade in services statistics, Jan. 20, 2018, http://english.mofcom.gov.cn/article/statistic/tradein services/201801/20180102706539.shtml.

Colombia

Bilateral Agreement for the Promotion and Protection of Investments between the Republic of Colombia and (blank), Colombian Model August 2007, www .italaw.com/documents/inv_model_bit_colombia.pdf [https://perma.cc/XGL8-NXSQ].

Ecuador

Constitution of Ecuador (2008).

India

AADHAAR (Targeted Delivery of Financial and Other Subsidies, Benefits and Services) Act, 2016 (March 26, 2016) (India) https://uidai.gov.in/legal-framework/acts.html.
Constitution of India (1950).
Department of Public Enterprises, Public Enterprises Survey 2015–16, Volume I, Statement 13 Ranking of CPSEs in Terms of Net Turnover/Revenue in 2015–16 (2016).
Directorate General of Commercial Intelligence and Statistics, India's Foreign Trade by Economic Region (2017), Table 2A, www.dgciskol.nic.in/pdfs/ emsft_2a.pdf.
Indian Model Text of BIPA, www.italaw.com/sites/default/files/archive/ita1026 .pdf [https://perma.cc/L2YK-3Z95].
Law Commission of India, Analysis of the 2015 Draft Model Indian Bilateral Investment Treaty, Report No. 260, http://lawcommissionofindia.nic.in /reports/Report260.pdf.

Ministry of Finance, Department of Economic Affairs, Office Memorandum, F. No. 26/5/2013-IC, Annex, Dec. 28, 2015.

Ministry of Heavy Industries & Public Enterprises, Department of Public Enterprises, Annual Report 131 (2016).

Ministry of Heavy Industries and Public Enterprises – Department of Public Enterprises, Office Memorandum No. 18(8)/2005-GM (2010).

Ministry of Heavy Industries & Public Enterprises, Department of Public Enterprises, Public Enterprises Survey 2015–16, Volume I, Statement 14 Ranking of CPSEs in Terms of Employment in 2015–16 (2016). Ministry of New and Renewable Energy, Jawaharlal Nehru National Solar Mission – Towards Building SOLAR INDIA (2012), https://mnre.gov.in/file-manager /UserFiles/mission_document_JNNSM.pdf.

Model Text for the Indian Bilateral Investment Treaty, www.jurisafrica.org/html/ pdf_indian-bilateral-investment-treaty.pdf.

Kenya

Ministry of Industrialization and International Development, Kenya's Industrial Transformation Programme (2015).

South Africa

Constitution of the Republic of South Africa Act, 1996.

Department of Trade and Industry, Industrial Policy Action Plan – IPAP 2016/17 – 2018–19 (2016).

Department of Trade and Industry, Bilateral Investment Treaty Policy Framework Review (Government Position Paper, June 2009), http://pmg-assets.s3-website-eu-west-1.amazonaws.com/docs/090626trade-bi-lateralpolicy.pdf.

Mineral and Petroleum and Resources Development Act No. 28, 2002, Government Gazette Vol. 448, No. 23922, Oct. 10, 2002.

Promotion of Investment Act No. 22 of 2015, Government Gazette Vol. 606, No. 39514, Dec. 15, 2015.

United States of America

Central Intelligence Agency, The World Factbook: Country Comparison, Stock of Direct Foreign Investment, www.cia.gov/library/publications/the-world-factbook/rankorder/2198rank.html.

National Security Strategy of the United States (2017), www.whitehouse.gov/wp-content/uploads/2017/12/NSS-Final-12-18-2017-0905.pdf.

Office of the United States Trade Representative, 2017 Special 301 Report.

United States Trade Representative, 2016 Report to Congress on China's WTO Compliance (2016).

U.S.–China Economic and Security Review Commission, *Fentanyl: China's Deadly Export to the United States*, Feb. 1, 2017, www.uscc.gov/sites/default/files/ Research/USCC%20Staff%20Report_Fentanyl-China%E2%80%99s%20Deadly %20Export%20to%20the%20United%20States020117.pdf.

U.S.–China Economic and Security Review Commission, 2016 Report to Congress of the U.S–China Economic and Security Review Commission.

International Organizations Sources

Africa Mining Vision, www.africaminingvision.org/, (Oct. 27, 2017).

African Development Bank Group, Industrialize Africa (2017).

ASEAN, *Thinking Globally, Prospering Regionally – ASEAN Economic Community 2015* (March, 2015), http://asean.org/storage/2016/06/4.-March -2015-Thinking-Globally-Prospering-Regionally-%E2%80%93-The-AEC -2015-Messaging-for-Our-Future-2nd-Reprint.pdf.

Bolivarian Alliance for the Peoples of Our America [ALBA], Fundamental Principles of the Peoples' Trade Treaty, http://alba-tcp.org/en/contenido/gov erning-principles-tcp.

South African Development Community, SADC Model Bilateral Investment Treaty Template with Commentary, July 2012, www.iisd.org/itn/wp-content /uploads/2012/10/SADC-Model-BIT-Template-Final.pdf.

WORLD BANK, AFRICA: ECONOMIC PARTNERSHIP AGREEMENTS BETWEEN AFRICA AND THE EUROPEAN UNION, WHAT TO DO NOW? SUMMARY REPORT (2008).

WORLD BANK, WORLD DEVELOPMENT STATISTICS INDIA (2016).

World Intellectual Property Organization, Record Year for International Patent Applications in 2016; Strong Demand Also for Trademark and Industrial Design Protection (2017).

African Union

African Union Commission, Africa Action Plan on Development Effectiveness (2011), www.nepad.org/resource/africa-action-plan-development- effectiveness.

African Union Commission, Agenda 2063: First Ten-Year Implementation Plan 2014–2023, September 2015, www.nepad.org/resource/agenda-2063-first-ten- year-implementation-plan-2014–2023.

Launch of Continental Free Trade Area Negotiations (Assembly/AU/Dec.569 (XXV)) [2015] AUDECISIONS 9, www.saflii.org/au/AUDECISIONS/2015/9.html.

Asia–Pacific Economic Cooperation

APEC Blueprint for Action on Electronic Commerce, 6th APEC Economic Leaders' Meeting, APEC Doc. 1998/AELM/DEC/3 (Nov. 17, 1998).

APEC Data Privacy Pathfinder, APEC Doc. 2007/CSOM/019 (Sept. 2, 2007).

Committee on Consumer Protection, Consumer Protection in ASEAN (2010).

Electronic Commerce Steering Group, Meeting Summary Report – 2002, APEC Doc. 2002/ECSG2/SUM (Aug. 17, 2002).

European Union

Commission Regulation No 978/2012, 2012 O.J. (L 303/1) (EU).

Commission Regulation No 1421/2013, 2013 O.J. (L 355/1) (EU).

Commission Regulation (EU) No 1016/2014, 2014 O.J. (L 283/23) (EU).

Commission Regulation (EU) No 2015/1979, 1979 O.J. (L 289/3) (EU).

Council of the European Union, IV EU–Mercosur Summit, "Joint Communiqué" (May 17, 2010) 9870/10 Presse 129.

European Commission, Overview of Economic Partnership Agreements, http://trade.ec.europa.eu/doclib/docs/2009/september/tradoc_144912.pdf.

European Commission, *Report from the XXIXth round of negotiations of the Trade Part of the Association Agreement between the European Union and Mercosur*, Brasilia (October 2–6, 2017), http://trade.ec.europa.eu/doclib/docs/2017/october/tradoc_156336.pdf.

European Commission, *Report from the XXXth round of negotiations of the Trade Part of the Association Agreement between the European Union and Mercosur*, Brasilia (November 6–10, 2017), http://trade.ec.europa.eu/doclib/docs/2017/november/tradoc_156408.pdf.

European Commission, *Report from the XXXIth round of negotiations of the Trade Part of the Association Agreement between the European Union and Mercosur*, Brussels (Nov. 29–Dec. 8, 2017), http://trade.ec.europa.eu/doclib/docs/2018/january/tradoc_156529.pdf.

European Commission, *Report from the XXXIIth round of negotiations of the Trade Part of the Association Agreement between the European Union and Mercosur*, Asuncion (Feb. 21–March 2, 2018), http://trade.ec.europa.eu/doclib/docs/2018/march/tradoc_156641.pdf.

European Commission, *Report from the XXXIIIth round of negotiations of the Trade Part of the Association Agreement between the European Union and*

Mercosur, Montevideo (June 4–8, 2018), http://trade.ec.europa.eu/doclib/docs/
2018/june/tradoc_156963.pdf.

United Nations Conference on Trade and Development

Bilateral Investment Treaties in the Mid-1990s, UN Doc. UNCTAD/ITE/IIA/7
(1998).
Investment Policy Framework for Sustainable Development, UNCTAD/DIAE/
PCB/2015/5 (2015), http://unctad.org/en/PublicationsLibrary/diaepcb2015
d5_en.pdf.
Report of the Expert Meeting on the Transformation of the International
Investment Agreement Regime: The Path Ahead, TD/B/C.II/EM.4/3
(UNCTAD, ed., 2015), http://unctad.org/meetings/en/SessionalDocuments/
ciiem4d3_en.pdf.
Report of the Investment, Enterprise and Development Commission on Its
Seventh Session, TD/B/C.II/31, (2015), http://unctad.org/meetings/en/
SessionalDocuments/ciid31_en.pdf.
United Nations Center on Transnational Corporations, Bilateral Investment
Treaties, U.N. Doc. ST/CTC/65 (1988).
UNITED NATIONS ECONOMIC COMMISSION FOR AFRICA, GREENING AFRICA'S
INDUSTRIALIZATION – ECONOMIC REPORT ON AFRICA (2016).

World Trade Organization

Council for Trade in Goods – Africa Growth and Opportunity Act Request for
a Waiver, G/C/W/713, July 16, 2015 (Request from the United States).
General Council – Decision on Waiver Relating to Special Treatment for Rice of
the Philippines – Waiver Decision of July 24, 2014, WT/L/932.
General Council – Preferential Tariff Treatment for Least-Developed Countries –
Decision on Extension of Waiver – Adopted on May 27, 2009, WT/L/759.
General Council – Senegal – Waiver on Minimum Values in Regard to the
Agreement on the Implementation of Article VII of the General Agreement
on Tariffs and Trade 1994 – Decision of July 31, 2008, WT/L/735.
International Trade Statistics 2015, www.wto.org/english/res_e/statis_e/its2015_e/
its2015_e.pdf.
Joint Ministerial Statement on Investment Facilitation for Development, WT/MIN
(17)/59, Dec. 13, 2017.
Ministerial Conference – Ninth Session – Bali, Dec. 3–6, 2013 – Operationalization
of the Waiver concerning Preferential Treatment to Services and Service

Suppliers of Least-Developed Countries, Ministerial Decision of December 7, 2013, WT/L/903.

Ministerial Declaration [Doha Declaration], Nov. 14, 2001, WT/MIN(01)/DEC/1; 41 I.L.M. 746 (2002).

Report by the Secretariat, India – Trade Policy Review, at ¶ 2.14, WT/TPR/S/313 (April 28, 2015).

INDEX